BUREAUCRATIC DEMOCRACY

Bureaucratic Democracy

The Search for Democracy and Efficiency in American Government

DOUGLAS YATES

HARVARD UNIVERSITY PRESS
Cambridge, Massachusetts, and London, England
1982

Library of Congress Cataloging in Publication Data

Yates, Douglas, 1944-
    Bureaucratic democracy.

    Includes index.
    1. Bureaucracy—United States. 2. United States—
Politics and government. 3. Democracy I. Title.
JK421.Y37   353'.01   81-7235
ISBN 0-674-08611-2   AACR2

For my mother and father

Preface

WHEN I TOOK ON THE ASSIGNMENT of teaching the introductory American government course at Yale, I encountered a problem that I am sure most others assigned to this pedagogical "beat" also face. That is, teaching introductory American government to a class of smart freshmen is a tough job.

By trial and error, through three years of trying to find a solution to the great American government problem, classroom division, I concluded that the best way to avoid describing institutions on parade or inflicting too much professional methodology on students was to develop a sustained theme reflecting what I thought to be a fundamental and increasingly serious problem in our governance. The theme I chose was the conflict between the competing values of democracy and efficiency. This conflict finds its way into this book as an analytical framework for thinking about the present performance of our government and about what choices and trade-offs we face today. A second theme that emerged from that undergraduate class and that pointed the way toward this book was that our democracy, the American policymaking system, is increasingly embedded in bureaucratic structures of various kinds.

In 1975, I became Associate Dean of Yale's new School of Organization and Management, whose mission is to train professional managers for government and business. Again I found that demanding students and the process of teaching challenged me to deepen and clarify my thinking about the workings of bureaucracy in American government. My management students forced me to examine the implications of policymaking in a bureaucratic democracy for the art and practice of governance. This meant thinking not only about how political actors behave and administrative environments vary but also about how policymaking and management might be improved in different settings.

My first debt of gratitude is therefore to the hundreds of students who have prodded and questioned me in the development of the ideas that have gone into this book. A second obvious debt is to those scholars who are writing in the burgeoning field of public policy. I have benefited greatly from the writings of many current students of public policy and have frequently taken the liberty of drawing connections and contrasts from their work.

Closer to home, I have benefited from the institutional support provided in so many different ways by Yale's School of Organization and Management, its Political Science Department, and its Institution for Social and Policy Studies. In addition, ten to fifteen persistent souls, under the leadership of C. E. Lindblom, have been holding a weekly seminar on American Democratic Institutions for at least six or seven years. The seminar has been a powerful source of intellectual stimulation for me.

I have received helpful comments on successive drafts of this manuscript from numerous scholarly colleagues. They include Martha Weinberg, Aaron Wildavsky, Richard Hackman, Dick Nelson, Garry Brewer, Dwight Waldo, Allan Sindler, and Barbara Ankeny. Robert Katzmann variously aided me as research assistant, critic, and editor. I also benefited greatly from the stylistic judgment and analytical clarity of my editors at Harvard University Press, Aida Donald and Camille Smith. Most of all, I am enormously indebted to three colleagues at Yale, Geoffrey Hazard, Douglas Rae, and James Fesler, who through extended discussions, criticisms, suggestions, and support have made this a far better book than it otherwise would have been. Finally, as one whose handwriting is nearly illegible, I would still be on square one were it not for the deciphering abilities and sheer determination of Marie Avitable and Chris Anastasion.

Contents

BUREAUCRATIC DEMOCRACY

1

Bureaucracy and American Democratic Theory

THIS BOOK IS ABOUT the role of bureaucracy in American government. It is about the causes and consequences, the strengths and weaknesses of bureaucratic policymaking. It is about the difficulties that bureaucracies present for the functioning of a democratic society. It is about the similarities and differences among different bureaucratic institutions. And finally, it is about possible solutions to the "bureaucracy problem."

Discussions of bureaucracy operate at a high level of rhetoric and feeling. The government bureaucracy has become a favorite whipping boy of commentators and public officials across the American political and ideological spectrum. Jimmy Carter ran for the presidency in 1976 on a campaign pledge that he would tame and control the bureaucracy, and presidential candidates in 1980 were quick to mount the same attack.

All of this political rhetoric and controversy is rooted in a valid concern. American government has increasingly become a "bureaucratic democracy"; that is, democratic decisionmaking takes place more and more in bureaucratic settings. This pattern is most obvious in the workings of the national bureaucracy, but it is also evident in the bureaucratization of the White House staff, congressional staffs, and state and local governments, as well as in the proliferation of local bureaucracies.

There are many reasons for the rise of bureaucratic democracy, and not all of them are "bad" by any means. Yet this snapshot picture of bureaucratic democracy is at such variance with our normal understanding of the workings of the American system of government that it calls for sustained analysis and appraisal. Bureaucratic democracy is a politico-administrative system quite different from the one in the minds of the founding fathers or in more recent writings on democratic theory. My task in this book is to dissect the elements of bureaucratic democracy—to see how this politico-administrative arrangement works. I will look at how it functions administratively, at how democratic it is, and most important, at the relationship between its administrative and democratic features.

The Neglect of Bureaucracy in American Democratic Theory

Given the contemporary importance of bureaucracy, it is surprising to find how little attention was paid to the administrative side of government either by the first designers of our political order or by more recent democratic theorists. As James Q. Wilson has written,

> The founding fathers had little to say about the nature or function of the executive branch of the new government. The Constitution is virtually silent on the subject and the debates in the Constitutional Convention are almost devoid of reference to an administrative apparatus. This reflected no lack of concern about the matter, however. Indeed, it was in part because of the founders' depressing experience with chaotic and inefficient management under the Continental Congress and the Articles of Confederation that they assembled in Philadelphia.[1]

Administration was recognized as an issue in the earliest days of the republic. It was simply deemed less important than the broad questions of constitutional design facing the Convention, and thus the Founding Fathers gave it only fleeting attention.

James Madison, for example, appeared to consider the problem of administration as part of the general problem of how to check and balance power in a democracy. The notion of pitting one administrative structure against another in the interests of the citizen's liberty appears in Federalist 46, where Madison argues that healthy conflicts may arise between state and federal governments—the one offsetting and balancing the other.

The matter of administration appears to have aroused two conflicting sentiments in Alexander Hamilton. On the one hand, Hamilton was manifestly in favor of creating an energetic presidency.

Much of his writing in Federalist 70 and 72 is devoted to that objective. As he put it, "Energy in the Executive is a leading character in the definition of good government."[2] But that is not an especially lofty theory of government. It turns, at least in the *Federalist*, on the advantages of having a single executive, of giving that executive the clear power to appoint his major administrators, and of allowing that executive to serve more than one term. Hamilton's concern is largely with creating a viable presidency. His comments on the general conduct of administration are brief and perfunctory. On the other hand, Hamilton was also mindful, in the Madisonian spirit, of the advantage of balancing one level of government against another to prevent abuses of executive power. It is particularly significant to find this concern for administrative checks and balances in the writings of such an advocate of a strong presidency and a centralized administration.

Another strand of early American political thought appears in the work of Thomas Jefferson, who emphasizes democratic processes above all and treats administration as a political stepchild. Jefferson believed that in a republic, especially in his "little republics," citizens should bear a great part of the administrative burdens of the state. This view collapses the problem of administration and bureaucracy into the prior and fundamental problem of democracy—how to manage democratic procedures to establish popular control.

As any student of American government knows, Jefferson wanted to implement his democratic vision by relying on decentralized limited governments. He envisioned the system of federalism as a chain of governments building up from the smallest unit, the level at which citizens conducted their own affairs, to the national government. As Lynton Caldwell has written,

> Jefferson believed that a federal organization of the state was the way to combine public strength with individual freedom. He described a graduation of authorities, the elementary republics, the state republics, and the Republic of the Union forming a comprehensive political system. Good government, he declared, was effected not by the consolidation or concentration of powers but by their distribution, each division of the country to do for itself what concerns itself directly.

In Jefferson's dictum, "Were we directed from Washington when to sow and when to reap, we should soon want bread."[3]

As should be plain from the above, Jefferson was in no way a positive theorist of administration. His views ranged from a hostility to centralized administration to a considerable skepticism about the importance of the administrative enterprise. He declared himself in favor of a "government rigorously frugal and simple," and added, "I think, myself, that we have more machinery of government than is necessary, too many parasites living on the labor of the industrious."[4] With adjustments for modern vernacular, these words might well have been spoken by any one of numerous American politicians in recent years, including a latter-day southern president.

More important, Jefferson seriously doubted whether administration would prove to be much of a practical problem in his democratic republic: "The accounts of the United States ought to be, and may be made as simple as those of a common farmer, and capable of being understood by common farmers." As Caldwell puts it, Jefferson believed that "there are no mysteries in public administration." Or in Jefferson's words, "The ordinary affairs of a nation offer little difficulty to a person of any experience."[5]

Of course, in the early stages of the republic, administration was a very small undertaking — and thus perhaps easy to overlook. There were only about three thousand appointed civilian officials at the end of the Federalist period.

Even if the Founding Fathers do not seem to have recognized bureaucracy as a problem, we might expect to find such a recognition in more recent writings on democracy. In the period since World War II, American governmental theory has been dominated by the concept of pluralist democracy. The writers who have developed this concept, like the Founding Fathers, treat bureaucracy as a fairly inconspicuous feature of our political system.

In *The Governmental Process*, one of the first postwar studies of pluralism, David Truman depicts a political society characterized by competition and compromise among governmental and non-governmental interest groups. In Truman's buoyant portrait, the American political world is composed of myriad groups balancing and checking each other as they press their claims on government. This government by energetic factionalism is a positive version of Madison's more negative concern for pitting faction against faction to ensure liberty. As Truman puts it, "The behaviors that constitute the process of government cannot be adequately understood apart from the groups, especially the organized and potential interest groups."[6]

What are the roles of government and bureaucracy in the context of group pluralism? According to Truman, "government functions to establish and maintain a measure of order in the relationship between groups." Specifically, government provides a "multiplicity of points of access" for interest groups seeking to influence public policy. In this account, the role of bureaucracy simply reflects this basic function of the government as a whole. "The executive branch of government in the United States normally exhibits a diffusion of leadership and a multitude of points of access comparable to that in the legislature . . . Dispersed leadership and multiple points of control within one branch reflect and reinforce similar patterns in the other." From Truman's perspective, the bureaucracy falls within the confines of the normal processes of group pluralism. Congress, the presidency, the bureaucracy, all are mutually reinforcing actors in the political system.[7]

The view that bureaucracy is just another part of the ordinary American political process is also stated clearly by Robert Dahl, undoubtedly the most influential modern contributor to the doctrine of pluralist democracy. After rigorously dissecting the democratic theories of Madison and Jefferson, Dahl presents an American hybrid that extends Truman's optimism about group pluralism and points of access. He defines the "normal" American political process as "one in which there is high probability that an active and legitimate group in the population can make itself heard effectively at some crucial stage in the process of decision." Government again provides needed points of access. In Dahl's words, "When I say that a group is heard 'effectively' I mean more than the simple fact that it makes a noise; I mean that one or more officials are not only ready to listen to the noise but expect to suffer in some significant way if they do not placate the group, its leaders, or its most vociferous members." On the same page, Dahl defines the bureaucracy as part of the normal political process.

The subsequent growth of bureaucratic organizations under the nominal control of the President or of President and Congress together has been powerfully shaped by the legacy of Congressional government and the political habits and outlooks it gave rise to. In the context of decentralized bargaining parties and a decentralized bargaining legislature, it was perhaps inevitable that despite the powerful efforts of many Presidents and the somewhat Utopian yearnings of many administrative reformers, the vast apparatus that grew up to administer the affairs of the American welfare state is a decentralized bargaining bureaucracy. This is merely another way of saying that the bureaucracy has become a part of what earlier I called the "normal" American Political Process.[8]

As far as Truman and Dahl are concerned, there is no apparent reason to single out bureaucracy for special consideration and analysis. It is just one element among many in the normal political process.

One writer in the pluralist tradition who does accord a distinctive quality to bureaucracy is Charles E. Lindblom. In *The Intelligence of Democracy*, Lindblom describes a decisionmaking process characterized by partisan mutual adjustment. This sounds very much like decisionmaking by decentralized bargaining as presented by Truman and Dahl. Lindblom does recognize, however, that there are important structural limitations to the bargaining process. He sees bureaucracies as an integral part of the process of partisan mutual adjustment, but he also points out that bureaucracies possess authority over particular areas of policymaking, and that the use of governmental authority is a different process from mutual adjustment: "Each agency possesses and employs governmental authority over some participants in the governmental process (officials, agencies, non-official leaders, citizens), restricted and specialized, however, to its policy-making area . . . mutual adjustment is not a contest of naked power, but a ritualized process in which the principal counter is authority."[9] This emphasis on mutual adjustment places Lindblom squarely within the pluralist tradition, but his recognition of bureaucratic authority raises a new dimension and calls for a particular scrutiny of bureaucracy.

The theory of pluralist democracy envisions a political model in which there are multiple centers of power, which bargain and compromise in a way that represents myriad interests and produces decisions that are acceptable to many such interests. A central question, therefore, is whether bureaucracies should be viewed as just another center of power in the normal political process of bargaining and compromise. Obviously I do not think so. But this is not a matter of simple assertion.

The relationship between bureaucracy and democracy is not a completely unattended subject. There is a large corpus of literature on the problem of how to control bureaucratic activities in a democratic society. Writers such as Charles Hyneman, Carl Friedrich, and Herbert Finer have made significant contributions. More recently, Vincent Ostrom has thoughtfully raised matters of bureaucratic theory as they relate to democratic governance.[10] My point is that the problem of bureaucracy has not often been placed squarely within the tradition of American democratic theory. To do so requires theoretical accounts of both bureaucracy and democracy and an assessment of their interrelationship. Providing such accounts and such an assessment is the task of this analysis.

2

The Rise of Bureaucratic Democracy

THE FOUNDING FATHERS played the role of architects of an entire government. Their first task was to choose from among competing political values the values they wished to emphasize in their new nation. Then they had to design a structure for their government: a set of institutions that would support the values they had chosen.

Any group considering possible reforms of American government today faces the same tasks. First they must select some set of values around which they wish to build their structure, and define what they mean by those values. To do this, they must develop a conceptual model—however simple—of their objectives. This model will guide them in designing institutional arrangements to bring about their desired ends.

Questions of value are seldom straightforward. One reformer might decide, for example, that democracy is the most important value in American government. But democracy how understood? Someone else might declare that the government should be devoted to advancing equality. But what kind of equality, and for whom? Others might value efficiency in government above all, or personal liberty, or justice. The list could go on. These concepts, however, have vague and debatable meanings, and once they are defined they are likely to conflict with one another.

Governmental reformers operating today have opportunities that were not open to the Founding Fathers. They can assess how far past objectives were achieved and how institutional arrangements actually worked to fulfill their purposes. They can also learn whether political values and objectives have changed over time and whether institutions have shifted in character from their original design. Present-day architects of government not only can read historical blueprints of institutional forms but also can look at the evolution of particular objectives and institutions. For example, as we saw in Chapter 1, there was little bureaucracy at the founding of the American republic. Today there is a large bureaucracy, and many observers suspect that it is becoming increasingly powerful. Many suspect also that it is often ineffective. The question for present-day architects is: How did we get from there to here? More precisely, what were the predominant values and objectives, institutional arrangements, and evolutionary patterns that accompanied the rise of bureaucratic democracy?

Pluralist Democracy and Administrative Efficiency

An examination of American public policy in recent decades might well focus on the conflict between the values of equality and liberty in the formation of public policy. That conflict might prove to be the touchstone for understanding the direction that the government has taken in a large number of policy arenas, such as education, welfare, and tax policy.

But I believe that the best way to understand the design of American governmental institutions is to pay primary attention to two other normative concepts: pluralist democracy and administrative efficiency. It should come as no surprise that concepts like democracy and efficiency appear on a list of guiding concerns for government operations. Democracy, however defined, is a cardinal political virtue in most Western societies, and efficiency is a main virtue in any managerial or administrative setting.

So it makes sense to put democracy and efficiency high on our list of guiding objectives for American government and to assert that government should be *both* democratic and efficient. The problem is that the particular American understanding of democracy and administrative efficiency causes the two objectives to come sharply into conflict, and this conflict creates deep-seated disagreements about the design of institutions.

In order to understand the "bureaucracy problem," we must

examine the ways earlier designers of government attempted to re-
concile democracy and efficiency — that is, to create an efficient
administrative system within a democratic political order. Two conceptual models will be useful: the model called pluralist democracy,
and that called administrative efficiency. Obviously, democracy
and efficiency can be defined in various ways — so many indeed that
an ingenious analyst could undoubtedly produce many different
relationships between them, depending on their initial definitions.
The two models discussed here reflect only the conceptions of two
groups of designers and reformers of American governmental institutions.

The first group, the theorists of pluralist democracy, includes
some of the Founding Fathers, namely Madison and Jefferson, along
with Tocqueville and a more recent analyst, Robert Dahl. The second group of government designers is a more eclectic one and includes Woodrow Wilson and many more recent contributors to the
literature of administration. Their conception of how American
government ought to work and how it should be structured is captured in the model of administrative efficiency. It is important to
realize that the advocates of pluralist democracy and administrative
efficiency have not merely been academic analysts of government.
Both groups have had a significant effect on the shaping of our institutions. This is obvious in the case of the Founding Fathers, but it is
also true that the proponents of administrative efficiency have had a
major impact on the design of American bureaucracy.

The Pluralist Democracy Model

Pluralist democracy provided the initial design of our political order
at the time when the Founding Fathers sought to realize their values
in particular institutions. The conceptual model of pluralist democracy is based on the role of multiple centers of governmental power
and multiple interest groups in the political process. It provides that
government should and will offer groups an opportunity for direct
involvement in democratic decisionmaking. As one Madisonian
scholar, Andrew Hacker, has put it, "If [Madison] acknowledged
that political power must be used to regulate the activities of groups
in the society, he also wanted groups to have a positive role in making governmental policy. In other words, groups must not only be

regulated, they will also be represented in the government of the republic." This appraisal of Madison squares with Dahl's analysis of American pluralism at the point where Dahl speaks of the high probability in the normal American political process that "an active and legitimate group in the population can make itself heard effectively at some crucial stage in the process of decision." In addition, this positive view is echoed by David Truman's belief, noted in Chapter 1, that government will provide multiple "points of access" for various group interests.[1]

This positive view of group pluralism is less familiar than Madison's desire to create a governmental system of checks and balances in which factions would be effectively controlled. On this account, we have the same field of groups pursuing their interests, but the issue is given a negative complexion. Madison is drawn to the divison of institutional and political power to ensure that "ambition counteract ambition" and thereby bring about a balance of power (and prevent a possibly oppressive concentration of power).

Madison makes his point in the following language:

> To what expedient then shall we finally resort, for maintaining in practice the necessary partition of power among the several departments, as laid down in the Constitution? The only answer that can þe given is that as all these exterior provisions are found to be inadequate, the defect must be supplied, by so contriving the interior structure of the government as that its several constituent parts may, by their mutual relations, be the means of keeping each other in their proper places.

And further:

> The great security against a gradual concentration of the several powers in the same department consists in giving to those who administer each department the necessary constitutional means and motives that resist encroachments of others.[2]

Another key proposition in the conceptual model of pluralist democracy relates again to the hoped-for system of checks and balances and concerns the role of federalism in taming power in the American system. Madison was careful to note that "the proposed constitution is, in strictness, neither a national nor a federal constitution but a combination of both."[3] He made this point to assure state officials and citizens whose primary allegiance was to the state that the new constitution had provided a center of power (the state governments) through which their local interests would be articulated. State government would reinforce the dispersion of power and create an additional mechanism for balancing power centers. In short, Madison linked a vertical fragmentation of power to a horizontal fragmentation of power among the branches of national government to further ensure that it would be very hard to seize, concentrate, and abuse power in the new republic.

Tocqueville strongly approved of this emphasis on decentralized administration and added importantly to this strand of pluralist democracy. In his account, "In the American townships, power has been disseminated with admirable skill, for the purpose of interesting the greatest number of people in the common weal. Independently of the voters, who are from time to time called into action, the power is divided among innumerable functionaries and officers."[4]

The other proposition in the conceptual model of pluralist democracy is that the social and economic diversity of our nation will make it difficult to concentrate and abuse political power. On this point Madison and Dahl are in strong agreement. According to Madison, the society itself will be "broken into so many parts, interests, and classes of citizens, that the rights of individuals of the minority will be in little danger from interested combinations of the majority." According to Dahl's view of pluralism:

> The making of governmental decision is not a majestic march of great majorities united upon certain matters of basic policy. It is the steady appeasement of relatively small groups . . . For to an extent that would have pleased Madison enormously, the numerical majority is incapable of undertaking any co-ordinated action. It is the various components of the numerical majority that have the means for action.[5]

In sum, the model of pluralist democracy presents the following main propositions: (1) Governmental authority is and ought to be divided within the national government and between national and local governments; power is thereby dispersed and concentrations of power are prevented. (2) Government will actively seek to facilitate the representation of group interests and by virtue of its divided structure will provide multiple points of access to such groups. (3) American politics is composed of a mosaic of competing social interests. (4) American government and politics can therefore be best understood as a competition among minority interests. (5) The competition among governmental institutions and nongovernmental interest groups leads to bargaining and compromise and produces, it is hoped, a rough balance of power in the society. As Dahl puts it, "it is a markedly decentralized system; perhaps in no other national political system in the world is bargaining so basic a component of the political process." In a statement that foreshadows the tensions about governmental design, Dahl continues: "In an age when the efficiencies of hierarchy have been re-emphasized on every continent, no doubt the normal American political system is something of an anomaly, if not, indeed, at times an anachronism."[6] It follows from the above propositions that the pluralist process will be an open and participatory one—especially from the vantage point of citizens and interest groups, but also for different cadres of public officials.

A corollary theme is that if American bureaucracy is a normal part of the pluralist model, it constitutes, as Dahl indeed states, a "decentralized bargaining bureaucracy."[7] On a strong interpretation of this logic, bureaucracy would (1) present multiple centers of power (by means of which concentrations of power would be checked), (2) facilitate the representation of interest groups by providing multiple points of access (especially to minority interests), (3) have strong elements of decentralization, (4) be internally competitive, (5) be open and participative, (6) produce widespread bargaining. A weaker interpretation of the pluralist model would be that bureaucracy displays some but not all of these structural design characteristics or that it displays these basic characteristics but less strongly. In developing a portrait of the political behavior of bureaucracies in Chapter 3, I will attempt to determine how closely actual, observable bureaucratic functioning fits the pluralist model.

There is one further point to be made about the normative character of the pluralist model of the American political order: a far-reaching suspicion of power and especially of executive power. As Bernard Bailyn has shown, the American colonists' experience of British rule and their perception of tyranny in other countries led to a negative view of political power. According to Bailyn,

Most commonly the discussion of power centered on its essential characteristic of aggressiveness; its endlessly propulsive tendency to expand itself beyond legitimate boundaries. In expressing this central thought, which explained more of politics, past and present, to them than any other single consideration, the writers of the time outdid themselves in verbal ingenuity. All sorts of metaphors, similes, and analogies were used to express this view of power. The image most commonly was that of the act of trespassing.

James Q. Wilson underscores this early distaste for executive and administrative power in more concrete terms:

> What made political authority problematic for the colonists was the extent to which they believed Mother England had subverted their liberties . . . The evidence of usurpation is now familiar: unjust taxation, the weakening of the independence of the judiciary, the stationing of standing armies, and the extensive use of royal patronage to reward office-seekers at colonial expense. Except for the issue of taxation, which raised for the colonists major questions of representation, almost all of their complaints involved the abuse of *administrative* powers.[8]

The upshot of this reaction is that the American political executive began life under a considerable pall. Governors and mayors were given deliberately small powers and virtually no mandate to govern. The pluralist emphasis on representativeness led a strong value to be placed on legislative control, political competition, partisan elections (for everything from president to dog catcher), interest-group activity, political appointments, and other forms of popular involvement in government.

Although not every writer in the pluralist tradition, from Madison to Dahl, offers exactly the same theory of democracy, I believe that the central themes in the tradition add up to a coherent model of government. A further question is: How distinctive is the model of pluralist democracy? At the level of formal structural differences, the pluralist design can be easily distinguished from political systems that Dahl terms "hegemonic," which are characterized by a concentration of power and authority in a single center. These systems typically do not have free elections or party competition.[9] Such regimes may be monarchies, military dictatorships, theocracies, or communist systems with power concentrated in a ruling central committee (for example, the Soviet Politburo). At another level of structural difference, the design of explicitly divided power is easy to distinguish from parliamentary systems that make executive leadership dependent on majority control in the legislative branch. A governmental design like DeGaulle's Fifth Republic might appear to resemble the pluralist design more closely than most other systems; but even in this case the larger powers granted to the president — giving rise to what has often been termed "plebiscitary democracy" — violate the pluralist design's concern to balance and check power and its fear of concentrated power, especially strong executive power.

The pluralist design is also easily distinguishable from "corporatist" structures in which the state charters certain nongovernmental institutions, such as the church, trade unions, or corporations, to exercise authority in their functional domains. In Philippe Schmitter's definition:

> Corporatism can be defined as a system of interest representation in which the constituent units are organized into a limited number of singular, compulsory, noncompetitive, hierarchically ordered and functionally differentiated categories, recognized or licensed (if not created) by the state and granted a deliberate representational monopoly.[10]

This definition of corporatism, as found in various Latin American and Iberian states as well as in earlier historical versions, violates the pluralist design's concern with the competition between governmental and nongovernmental groups and with opening government to a wide range of interest groups (by offering multiple points of access in government). In short, the pluralist design can be distinguished from most other recognizable political systems by the use of a small number of simple structural distinctions.

This is not to assert that there can never be multiple centers of power or, more simply, even multiple competitors for power in nonpluralist systems. We have already seen that multiple centers of power are designed to exist in certain corporatist structures but are designed to be noncompetitive and indeed heavily controlled by the main center of power, the state. To take a recent example, organized interests in Mao's China, including the bureaucracy, the military, and the professoriat, apparently sought a degree of autonomy as institutional power centers. If successful they would have increased the level of de facto political pluralism in China. Mao bitterly fought these efforts, and it would be difficult to view the ensuing Cultural Revolution as an endorsement of or a triumph for pluralism. In addition, it is easy to find examples of opposition parties trying to mobilize in one-party states or labor unions or newspapers attempting to establish freedom of association or of expression in systems designed not to permit such freedoms. There is also recurrent discussion of movement toward political pluralism — especially in terms of organized interest groups — in certain Eastern European states. But what is interesting about this nascent pluralism is precisely that it is seeking to emerge in the face of explicitly nonpluralist or antipluralist governmental designs.

At the level of ordinary political competition, the absence of an explicitly pluralist design certainly does not prevent political conflict among individuals, factions, cabals, and so forth. Palace intrigues and infighting, coups, disputes between emperors and their advisers, generals, or bishops, and competition among bureaucratic officials are the essential stuff of political history, observed as long as anyone has bothered to write about politics. We can safely assume that such de facto political competition will always exist. The central point about the pluralist design is that it makes multiple centers of power and the competition and bargaining that they create an explicit de jure foundation of its governmental architecture.

Adding in the pluralist emphasis on decentralized government and decentralized bargaining makes it possible to distinguish pluralist democracy even more sharply from other political systems. Although a variety of political systems do contain some elements of federalism, defined as the decentralization of power and functional authority to subnational units, few have decentralized extensive power and authority. And few combine this vertical division of power with a deliberate horizontal division and separation of power at the national level. Moreover, at the subnational level in the pluralist design, the horizontal pattern of divided power between executive and legislatures still obtains — adding still more dimensions of competition and bargaining. The horizontal and vertical dimensions of the pluralist design together add up to a structure that may not only be anomalous, as Dahl puts it, but is, I believe, highly distinctive. Considering, finally, the array of competitive interest groups and bureaucracies at all levels makes the design even more distinctive.

The full blueprint for pluralist democracy is depicted in table 2.1. Taken on its face, this map indicates a great number of different power centers and suggests an extraordinarily intricate and multi-dimensional pattern of competition and bargaining. Again assuming no discrepancy between theory and practice, Dahl's observation seems justified: "perhaps in no other national political system in the world is bargaining so basic a component of the political process."

Some Questions about Pluralism

It is important not to accept this relatively simple model of the pluralist design for government at face value. A mere glance at table 2.1 might suggest that pluralism must be an impossibly complex

Table 2.1 A blueprint of American pluralism.

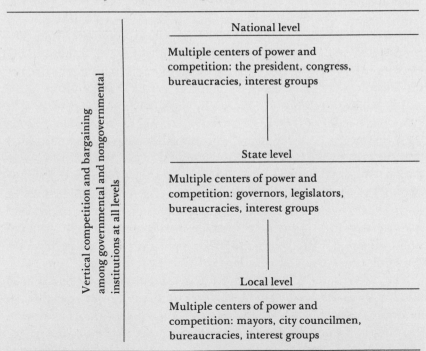

and interactive political system. It is obvious that not all of the multiple power centers—the president, the Congress, numerous national bureaucracies, fifty states, thousands of local governments (and their own numerous bureaucracies), and hundreds if not thousands of different interest groups—could or would compete and bargain on every given issue. Bargaining on such a scale is plainly impossible, although different subsets of bargainers might well be linked vertically and horizontally across the system. The question is how many centers of power must compete and bargain on any given policy issue to fit the pluralist design. Two, ten, twenty? A more practicable way of describing the pluralist design is to say that the policymaking process is divided into numerous policy arenas, each containing multiple centers of power and displaying competitive bargaining behavior. This arrangement would obviously check absolute concentrations of power but would not necessarily ensure competition and bargaining in the system as a whole or satisfactory "balanced" outcomes of bargaining for most groups and especially minority interests.

The question of how to ensure that the system as a whole is characterized by competition and bargaining brings up an important problem of appraisal and evaluation. What if stable alliances develop among separate power centers in a particular arena? If a legislative committee allies with one interest group against another, or if a bureaucracy establishes mutually supportive relationships with some but not all of the interest groups seeking to press their claims, then the bargaining feature of the pluralist design is undermined and the existence of multiple centers of power within multiple policy arenas will not fully satisfy the pluralist design. In such a case, as various critics have pointed out, the *appearance* of a vast pluralist bargaining system and a multiring circus of policy arenas might well mask many noncompetitive arrangements: perhaps an array of small oligopolies or even monopolies within the overall policymaking structure.

The question of how to ensure balanced outcomes of bargaining also brings up difficult analytical issues. The notions of competition and bargaining, tightly bound up with the core pluralist notion of dividing and checking power, can be interpreted in various ways, and the simple model of pluralism does not give us many precise clues to interpretation. One obvious interpretation of the intended relationship of multiple centers of power to the bargaining process is that no gross imbalance should exist in bargaining outcomes such that, for example, group A receives 95 units of the good that is being allocated, group B 3 units, and group C 2 units (or for that matter that group A receives all 100 units). In many pluralist writings the idea of bargaining is linked to notions of balance and equilibrium. For example, Arthur Bentley speaks, albeit inelegantly, of "equilibriation," John Kenneth Galbraith refers to "countervailing power," and V. O. Key describes the pluralist politician as a weigher and juggler of group claims.[11] But what does the idea of balance require? Equal outcome in aggregate so that groups A, B, and C receive exactly the same amounts? Or equal division at the margin so that groups A, B, and C each receive one new unit, even if they previously possessed 70, 40, and 3 units respectively? In the former case, the test of bargaining is quite strict. In the latter case, the test of bargaining is quite weak since group C, though better off than before with the additional crumb achieved in bargaining, still stands in sad comparison with groups A and B which already own fairly large cakes (plus their new crumbs). Again, considering only bargains at the margin, what if group C receives a smaller share than groups A and B in two-third of the bargains struck over a period of time?

Finally, what if different policy arenas, each with its multiple contestants, contain vastly different quantities of whatever units are being allocated? Imagine that the pluralist players in policy arena A — be they governments or nongovernmental organizations — are competing and bargaining over 500 units of allocation, whereas the contestants in policy arena B are bargaining over only 50 units of allocation. Given this disparity, and assuming the same number of contestants per arena, contestants in policy arena A would consistently tend to receive more units of allocation than contestants in policy arena B. In this case, the existence of multiple centers of power and multiple policy arenas would again disguise systematic and substantial inequalities in the bargaining process. In sum, the question arises whether, if certain bargainers frequently receive a consistently smaller marginal share than their competitors or if some bargainers play for very small stakes as compared to contestants in other arenas, the pluralist norms concerning bargaining and balance are fulfilled. How strong, weak, or elastic are the structural specifications of the pluralist design in the first place?

Another question, which will be addressed in Chapter 3, is how, if at all, the structure of public bureaucracies fits into the pluralist design. After all, hierarchically structured bureaucracies are not instantly thought of as pluralist bargainers. In fact Dahl alludes to the appeal of the "efficiencies of hierarchy," a presumed feature of bureaucracy, as a powerful rival to the virtues of decentralized bargaining processes.

Every design for government has its disadvantages and limitations, including the model of pluralist democracy with its deliberate emphasis on representativeness and on fragmenting government institutions to curb concentrations of power. The Founders' design for a pluralist, representative republic quickly encountered two sorts of difficulties in later political experience. The first problem was that the doctrine of representativeness and political control of government permitted other kinds of abuse of power, particularly by political factions that used political office to reward loyal followers. This abuse was apparent, for example, in the depredations of the big-city machines in the nineteenth century, which used patronage resources to build impressive political empires. The other difficulty was that a republic designed to be divided was a government difficult to govern. The executive or administrative leader was the head of only one branch of government. Could the president be a uniting and coordinating force? Hamilton, early on, recognized the confusion that was created by the pluralist design and initiated the practice of having the president submit bills to the Congress, a practice not envisioned in the original design (with its emphasis on the primacy of representative legislatures).

The Administrative Efficiency Model

It is in part as a response to these apparent defects in pluralism that the model of administrative efficiency came into being. This model of governance stresses a different set of values and objectives and stands in almost direct opposition to the model of pluralist democracy. I should indicate how I use the term "efficiency," because it is a loaded word. It would be hard to find many citizens who would come out in favor of *inefficiency* on its merits. In discussing the conceptual model of administrative efficiency as it is found in American political ideas, I do not wish to assert that this model is necessarily the most efficient, or indeed that it is necessarily efficient at all. Rather, I wish to describe a model that, like pluralist democracy, was designed by its architects to produce what they considered to be the proper sort of government for the American political system. The question of whether the model of pluralist democracy is necessarily "democratic" or that of administrative efficiency necessarily "efficient" will be discussed later.

There have been many reform movements in American government. Many of these have had in common an intent to make public decisions on something other than a political basis—whether that calls for nonpartisan elections, experts, bureaucrats, city managers, or the merit system in government appointments. The negative case for concentrating on administrative efficiency is that pluralist democracy has failed to provide rational, objective decisionmaking or strong executive or administrative leadership and that it has been susceptible to political abuses of various sorts. But the case for administrative efficiency is not just negative; it is based on strong beliefs about how a government ought to be run under any conditions. The model of administrative efficiency is not merely a reaction to perceived problems with democracy; it carries a long history of fervent commitment to notions of "good," energetic, and professional government.

The doctrine of administrative efficiency begins with a celebration of the word "efficiency" itself; its elevation to the position of primary administrative value. For Woodrow Wilson, administration involves the discovery "of what government can properly and successfully do, and, secondly, how it can do these proper things with the utmost possible efficiency and at the best possible cost either of money or of energy." Summarizing the early movement to efficiency in public administration and among government reformers, Dwight Waldo observed: "It is yet amazing what a position of dominance 'efficiency' assumed, how it waxed until it had assimilated or overshadowed other values, how men and events came to be degraded or excelled according to what was assumed to be its dictate. It became a movement, a motif of Progressivism, a 'Gospel.' "[12]

Wilson and other contributors to the doctrine of administrative efficiency were clearly impressed by what they took to be the efficient methods of business and industry. Wilson wanted administration in government to be "businesslike." Hence his famous observation:

> The field of administration is a field of business. It is removed from the hurry and strife of politics; it at most points stands apart even from the debatable ground of constitutional study. It is a part of political life only as the methods of the counting-house are a part of the life of society; only as machinery is part of the manufactured product.

Much has been made of the fact that this observation appears to draw a sharp distinction between the realms of politics and administration. It is perceived by many scholars to provide a foundation for the much maligned dichotomy between politics and administration. Indeed, Wilson goes on to say, "Administrative questions are not political questions. Although politics sets the tasks for administration, it should not be suffered to manipulate its offices."[13]

I read these comments as being more normative than descriptive, for at other points Wilson notes the practical difficulty of administering government in a democracy where there are so many different voices. What Wilson offers, I believe, is a vision and a doctrine of administration, not an empirical account. His vision is of a model of administration in which efficiency is the guiding objective and certain institutional features are required for the sake of efficiency.

If we see Wilson as presenting primarily a normative model, then we need not worry much about whether he was naive in believing politics to be empirically separable from administration. The point is that Wilson thought politics *ought* to be separated from administration; in his view, "administration lies outside the *proper* sphere of politics."[14] For Wilson, efficient administration is and ought to be like a business, a countinghouse. Administration requires the same institutional qualities as business: autonomy, centralized authority, objective rationality, professionalism, and so forth. The reason that the normal workings of the political process are not compatible with this normative model of administrative efficiency is that the political (and democratic) world has very different normative concerns, such as a balancing of many diverse interests.

Wilson's essay on administration points up the conflict between the models of pluralist democracy and administrative efficiency. The implication is that if you wish to organize a polity around the principles of pluralist democracy you adopt one kind of institutional design, and if you want to organize a government around the doctrine of administrative efficiency you follow a quite different institutional design. Recall, for example, that pluralist writers display a skeptical if not hostile view of power and design their institutions to prevent concentrations of power. By contrast, Wilson sees power as necessary for achieving efficient administration: "large powers and unhampered discretion seem to me the indispensable conditions of [administrative] responsibility . . . There is no danger in power, if only it be not irresponsible."[15]

A related theme in Wilson's essay, again directly opposed to the pluralist model, is that power should be strongly centralized: "If [power] be divided, dealt out in shares to many, it is obscured; and if it is obscured, it is made irresponsible." Wilson was highly critical of the doctrine of checks and balances: "those checks and balances have proved mischievous just to the extent to which they have succeeded in establishing themselves in realities." Other scholars who support doctrine of administrative efficiency also emphasize centralization of power in the executive. The President's Committee on Administrative Management, for example, reporting in 1937, in discussing its "canons of efficiency," urged the strengthening of the chief executive and his lines of command to make the president "the center of energy, direction and administrative management."[16] Various waves of urban and state government reformers have also recommended the centralization of power in governors and mayors as a way of increasing government efficiency.

A final theme in Wilson's writings on administration is that, quite apart from relying entirely on group pluralism to carry out the work of government, he placed substantial importance on the role of expert civil servants, civil servants who would be "prepared by a special schooling and drilled . . . in a perfected organization, with an appropriate hierarchy and characteristic discipline."[17]

In addition to concentrated power and strong executive leadership, there are a number of other design features in the general model of administrative efficiency in government.

Merit Appointments

It has been an article of faith in the movement for administrative efficiency, since Wilson's time that government officials should be selected on the basis of competence and protected both at the appointment stage and thereafter from the vagaries of politics. This emphasis arose, in large part, as a reaction against the abuse of patronage power. It led to the development of the Civil Service system and to the creation of independent boards and commissions designed to be controlled by professional, nonpartisan administrators concerned with "efficient" management and insulated from the political process. Herbert Kaufman aptly calls this feature of institutional design "the quest for neutral competence":

> And at every level, reformers began to cast around for new governmental machinery that would provide a high level of responsible government service while avoiding the high costs of unalloyed representative mechanisms. Thus began the quest for neutral competence in government officials, a quest which has continued to the present day. The core value of this search was ability to do the work of government expertly, and to do it according to explicit objective standards rather than to personal or party or other obligations. The slogan of the neutral competence school became, "Take administration out of politics."[18]

This is a crucial aspect of institutional design, for in contrast to the doctrine of pluralist democracy, "neutral competence" gives substantial political power and authority to administrators rather than to citizens and elected officials.

Expertise and Professionalism

The efficiency model also emphasizes expertise and professionalism. This is logically the next step to take in institutional design after establishing merit appointments. First you make sure that public officials are appointed for competence, not on political grounds; this is a negative, defensive tactic, to keep out political hacks. Then, more positively, you try to enhance the caliber of government service by recruiting trained, often technically trained officials.

The drive for experts and professionals was an integral part of the early administrative efficiency movement—indeed another article of faith for generations of government reformers. At the turn of the century, as Dwight Waldo has written,

> professionalism was becoming a prominent characteristic of American life and specialization a key to prestige. Slowly at first, then with over-

whelming force, it was borne in upon those interested in administrative personnel that morality in government is not enough. That no amount of simple honesty will enable a person to keep accounts, design a bridge, or manage a business. Not only must persons not be given positions as party plunder, not only must they be honest: they must be trained and capable . . . This growing current of thought became a part of Progressivism, and upon the advent of the first great war, Science was a cult and Expert a fetish.

This belief in experts was expressed vividly by the progressive and government reformer A. Lawrence Lowell in 1915: "Democracies may be honest, they may be noble, but they cannot be efficient without experts; and without efficiency, nothing in this world can endure."[19]

The introduction of professionalism into government was not merely a fetish of fervent reformers; it filled a real need. In the nineteenth century urban public services, for example, were a rag-tag affair. Police work was performed by untrained night watchmen, fire protection was provided by unruly volunteer companies, "sanitation" was handled by scavengers, and teachers were usually patronage appointments. In this context, applying the professionalism doctrine of the efficiency model led to a complete restructuring of urban public services around the appointment of technically trained administrators who, in turn, worked to develop standards of professional conduct for their employees.

The drive for expertise and professionalism has proceeded unabated up to the present, and as a consequence the professions have come to dominate many segments of the bureaucracy. Frederick Mosher calls professionalism "the characteristic of the public service . . . which seems to me most significant today," and he adds:

Professionalism rests upon specialized knowledge, science, and rationality. There are *correct* ways of solving problems and doing things. Politics is seen as constituting negotiation, elections, votes, compromise — all carried on by subject-matter amateurs. Politics is to the professions as ambiguity to truth, expedience to rightness, heresy to true belief.[20]

If this evidence does not suffice, consider the recurrent inclination of presidents to try to improve their policymaking capability by recruiting professional advisers, as in the case of the Council of Economic Advisers, science advisory boards, and the often-discussed Council of Social Advisers.

Bureaucratic Organization

After merit appointment and professionalism, the next step in design of the administrative efficiency model was the ordering of individual activity into effective organization. The mechanism for this organization, the chosen instrument, was bureaucracy. By bureaucracy, the apostles of administrative efficiency meant merit and expertise, certainly, but merit and expertise organized in such a way as to provide for strong hierarchy and a specialization of functions.

Urban government furnishes a clear example of the attempt to use bureaucracy to improve efficiency. And again the logic of bureaucratic organization was drawn, in part, from the experience of private enterprise. In urban school systems, as Michael Katz has written,

> Schoolmen over and over again used the example of industry as an idealized standard that formed the basis for their justifications of the superintendency. They often described their school systems as factories . . . Modern industry, they could see, had developed its remarkable capacity through a rational organization that stressed hierarchy, the division of labor, and intensive professional supervision. If those methods worked in industries as diverse as textiles and railroads, why would they not work in education?[21]

The emphasis on bureaucratic organization and its hoped-for hierarchical efficiencies has not been a fleeting inspiration. According to Dahl and Lindblom, "the world of the modern American rushes headlong toward bureaucratization." As reasons for this trend they cite bureaucracy's capacity to serve as an "economizing device" in fulfilling administrative needs to coordinate large numbers of people, to make complex decisions "beyond the competence of one person to make," and to bring about "the advantages of the division of labor."[22]

Since the start of the New Deal, public officials have had an easily observable propensity, when faced with a new or complex problem, to create a new bureaucracy. When they are not creating new bureaucracies in this manner, public officials can often be observed hard at work on reorganization projects designed to improve government efficiency by improving the formal structure of bureaucracy. Given the hierarchical logic of bureaucracy, it is no surprise that such reorganization often leads to the creation of superagencies, such as the Department of Housing and Urban Development. On this logic, if bureaucracies have not produced sufficiently efficient administration, the solution is to try "bigger and better" bureaucracies. Whatever the merits of this logic, it cannot be denied that the idea of bureaucracy is a strong and persistent driving force in the administrative efficiency model.

Planning and Fiscal Management

An administrative system that provides for merit appointment, professionalism and expertise, and bureaucratic organization, also needs the tools of "efficient" administrative management. Thus another central design feature of the model of administrative efficiency is an emphasis on planning and centralized fiscal management. In this context, planning may be understood as the antithesis of short-term political accommodation and bargaining. It is an attempt systematically to develop policy alternatives and to work out a long-run strategy for governmental activity. The emphasis on planning has led to the development at the local level of research bureaus designed to provide the analytical foundations for long-range planning. At the national level there have been scores of proposals for national planning whose goal, as Otis Graham puts it, is to bring about a "planned society."[23] Most cities have city planning departments, and metropolitan and regional planning bodies have sprung up in large numbers as well. Many of the planning documents that are written may be shelved, but that does not deter advocates of the administrative efficiency model. As recently as 1975, Senators Hubert Humphrey and Jacob Javits cosponsored a bill calling for the establishment of national economic and social planning. The hope is that planning will place governmental policymaking on a rational, scientific basis and provide coherence and persistence in policy, qualities that planning advocates believe would never result from the bargaining processes of the pluralist model.

A somewhat more common feature of the administrative efficiency model is a strong reliance on techniques of centralized financial management. One such technique that was widely used in attempts to reform city governments involved financial and managerial accounting. Another involved the development of centralized budgeting systems, as in the federal Budgeting and Accounting Act of 1921. Budgeting was introduced to provide coordination and control of public expenditures, and the essence of the "budget idea" has persisted unchanged through this century. In 1906, for example, the New York Bureau of Municipal Research made budgeting proposals designed to inject "uniformity and responsibility into the fiscal tissues of the government." In a direct foreshadowing of program budgeting, as introduced in the 1960s by the Kennedy and Johnson administrations, the bureau proposed a "segregated budget" which would classify the activities of departments into integral parts.[24] This emphasis on centralized financial management has proved to be a persistent response among efficiency-oriented public managers. When Robert McNamara set out to improve decision-making in the Defense Department, he introduced systems analysis. When "efficiency experts" were called in to save New York City from fiscal crisis, their immediate response was to reorganize the city's entire accounting system. They also established an extraordinarily powerful financial control board as a way of remedying the perceived "management mess." When Jimmy Carter arrived in to Washington, he set out to implement "zero-based budgeting." Financial management reform has a remarkable capacity to reincarnate itself whenever anyone sets out to improve efficiency in government.

Strengthening the Chief Executive

The capstone of the system built on merit, professionalism and expertise, bureaucracy, and the tools of management is a powerful chief executive. The logic of the administrative efficiency model is that there must be a strong overall administrative capability to coordinate and energize the other parts of the system. This belief in the transforming powers of the chief executive has many manifestations in American administrative reform efforts of the past century. At the city and state level, it was expressed in reforms that lengthened the terms of mayors and governors and gave them executive budgets and line-item veto powers, as well as greatly increased powers to hire and fire department heads. At the federal level, efforts to strengthen the role of the president have been in evidence for forty years. Indeed, the hallmark of the "textbook presidency," which is Thomas Cronin's term for the standard picture of the presidency in recent political and historical writing, is the abiding faith in the ability of a strong president and an expanded executive office to provide focus and initiative in national policymaking. This view of the presidency was captured by the President's Committee on Administrative Management in 1937, as Kaufman points out:

> Few clearer statements of the executive leadership value than the Report . . . have ever been published, with its recommendations on pulling the administrative functions of the independent regulatory commissions back under the President, on drawing the government corporations back into the hierarchy, on bringing personnel management under close direction by the President, on strengthening the White House Staff . . . the Committee offered the classic presentation of the reorganization aspects of the executive leadership school.[25]

In the final analysis, the test of the administrative efficiency model is whether having a powerful chief executive who will harness and channel the energies of civil servants and experts in the context of a hierarchically ordered bureaucracy will increase efficiency in government. At present, the test is still under way, although some would say a full test has never been made since a pure version of the administrative efficiency model's ideal system has never been created.

Whereas pluralist democracy appears to have particularly strong roots in American experience and public values, it seems likely that most political systems would be concerned with administrative efficiency. Yet there are some distinctively American features in the combination of elements found in the administrative efficiency model. First, many societies are less concerned than the United States to "take administration out of politics." Americans seem to have a general distrust of political power or a cultural tendency to view politics as a dirty business. In many countries, bureaucrats are expected to be highly political and partisan and would not survive long if they were not. The American emphasis on professionalism is also quite distinctive. Countries like Britain and France pursue a quite different course, recruiting a corps of well-educated generalists for public service. Of course, public service has rarely conferred high social status, and the emphasis on professionalism may be seen as a way of increasing social esteem for public service and thus of making such service more attractive. The emphasis on a strong chief executive is not unique to the American experience, but it has a special force in a political contest of such widely divided governmental authority. The emphasis on strategies of efficient management has a distinctively American flavor in that these strategies, including hierarchical bureaucracy, have been influenced by a cultural glorification of private-sector experience.

Some Questions about the Efficiency Model

The elements of the administrative efficiency model seem to add up to a coherent approach to government. But there are some tensions in the model that are important to keep in mind as we consider the development of government structures—especially bureaucracies—to which the model has been applied. For example, if administrative power is to be neutral and sometimes walled off in separate commissions, how can it respond to the chief executives' political needs, and how can it be coordinated at the top? If professionals have a tendency toward autonomy and self-governance, as Mosher has argued, how can they be fitted smoothly into a strongly hierarchical bureaucracy?[26] Finally, if civil servants are given a high degree of security via the merit system, how can they be easily directed or redirected by the chief executive, who is supposed to take charge of his entire administrative system?

Public and Private Management

At this juncture, a further significant difference between the models of pluralist democracy and administrative efficiency comes more clearly into view. The pluralist model is a *political* model par excellence with its roots in constitutional theories of the state as well as in theories of liberty and rights. Its intellectual forebears include political philosophers such as Locke and Montesquieu. For points of comparison, pluralist writers typically look to the constitutional and political experience of other governments, past and present, as they explore the classic question of the relationship of the citizen to the state. The model of pluralist democracy partakes of the central and abiding concerns of democratic theory. It is concerned with the abuse of power by leaders and with devices, such as competitive elections, for establishing citizen control of leaders (what Dahl and Lindblom term "polyarchy"). It is concerned to ensure that citizens have their voices heard and their interests recorded by government in fair and open procedures of public decisionmaking. It is concerned with citizen participation in government—as a means of strengthening polyarchy and interest-group representation and because participation is believed to provide the necessary education for citizens to perform as effective political actors.

The model of administrative efficiency has quite different roots and a different angle of vision. It is in some sense a partial theory because it focuses more on the administrative process per se than on the entire politico-administrative system. It is more concerned with "government in action," in Wilson's term, than with broad constitutional design. As Wilson noted, "It is getting to be harder to run a constitution than to frame one."[27]

More important, the model of administrative efficiency bears the strong imprint of the experience of business organizations in the United States. Wilson alerts us to this fact when he calls administration "a field of business." Waldo has written of the impact of business on the concept of efficiency in government:

> The contribution of business . . . has been very great . . . Business organization, for example, and particularly the corporate firm, was used to justify the tenets of reorganization. It was used to depreciate separation and balance of powers. It was used to aggrandize the chief executive. It was used to justify hierarchy.[28]

The conflict between the models of pluralist democracy and administrative efficiency is a conflict not only between two institutional designs but also between two historical traditions. Although the traditions have very different points of origin, they do address and offer recommendations on the same issue—how best to organize a politico-administrative system. One question that arises is whether the pluralist treatment of the political system is adequate to deal with the problems of large-scale administration. The parallel question is whether the administrative efficiency model's emphasis on businesslike procedures and rational decisionmaking is adequate to deal with the problems of administration in a *political* and *democratic* setting. It is often asked what the relevant similarities and differences are between public and private management. There are many different opinions on this point. In what follows we will implicitly be required to ask whether private-sector traditions of organization and management are desirable and effective in public settings, as we consider not only the conflicts between the two models but also what problems and limitations each model, taken separately, presents for the current workings of bureaucratic democracy in America.

Pluralist Democracy and Administrative Efficiency: The Trade-Off

How serious and how unavoidable is the trade-off between pluralist democracy and administrative efficiency? I will approach this question in two ways: first in terms of conflicts between the *stated* design features of the two models and second in terms of basic *analytical* conflicts — which may or may not coincide with or confirm the apparent conflicts in design.

A first step is to summarize the main conflicts between the normative models of pluralist democracy and administrative efficiency.

1. In the pluralist model, power is dispersed and divided; in the efficiency model, power is concentrated. Related to this, in the pluralist model, governmental policymaking is decentralized; in the efficiency model, it is centralized.

2. In the pluralist model, there is a suspicion of executive power (in fact of any concentration of power); in the efficiency model, great emphasis is placed on centralizing power in the hands of the chief executive.

3. In the pluralist model, power is given to politicians, interest groups, and citizens; in the efficiency model, much power is given to experts and professional bureaucrats.

4. In the pluralist model, political bargaining and accommodation are considered to be at the heart of the democratic process: in the efficiency model, there is a strong urge to keep politics out of administration.

5. The pluralist model emphasizes individuals' and political

actors' own determination of interest and utility; the efficiency model emphasizes technical or scientific rationality (which can be better discovered by detached expert analysis than by consulting the desires of voters and politicians).

In all, at the design level, the models of pluralist democracy and administrative efficiency conflict systematically on such dimensions as centralization versus decentralization, dispersion versus concentration of power, and the allocation power to citizens and politicians versus experts and bureaucrats. But do these conflicts and trade-offs stand up analytically? Here the test is whether the conflicting design features are in basic analytical and structural opposition.

Viewed in this way, some of the trade-offs are easy to confirm. It is impossible to concentrate and disperse power simultaneously. It is impossible to centralize power in a chief executive and also curtail that power simultaneously. It is impossible to admit political bargaining into administration and at the same time to isolate politics from administration. More subtle relationships exist as well. For example, most structures of government include elements of both centralization and decentralization; hence there is no clear dichotomy in this case. Yet the pluralist emphasis on decentralization and the administrative efficiency model's emphasis on centralization clearly point in opposite directions. Similarly, it would be possible to imagine a political system in which substantial power was given to both citizens and politicians, on the one hand, and experts and bureaucrats, on the other. Yet since power is a relative commodity, the critical question is which group gains an advantage in the balance of political power. The model of pluralist democracy would give that advantage to citizens and politicians; the administrative efficiency model would give it to experts and bureaucrats. Note too that it is implicit in the idea of expertise and professionalism that professional standards be given primary emphasis over the preferences of clients (and citizens). That much we have learned from the medical profession. Thus although it is possible to imagine a political order in which individual preferences and technical rationality are both given strong weight, there comes a point when one has to choose between the two criteria. To take a caricatured example, one can build a highway along the straight line favored by engineers or according to adjustments suggested by affected neighborhoods. But one cannot build it both ways at once.

Program Planning Budgeting Systems (PPBS)

One instance in which the two models can be seen analytically to be in sharp conflict occurred in the introduction of the PPBS in the national government as a part of the Kennedy-Johnson drive for increased efficiency in public decisionmaking. In the view of pluralist democracy, budgeting is an integral part of the political process and political values should be given weight along with efficiency values. Pluralists would argue that elected officials should be the primary actors (certainly more than systems analysts) in determining desirable public expenditures. By contrast, according to the administrative efficiency model, government expenditures can and should be subjected to a rigorous benefit-cost analysis that treats expenditures on the merits of efficiency. Political considerations and interests are, on this view, an impediment to rational decisionmaking. In the pluralist model, involvement in the budgetary process is decentralized among many interest groups and political actors. In the efficiency model, the attempt is made to centralize policymaking in the hands of the president and expert analysts. Allan Schick has aptly described the conflict as one between "process politics" and "systems budgeting."[29] The central question is whether to rely on the judgment and preferences of political actors or on the findings of professional policy analysts. This is not merely a question of whose judgment one prefers; it is also a question of how decisionmaking power is allocated.

Energy Policy

A second instance of the analytical conflict between pluralist democracy and administrative efficiency is manifest in the debate over energy policy. In October 1979 the Senate voted to create an Energy Mobilization Board. In the debate over the proposal, arguments for democracy and efficiency came into sharp opposition. The proponents of the board, which was to possess unusual powers, argued on efficiency grounds that a "small elite group" was needed with "real powers to cut some red tape." A supporting argument in an anti-pluralist spirit was that "Everyone has the power to delay decisions on energy projects, and too many decision-makers are unwilling to decide." The objection to the Energy Mobilization Board was based, predictably, on the grounds of pluralist democracy. Would not such a board be "an unresponsive, untouchable, and uncontrollable power in itself"? Would it not be dangerous to permit the board to "alter federal, state, and local laws, and in some instances to act in place of federal, state, and local agencies, all in the name of the energy emergency"?[30] This conflict by no means exemplifies every struggle over government organization. But it does stand for a class of cases — a growing one, I believe — in which policymakers are faced with the complaint that government is not moving fast enough or "getting things done" on a given problem.

The Report on Administrative Management

Another instance of the conflict between the models of pluralist democracy and administrative efficiency is found in the reaction of various political actors and analysts to the report of the President's Committee on Administrative Management in 1937. We will recall that this committee hewed closely to the doctrines of administrative efficiency and, in particular, urged a strengthening of a centralized presidency as well as of the hierarchical chain of command in bureaucratic organization. The proponents of pluralist democracy reacted strongly against the committee's proposals for reorganization. A National Committee to Uphold Constitutional Government was formed which accused the efficiency-oriented reforms of being a "colossal snatch . . . for Presidential power" and a scheme to impose "one man rule" on a free people. Prominent journalists and congressmen echoed this view. Walter Lippmann warned that the reorganization plan would constitute a "rapid descent into personal government." And Bernard DeVoto, the editor of *Harper's Magazine*, claimed that the reform proposals would "destroy all the effective barriers to totalitarianism that exist."[31] Notice that these men were not discussing any attempt to invoke emergency powers for the president; they were talking about the reform of administrative organization. This makes all the intense feeling about potential executive tyranny all the more revealing.

New Haven

In actual practice, the workings of pluralist democracy often appear to interfere with and undermine the workings of administrative efficiency, and vice versa. The effects of the administrative efficiency model on pluralist democracy can be examined using the example of politics and administration in New Haven in the last two decades. Robert Dahl, who studied New Haven in the early 1960s, concluded in his landmark study, *Who Governs?*, that there was a flourishing system of pluralist democracy operating in the city. Dahl discovered multiple centers of power in New Haven and, in particular, found that different groups of political actors were active and influential in different policy arenas. He also concluded that there was an "executive-centered coalition" operating around the mayor at that time, Richard C. Lee, but that this coalition did not undermine the workings of a competitive, pluralist democracy.[32]

With this background in mind, it is instructive to trace political and institutional evolution in New Haven in the nearly twenty years since Dahl wrote about "democracy and power in an American city." One of Mayor Lee's strategies of governance was to centralize policymaking power in the mayor's office and to create new bureaucratic institutions to carry out his ambitious urban renewal and antipoverty programs. In short, Mayor Lee turned to the model of administrative efficiency, with its emphasis on centralization, bureaucracy, expertise, and planning, to provide the administrative capacity to rebuild his deteriorating city. He felt he could not rely on the existing bureaucratic structure to administer his programs.

As Phillip Singerman's recent research has shown, the consequences of this move to administrative efficiency were corrosive for pluralist democracy.[33] In the first stage, power and responsibility for policymaking flowed increasingly to the mayor's office and the bureaucracy. Lee's bureaucratic apparatus became politically and administratively dominant. During Lee's administration, the two-party system in New Haven was completely transformed. By 1969, when Lee, a Democrat, retired, there were no Republicans on the city's Board of Aldermen, and the party, which had elected a Republican mayor immediately before Lee, was in a shambles. Certainly Lee's personal popularity was a significant factor in reducing political competition in New Haven, but his bureaucracies also played a major role. For one thing, the urban renewal and antipoverty agencies produced a string of new programs, through successful grantsmanship, and these programs, especially the renewal projects, became the cornerstone of Lee's record in office. Thus the bureaucracy produced highly visible and tangible policy successes for which the mayor was able to take political credit. More important, as the renewal and antipoverty bureaucracies grew in power and responsibility they dominated an increasing sphere of policymaking in the city, so that other political actors and community groups had to come hat in hand to the bureaucracies if they wished to have any influence on renewal and antipoverty programs. In addition, Lee's administrative apparatus took on some trappings of a political machine, since the bureaucracy had a large number of benefits to bestow and jobs to fill. Many community leaders and some Republican opponents received jobs in the redevelopment agency and in Community Progress, Inc. (CPI), the antipoverty agency, and this added to Lee's political dominance of the city.

As the new bureaucracies expanded they came to be perceived by many community groups as unresponsive and remote. Organizations were formed to combat the redevelopment agency, and neighborhood corporations were created in reaction against the centralized structure of decisionmaking in CPI.[34] The centralized bureaucratic structures increasingly came to overshadow other centers of power in the city's political process. This is the imbalance, injurious to the competitive functioning of pluralism, that often seems to accompany the rise of bureaucratic democracy.

The Career of Robert Moses

Another instance of the undermining effects of the administrative efficiency model in pluralist democracy is found in the much-celebrated career of Robert Moses, New York's ambitious builder of public works.[35] There is no doubt that Moses produced an extraordinary record of achievement in constructing parks, highways, bridges, and other public facilities. To do this, he created a network of bureaucratic structures that were highly centralized under his personal leadership, highly expert with a plentiful supply of engineers and architects, and highly independent of and insulated from the normal political process. The problem with this public works empire was that as Moses's range of activities expanded, Moses and his bureaucratic structures became increasingly impervious to influence and criticism by other political actors. Governors, mayors, city councils, county boards, and neighborhood groups found themselves excluded from a substantial realm of public planning, and the competition and bargaining among such groups that would normally exist in a pluralist democracy was undermined. In short, because of the way he built his expert independent bureaucracies, Moses created a realm of silent politics in which, for the most part, the only voices that counted were his own and those of his professional bureaucrats. When Moses began to run new highways, such as the Cross-Bronx Expressway, through the centers of residential neighborhoods, the weakness of democratic participation and the absence of competing (and balancing) power centers became glaringly apparent.

The Port Authority

The structure and functioning of the Port Authority of New York and New Jersey also fit this pattern. The Port Authority was created to provide for efficient nonpolitical management of a large segment of metropolitan New York's air, land, and sea transportation systems. Though it was created by the two states, the Port Authority is heavily insulated from politics—both through the appointment of its own Board of Commissioners and through the establishment of obligations to and covenants with its bondholders. In particular, Port Authority covenants restrict the amount of debt it can legally incur on rail transit projects and thus serve to shelter the Authority from political demands that it play a greater role in providing mass transit in the area.

On the positive side, there is no doubt that the Authority runs a massive public "business" on a sound financial basis. The scale of the Authority's operation is impressive:

> The Port Authority has raised more than $3.5 billion from private investors, and it has a financial potential to raise as much as $1 billion more . . . A massive enterprise with over eight thousand employees, the authority's annual budget is larger than the operating budget of either of the state departments of transportation. Its net operating revenues were over $200 million in a bad year (1975) and rose 7 percent the next year.[36]

The price of this commitment to the administrative efficiency model is that, as with Moses, a substantial domain of public policymaking is strongly influenced by an insulated institution that does not enter into the competitive political process (or the debate about public priorities). When it comes to planning for rail transit, the governments of New York and New Jersey find that they have a substantially limited bargaining and decisionmaking position because of the Port Authority's range of independent "public" control. Governors have tried to persuade the Authority to pay attention to the public priorities of their state governments concerning the need to expand and upgrade rail transit, but the Authority has stood firm in its opposition to such projects because of their unprofitability. Frustrated, the state's legislators voted to repeal the bondholder covenants that the Authority used to avoid rail transit projects. However, the U.S. Supreme Court struck down state repeal of the covenants. The conflict between democracy and efficiency in the functioning of the Port Authority is strongly enunciated in a former New Jersey Governor's comment that Port Authority managers run it "as a business, but it is not a business."[37] That, of course, is the question at issue.

The examples of New Haven politics, Robert Moses, and the New York Port Authority suggest that the design features of centralization, expertise, and bureaucracy in the administrative efficiency model work to undermine the competitive functioning of pluralist democracy. And these examples stand for a more general class of cases in which an increase in bureaucratic power and resources has the effect of diminishing the competitive, pluralist balance in the rest of the political system.

The Undermining Process in Reverse

There are also cases in which the workings of pluralist democracy undermine the design and functioning of the administrative efficiency model. The most obvious examples are the bureaucracy and the independent regulatory commission. Recall that both the bureaucracies and the commissions were designed to stand apart from the political process. Insulation from political influence was a necessary condition of the rational, efficient, and neutral decisionmaking that these institutions were designed to produce.

This hoped-for isolation of administration from politics has not of course come to pass in actual political experience. Rather, it is plain that both bureaucracies and regulatory commissions operate in highly charged political environments in which many different interest groups routinely press their claims for available benefits and advantages. In addition, the bureaucracies and regulatory commissions often play a more active political role when they mobilize support among their constituencies, their interest-group "clients," and related congressional subcommittees in order to protect (and enhance) their institutional powers and policies. This pattern of "bureaucratic politics" is most evident in so-called clientele agencies like agriculture and labor, but this traditional American form of political bargaining has permeated bureaucratic and regulatory organizations at all levels of government.

From the perspective of the model of pluralist democracy, there is nothing objectionable in principle about interest groups lobbying and bargaining with government agencies. But the intrusion of political considerations into detached professional management is a clear violation of the administrative efficiency model. The weighing of political interests is not supposed to enter into rational decisions. This is the analytical point. But a perhaps more important criticism of bureaucracy and the regulatory commissions focuses on the close and allegedly compromising relationship between these administrative institutions and their constituent interest groups. When one or a few interest groups manage to establish such close relationships with the bureaucracy that they gain undue influence over policy decisions, both administrative efficiency and pluralist democracy are undermined.

The Two-Year Term

The impact of the pluralist democracy model on administrative efficiency is also manifest in the practice, found in many cities, of electing mayors every two years. This practice puts the mayor on a short political leash and works to increase the accountability of elected officials, which was the original intention of the two-year term of office. In this sense, it is a direct reflection of the suspicion of the chief executive in the pluralist democracy model. The consequence of this practice, in the view of generations of political reformers, is that mayors, forced to worry almost constantly about reelection, cannot perform their administrative roles as coherently and energetically as they might otherwise do. In particular, the two-year term works against the development of a professional administrative staff and the formulation of long-range programs and plans. It forces a short time-horizon on a mayor, many of whose policy problems call for a longer perspective. Two years is too short a time, for example, to deal with many problems in areas such as transportation, urban renewal, economic development, and public works, where projects tend to have long histories and where a long lead time is required to carry them out.

The same arguments can be made with some modifications in appraising the political and policymaking performance of congressmen. Faced with two-year terms, congressmen have been described as devoting themselves single-mindedly to gaining reelection. This "electoral connection," in David Mayhew's term, may well have the effect of making congressmen highly responsive to their constituents. To this extent, it enhances the political objectives of pluralist democracy concerning popular control. But at the same time, the orientation toward reelection has a deleterious effect on congressional performance in policymaking. For one thing, congressmen working on a two-year cycle have short time-horizons in thinking about the development and evolution of policy. According to Mayhew, congressmen focus on the kind of policymaking that will aid them in their quest for reelection. They emphasize activities like casework, position-taking, and symbolic proclamations that they can use as advertising back in their districts. More important, congressmen seek to deliver "particularized benefits" to their constituents. These might be new mental health centers or school lunch programs or any other programs that carry tangible benefits that can be parceled out to voters. Much of this policymaking activity may strengthen the democratic goals of representation and responsiveness (to the extent that congressmen do provide citizens with the benefits they desire). At the same time, all of those politically induced policymaking characteristics undermine the capacity of Congress as a whole to make sustained and systematic policy over time.[38] Many issues such as inflation and energy are not easily reducible to the politics of distributing particularized benefits; we can infer from Mayhew that Congress is not likely to perform effectively in those policy arenas. This inference certainly squares with recent experience.

Foreign Policy

The impact of the pluralist democracy on administrative efficiency is also found in the conduct of American foreign policy. Since World War II, decisionmaking power and responsibility in foreign policy have flowed to the president on the implicit premise that the administrative efficiency model is especially appropriate, indeed required, for dealing with fast-moving, complicated foreign policy problems. The conventional public philosophy about foreign policy is that the divided decisionmaking and the checking and balancing of pluralist democracy undermine speed in decisionmaking, unified leadership, and the need for secrecy in diplomatic activities. As Aaron Wildavsky has written, there have come to be "two presidencies":[39] most aspects of the president's job are embedded in the competitive political system of pluralist democracy, with its suspicion of centralized power, but in foreign policy we grant the president powers more congenial to the administrative efficiency model. Few would doubt that the arguments for strong presidential leadership in foreign affairs still obtain — but the underlying conflicts between the democracy and efficiency models have become far more intense in the last fifteen years. Criticisms of excessive presidential power during the Vietnam War led the Congress to reassert its democratic role in checking and overseeing presidential initiatives in foreign affairs. Similarly, criticisms of the CIA have led to proposals designed to place intelligence activities under increased public scrutiny and democratic control, again by the Congress.

Still, deep-seated tensions between the pluralist and efficiency models persist and come up over and over in policy dilemmas. For example, is it necessary for the president to conduct his Middle East diplomacy secretly in contexts like President Carter's Camp David summit? Can the government effectively negotiate a SALT Treaty with the Russians when members of the Senate begin to "get into the act"? Can a government run a competent intelligence service in the existing international environment when the work of the CIA is scrutinized by congressional committees? These questions are posed in a way that favors the values of the administrative efficiency model, but it would be just as easy to turn them around and state them in a way that emphasizes democratic values: by stressing the importance of ensuring that foreign policy decisions are not largely made outside a democracy's valued "public view" and that diverse interests are given weight in the conduct of foreign policy.

Cabinet Government

A final example of the effect of the pluralist democracy model on administrative efficiency occurs in the president's relationship with his cabinet secretaries. Several recent presidents, and most especially President Carter, proclaimed the intention to establish "cabinet government," meaning that individual cabinet secretaries and the cabinet as a whole would possess increased authority and independence. As advertised, cabinet government was designed to answer the objections of the pluralist democracy model as applied to presidential-level policymaking. Specifically, it implied greater openness in deliberations, greater representation of diverse opinions, a frank acceptance of competitive bureaucratic forces, and an intention to move from centralized White House control to greater authority and control at the departmental level. What happened was that the movement toward cabinet government also led to open disagreement and competition among cabinet officers, conflicting policy statements, and an appearance of inconsistency and disarray on the part of the administration.[40] As a consequence Presidents Nixon, Ford, and Carter concluded that cabinet government undermines orderly and coherent decisionmaking. They therefore moved to a stronger emphasis on the administrative efficiency model, centralizing policymaking power in the hands of a White House chief of staff and seeking concurrently to minimize administrative discord and competition at the cabinet level.

Whether this reaction against pluralism and in favor of the administrative efficiency model is fully warranted on the substantive merits is certainly debatable. The point to be stressed is that, in cabinet policymaking as well as in the examples given earlier, the models of pluralist democracy and administrative efficiency conflict not only in theory but also in practice. These examples do not demonstrate that the two models must *always* conflict in practice. But it is useful to see how the competing logical structures of the two models are borne out in the actual functioning of pluralist democracy and administrative efficiency.

The Problem of Governmental Design Reconsidered

Having outlined the conceptual models of pluralist democracy and administrative efficiency and the conflicts between them, we return to the central problem facing our hypothetical group of governmental designers. Is it possible to design a government that combines the features of pluralist democracy and administrative efficiency?

In the last hundred years, both positive and negative answers have been given to this question. The negative answer, which came earlier, is that there is no way to combine the values of pluralist democracy and administrative efficiency in an internally compatible governmental design. The solution then is completely to separate—to wall off—the political and administrative realms; in short, to take administration out of politics. This approach was expressed in the development of civil service systems and the creation of hundreds of independent boards and commissions at all levels of government. It also appears significantly in two other kinds of institutional design: independent regulatory commissions, and public authorities and government corporations. As Marver Bernstein has written, the regulatory commissions were created in large part to provide efficiency and expertise in decisionmaking in a setting that would be completely removed from congressional politics and interest-group influence.[41] As at the state and local level, the logic was to lock up administrative power in safety deposit vaults, where there could be no tampering with decisions presumably made on the substantive merits. The public authorities and government corporations were intended to carry out the public's business in a thoroughly "business-like" fashion—operating through the structure of a politically independent corporation. As we have seen, the New York Port Authority, with its emphasis on fiscal probity, is a classic example of this institutional design. The walled-off boards, commissions, and authorities constitute a highly pessimistic solution to the design problem of reconciling pluralist democracy and administrative efficiency. Here one value is chosen at the deliberate and complete expense of the other.

There is also a positive answer to this design dilemma, however. Throughout this century, government designers and reformers have seen in the instruments of the chief executive and the bureaucracy a way of combining the models of pluralist democracy and administrative efficiency.

Consider first the role of the chief executive. As I have noted, developing a presidency, governorship, or mayoralty with strong executive powers is the capstone of the administrative efficiency model's emphasis on centralized governmental organization. Furthermore, the proponents of the "textbook" president, governor, or mayor have argued that the chief executive—at whatever level of government—is well suited to represent a wide range of interests within a polity. The argument is that legislative branches, and the interest groups working through them, represent narrower, more segmented interests, but that the chief executive can blend and harmonize diverse interests. This argument is open to serious question, but for the moment let it stand. The point is that if the chief executive is the focus of administrative organization and simultaneously plays a central role in the resolution of interest-group conflict, then both pluralist democracy and administrative efficiency seem to be provided for in a powerful and appealing way. The only remaining conflict between the two models lies in the pluralist model's fear of concentrated power and suspicion of executives themselves. It should be plain that this suspicion, expressed in recent decades as a fear of an "Imperial Presidency," is not merely an outmoded relic of the days when Americans still had vivid and angry memories of life under a monarchy.

The second part of the positive answer to our design problem concerns the bureaucracy. Many government designers and reformers see bureaucracy as a magical way to provide for both democracy and efficiency. The origins of this solution are found in Wilson's essay on administration. Wilson believes that politics constitutes one kind of enterprise and administration another and that the two enterprises are compatible in a properly designed system. Recall Wilson's assertion: "Administrative questions are not political questions. Although politics sets the tasks for administration, it should not be suffered to manipulate its offices." The last phrase is the crucial one. Wilson believed that policy should be formulated by political actors and that administration should be a neutral instrument of implementation. The political system would handle the large questions, the administrative system the detailed ones. As Wilson put it, "The broad plans of governmental action are not administrative; the detailed execution of such plans is administrative."[42]

This means that in Wilson's envisioned politico-administrative system there would be no danger of bureaucrats (civil servants) becoming an independent class. Rather they would be responsive to politically responsible elected officials. Wilson took pains to make this point clear:

> I know that a corps of civil servants prepared by a special schooling and drilling . . . into a perfected organization, with appropriate hierarchy . . . seems to a great many very thoughtful persons to contain elements which might combine to make an offensive official class—a distinct, semi-corporate body with sympathies divorced from those of a progressive, free-spirited people, and with hearts narrowed to the meanness of a bigoted officialism. Certainly such a class would be altogether hateful and harmful in the United States.
>
> But to fear the creation of a domineering, illiberal officialism is to miss altogether the principle upon which I wish most to insist. That principle is that administration in the United States must be at all points sensitive to public opinion. A body of thoroughly trained officials serving during good behavior we must have in any case: that is a plain business necessity. But the apprehension that such a body will be anything un-American clears away the moment it is asked, What is to constitute good behavior? For that question obviously carries its own answer on its face. Steady, hearty allegiance to the policy of the government they serve will constitute good behavior. That policy will have no taint of officialism about it. It will not be the creation of permanent officials, but of statesmen whose responsibility to public opinion will be direct and inevitable.[43]

Here we have the basis of the magical resolution of democracy and efficiency. Policy and administration are separate yet related. Proper spheres are worked out so that democracy is provided by political actors and the daily operations of administration by bureaucrats.

This is, of course, the same structure proposed by those who would take administration out of politics. This dichtomy between politics and administration was given its most prominent expression in 1900 by Frank Goodnow. In Goodnow's view there are "in all governmental systems two primary or ultimate functions of government, viz. the expression of the will of the state and the execution of that will . . . These functions are, respectively, Politics and Administration." "Politics has to do with the guiding or influencing of government policy, while administration has to do with the execution of that policy."[44]

Much has been written about the dichotomy between politics and administration. Indeed, a generation of political scientists worked hard to show that there is a great deal of politics in administration (and vice versa) and that therefore one cannot distinguish the political and administrative realms as sharply or clearly as Wilson and Goodnow tried to do. Taken at face value, the dichotomy seems absurd: it implies that there could be in the empirical world two completely separate realms, one concerned with politics, the other with administration, and never the twain shall meet. This is doubtless a foolish proposition, and critics were right to show that conventional political processes pervade the world of administration.

What Wilson and Goodnow probably intended to convey, however, as Alan Altshuler usefully observes, is that there is an ideal type of administrative process (administration as efficiency) which is sharply different in character from political process (understood as democratic bargaining and group adjustment).[45] Indeed, these ideal types echo many of the themes of the models of pluralist democracy and administrative efficiency. It is important to understand that Wilson and Goodnow were writing in an essentially normative vein and recommending a particular politico-administrative system. In particular, they were offering a vision of the benign role they believed bureaucracy could play in a democracy. Their normative vision is of central importance, because it provides a theory of the relationship between bureaucracy and democratic institutions that appears to resolve many of the conflicts between democracy and administrative efficiency. It makes bureaucracy a positive instrument that serves to strengthen and fulfill the workings of the democratic process.

The next question to ask is how influential these considerations were in the development of actual political institutions in the United States. To offer one extreme answer, it would be hard to argue that the presidency and the bureaucracy grew powerful solely because they promised to provide both democracy and efficiency. Imagine rather that institutions are molded by two types of forces. One is the influence of the values around which the institutions are designed, particularly as these values enter into the American public philosophy. The second force is the way external events impinge on the functioning of government. I believe that the powers of the presidency and the bureaucracy expanded as a result of both these forces but that the two forces have operated very differently with respect to the values of pluralist democracy and administrative efficiency.

Consider first the influence of design values on the American public philosophy. It is clear that the idea of the textbook president as political leader and chief administrator has been dominant in American public philosophy at least since the Roosevelt administration (and until Watergate). This idealized view of the president as the source of political initiative and administrative energy was voiced widely and persistently in the 1950s and 1960s. The following, often florid appraisals are typical of the genre.

> Presidential government is a superb planning institution. The President has the attention of the country, the administrative goals, the command of information, and the fiscal resources that are necessary for intelligent planning . . . Better than any other human instrumentality, he can order the relations of his ends and means . . . calculate the consequences of different policies, experiment with various methods, control the timing of action, anticipate the reactions of affected interests, and conciliate them or at least mediate among them.[46]

> The [President] is the chief architect of the nation's public policy; as President, he is one who proposes, requests, supports, demands, and insists that Congress enact most of the major legislation that it does."[47]

> The President is the most strategic policy maker in the government.[48]

> He reigns but also rules, he symbolizes the people, but he also runs their government.[49]

The period between 1950 and 1980 also saw the publication of Thomas Cronin's textbook portrait of the presidency and of books by political analysts with titles like *Presidential Government: The Crucible of Leadership; Roosevelt: the Lion and the Fox; Presidential Greatness;* and *A Presidential Nation.*[50]

This philosophy of strengthening the chief executive to provide coherent leadership also influenced major design proposals of the mid-twentieth century, namely the President's Committee on Administrative Management in 1937 and the two Hoover Commissions in 1949 and 1955. As Francis Rourke has noted, the findings and recommendations of these groups "led the way toward a very substantial expansion of executive authority in national administration in the United States."[51]

The Wilson and Goodnow theory of the benign role of bureaucracy has also been a dominant strand in twentieth-century American administrative theory. Wilson's essay is the starting point for students of administration, and, as Waldo has written, Goodnow's analysis has achieved the status of a catechism in administrative writings:

> Most subsequent students of administration, even when they have not read it and even when they arrive at quite opposite conclusions with respect to the application of "politics" and "administration," have regarded [Goodnow's] *Politics and Administration* much as the eighteenth-century literati regarded Newton's *Principia*.[52]

In practice, the New Deal provides the archetypal expression of the solution to the conflict between democracy and efficiency that rests on the presidency and the bureaucracy. As Samuel Beer has written:

> Roosevelt called not only for a centralization of government, but also for a nationalization of politics. He not only said that the federal government would take the lead; he also urged the people to demand and shape that lead . . . A principal and persistent theme of the utterance of his administration was to assure the people that the federal government could solve their problems, would not harm them, was their agent, indeed consisted simply of the people themselves acting in their national capacity.[53]

Public support for bureaucracy was widespread and enduring. According to Altshuler, "from the beginning of Franklin Roosevelt's administration to the end of Dwight Eisenhower's, American liberals were generally united in defending the federal bureaucracy against its critics."[54]

While it is difficult to measure the effects of guiding values and a dominant public philosophy on institutional development, it is easier to discern the effects of external events on government. As should be plain even to casual observers of American government, external forces in this century have led to the strengthening of the presidency and the bureaucracy. These external forces have included the need to regulate a rapidly growing industrial structure early in the century, the Depression, the challenge of mobilizing to fight two world wars, the scientific and military demands of the Cold War, the War on Poverty, the long ordeal in Vietnam, the demands for regulation in environmental areas, consumer protection, and work safety, and the complex problems of energy and inflation.

In reactions to these events and pressures the American political system has turned repeatedly toward the model of administrative efficiency and away from the model of pluralist democracy in order to increase the problem-solving capabilities of government. Some of these problems appeared to call for special expertise; others appeared to require large-scale organizational mobilization of the sort promised by a hierarchical bureaucracy; some called for new organizational structures such as the Department of Energy. And most of the external problems appeared to call for strong, centralized executive leadership.

My argument is that, especially since the New Deal, the model of administrative efficiency has gained greatly in prominence at the expense of the model of pluralist democracy. When political and administrative actors have looked for institutional solutions to their problems, they have increasingly looked to the design features associated with the model of administrative efficiency.

The Structure of Bureaucratic Democracy

So far I have argued that the presidency and the bureaucracy experienced vast increases in power and responsibility for two reasons. First, these institutions provided the hope of producing both stronger pluralist democracy and greater administrative efficiency. Second, in response to the external pressures created by increasingly complex policy problems, the model of administrative efficiency has gained ascendancy in recent decades over the previously governing model of pluralist democracy, and as a consequence power has flowed to the president and the bureaucracy, where expertise, professionalism, and executive leadership are thought to reside.

I will now set out the main structural characteristics of bureaucratic democracy. To perceive its distinctive character, we must first recall the institutional relationships envisioned by the governing model of pluralist democracy. These relationships are rather easy to deduce from the theory of separation of powers, with its emphasis on the checking and balancing of political power and governmental authority. Simply, if power is to be checked, no single center can be dominant. For if one center of power were to grow disproportionately large, there would exist an imbalance in the mutual relationships which would, in turn, impede the smaller center's ability to check the larger. The institutional power relationships in pluralist democracy are depicted graphically in figure 2.1, with local governments considered to be one of the main balancing forces. (For the sake of simplicity, I will disregard the role of the judiciary in this illustration.)

As the figure indicates, no institutional center of power possesses disproportionate power resources, although particular power balances may differ from one issue or policy arena to another. I have included a center of power for bureaucracy but have drawn it with a dotted line, for bureaucratic power was not a factor in the institutional design created by the architects of pluralist democracy. I have also included center of power for the various interest groups in the polity. Interest groups are accorded substantial power in this schema because they are supposed to play a major role in balancing opposing forces and in producing accommodation and bargaining in pol-

Figure 2.1   Institutional power relations in pluralist democracy.

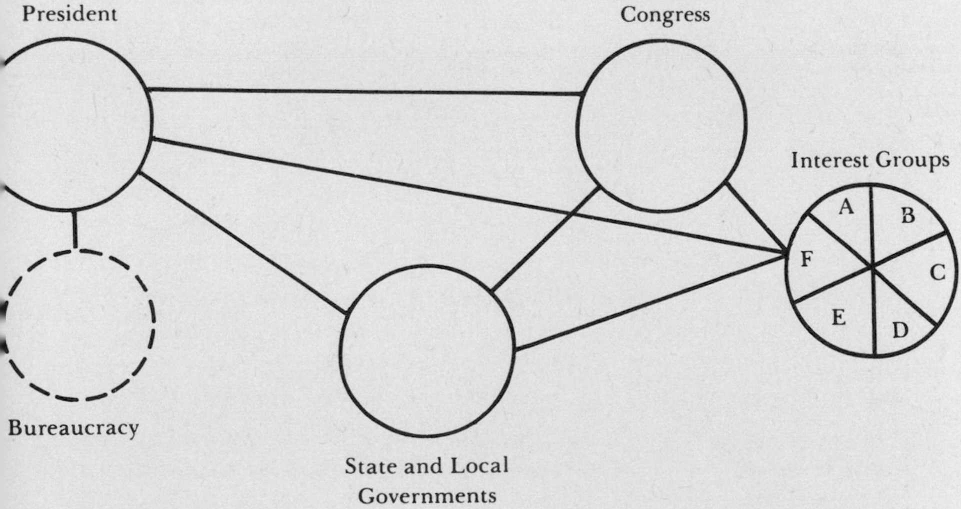

icymaking. But obviously the power of interest groups should not be disproportionate, for that would create another kind of power imbalance in the system. Moreover, I have indicated a number of roughly equal groups within the interest-group cluster since the theory of pluralism entails the proposition that various factions will check each other. There can be no disproportionately powerful interest group if the checking and balancing process is to work.

How does this original model of institutional power change in the course of the rise of bureaucratic democracy? In the first place, increased responsibility and range of activity flow to the presidency and the bureaucracy. In its first stage of development, bureaucratic democracy entails a disproportionate growth in the policymaking roles of chief executives, staff assistants of the executive, experts, and professional bureaucrats. As the government comes to rely more heavily on administrative specialists, the institutional power relations in the system change dramatically from those in the established model of pluralist democracy. The basic outline of power and responsibility relationships in bureaucratic democracy is presented graphically in figure 2.2.

Figure 2.2   Institutional power relations in bureaucratic democracy.

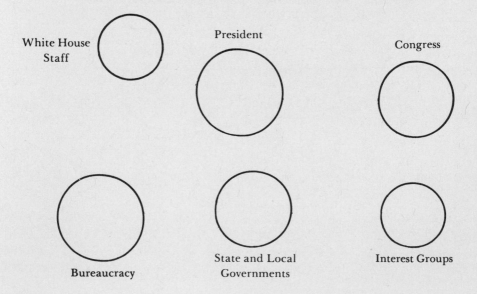

White House
Staff

President

Congress

Bureaucracy

State and Local
Governments

Interest Groups

In this figure the administrative side (the left side) of the politico-administrative system has grown greatly in relationship to the other main institutions in democracy: Congress, state and local governments, and interest groups. Further, the president has greatly increased his scope of activity and responsibility vis-à-vis the Congress, in large part because of the rise of the White House staff and the bureaucracy but also because more authority, especially in foreign policy, has been allocated to the president as an individual decisionmaker. The White House apparatus and the bureaucracy have come out of nowhere and constitute major centers of policymaking authority. Also because control over domestic policymaking has been greatly centralized in the hands of the White House and the bureaucracy, the relative power of state and local governments has declined significantly.

These evolving institutional relations obtain not only at the federal level but also at the state and local level. Institutional relations in subnational governments indeed reflect the changed national pattern, and can be depicted in figure 2.3. Thus the structure of bureaucratic democracy has a very different shape from the one envisioned by the model of pluralist democracy. This structure is not a static one, for the rise of bureaucratic responsibility brings about further changes in the structure of government.

Figure 2.3   Institutional power relations in subnational governments.

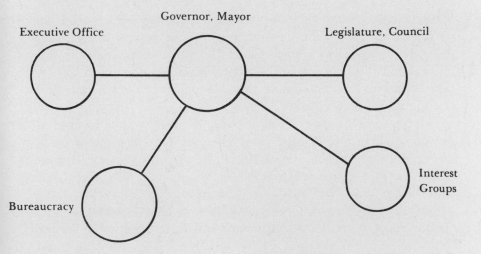

Institutional Interactions in Bureaucratic Democracy

In developing a simple model of bureaucratic democracy, I have treated the flow of power and responsibility to the president and the bureaucracy as occurring simultaneously. In fact, there is evidence that there has been a time lag between the growth of bureaucracy and the growth of the institutionalized presidency. That is, bureaucracy grew ahead of the presidency's institutional capacity to guide and control it, and many aspects of growth in the White House (and similarly in governors' and mayors' offices) came in reaction to the prior growth of bureaucracy and, in particular, to the problem of achieving executive control over bureaucracy. By the time the President's Committee on Administrative Management reported in 1937 that the president "needs help," at least two generations of new bureaucracies had already come into being: the regulatory commissions and the New Deal administrative agencies. As late as the early 1930s, there was an imbalance in the institutional capacities of the president and the bureaucracy. The president was operating with a small staff in the face of a bureaucratic structure that was mushrooming.

Since the 1930s, American presidents have adopted various new institutional mechanisms in their effort to get a grip on the bureaucracy. The role of the old Bureau of the Budget was expanded (and it was appropriately renamed the Office of Management and Budget), and with that expansion came the development of central clearance of the president's program. More important perhaps, presidents have built their own administrative apparatus within the White House in order to centralize control of policymaking in the executive branch. In foreign policy this institutional centralization is manifest in the National Security Council, in domestic policy in the Domestic Policy Council, and in economic policy in the Economic Policy Board.

More generally, the explosion in the size of the White House staff can be understood, in large part, as an effort to give the president increased oversight of administration in the bureaucracy. Increasingly, cabinet secretaries have had to channel their business through the White House staff structure. This presidential reaction to the problem of bureaucratic control may well have reached its high-water mark in the Nixon administration. In creating what Richard

Nathan has aptly called the "Administrative Presidency,"[55] Nixon not only sought to centralize control of administrative policymaking within the White House but also used an expanded White House to circumvent the bureaucracy directly. In addition, he expanded the management functions of the Office of Management and Budget to increase the administrative efficiency of the bureaucracies. He also insinuated large numbers of political loyalists into the bureaucracies in an effort to increase bureaucratic responsiveness to presidential programs and policies. In the light of this experience, it might be said that the first reaction of recent presidents has been to try to increase their control of bureaucracy. A second, more radical step has been to build a parallel administrative structure within the White House to give the president direct control of administrative policymaking. Both strategies are clear reactions to the growth of bureaucratic power. In terms of institutional evolution, what comes first is a growth in the bureaucratic system, followed by the rise of an institutionalized White House bureaucracy. At the end of this stage of evolution, we find a bureaucratic presidency struggling with a vast bureaucracy, both of which have come to possess great organizational resources relative to the other institutions of government.

This imbalance has led the other pluralist institutions of government, namely the Congress and state and local governments, to develop new bureaucratic institutions of their own in order to compete with the White House and the national bureaucracy. Let us briefly consider three sets of relationships of these institutional interactions in bureaucratic democracy: those between (1) the president and the Congress, (2) the bureaucracy and the Congress, and (3) the bureaucracy and state and local governments.

In response to increased presidential domination of national policymaking initiatives, the Congress has greatly bureaucratized its functioning in its effort to provide an effective counterforce. One manifestation of the rise of bureaucratic democracy in the Congress is the great increase in the size of congressional staffs. As one analyst has written:

> Congress, like the executive branch, has responded to the pressures by creating more specialists and topside staff. Since 1957 the total number of personal and committee staff on the Hill has climbed from 4,300 to 11,000 and over 20,000 more persons service the legislature

from institutional staff positions (the General Accounting Office, Congressional Budget Office, and so on). At the core of this blossoming congressional bureaucracy are bright, often remarkably young, technocrats who are almost indistinguishable from the analysts and subject matter specialists in the executive branch.[56]

Another more recent indication of the move toward a bureaucratic structuring of congressional life has been the creation of the Senate and House Budget Committees along with the Congressional Budget Office (CBO).[57] Again, these new bureaucratic instruments are designed in large part to give the Congress a greater ability to react to and appraise presidential budget initiatives and also to recapture some initiative for the Conress in the budgetary process.

Another reason for the creation of the budget committees was that reformers believed that the congressional spending process was out of control, that it was lacking any systematic evaluation of the overall package of congressional appropriations. Understood in this light, the budget committees are an attempt to import the central features of the administrative efficiency model into the heart of the workings of pluralist democracy. The establishment of the new budget institutions entailed a strong emphasis on efficiency values like expertise, long-range planning, financial management, and centralized control, all of which are quite foreign to the traditional operations of Congress. This emphasis fits squarely with the basic argument about the rise of bureaucratic democracy. Congress is caught in the same evolutionary currents as its rival institutions as it turns to the strategies of administrative efficiency (*a*) to deal with the external pressures presented by increasingly complex policy problems, (*b*) to bring coherence and control to the congressional policymaking process itself and (*c*) to enhance its ability to hold its own in policymaking with the executive branch.

The institutional interaction between Congress and the bureaucracy in bureaucratic democracy can be characterized in terms of the oversight function that congressional committees and subcommittees are supposed to perform with respect to the bureaucracy. As the bureaucracy has grown, congressional committees have been forced to try to keep up with its expertise and analytical resources. Without substantial analytical capabilities, the Congress's task of oversight becomes difficult to perform, to say the least. The institutional consequences of this reaction to bureaucracy have been twofold: (1) the Congress has greatly increased the number of its subcommittees in order to monitor the various new and evolving bureaucratic policy arenas; and (2) members of Congress have had to rely increasingly on the expertise of their expanded professional committee staffs as the work of the committees has increased in scope and complexity. Both of these consequences reinforce the institutional patterns of bureaucratic democracy: the congressional committees have become more specialized, expert, and bureaucratic in an effort to compete with the increased administrative resources of the bureaucracy. What we see is a kind of administrative arms race in which the escalation is triggered by growth in bureaucratic power and responsibility.

The centralization of domestic policymaking in the federal bureaucracy has had an enormous impact on subnational governments. First, as new social programs have proliferated at the federal level, lower-level governments have usually been given the responsibility of operating those programs on a day-to-day basis. That responsibility has required the creation of many new state and local bureaucracies designed to carry out the federal programs. Moreover, as soon as a state or local bureaucracy is established to implement a new federal program, for example the Comprehensive Employment and Training Act (CETA), the lower-level bureaucrats immediately become involved in a complex administrative relationship with their federal counterparts. The need to sort out and comply with federal guidelines, as well as to perform reporting and evaluation tasks for the "feds," requires that local bureaucracies devote a large part of their administrative resources to meeting the needs and requirements of their federal bureaucratic superiors.

Second, the fact that, even with revenue sharing, an overwhelming percentage of federal funds is distributed to state and local governments through grant-in-aid programs also leads to the enlargement of bureaucracy at the state and local level. If a governor or mayor wants to renew a grant or receive a new one, he must typically rely on professional grant writers and program evaluators. In the game of grantsmanship, the bureaucrats who know the ropes and the people—the regulations and the federal bureaucrats who hand out the money—are indispensable players.

Thus the federal bureaucracy not only induces the growth of local bureaucracies but also has the effect of increasing the power of local bureaucracies vis-à-vis governors and mayors. If a governor or mayor wants to expand his grants or maintain ones already in hand, he must depend on the skills and experience of his bureaucracy. And in this dependence lies a source of power for the local bureaucrats who know how to work the administrative levers in the federal government. This relationship between federal and local bureaucrats has been aptly termed "picket fence federalism" by former Governor Terry Sanford of North Carolina. Sanford is referring to the policymaking "connection" between bureaucrats at different levels, which leads, in his view, to the creation of policy subgovernments controlled by a network of bureaucrats running vertically from the federal to the local level (like a picket stake).[58]

Governors and mayors have often responded to this bureaucratic connection by increasing the administrative resources in the state house or city hall in order to control the operations of their own bureaucracies and to achieve some central coordination of the federal programs flowing into their state or city. This pattern is a parallel to that already noted at the national level in that the office of the chief executive has expanded (and greater centralization of policy is sought) in reaction to the problem of dealing with the bureaucracy — in this case with both federal and local bureaucracies. As at the federal level, this building up of first the bureaucracy and then the chief executive leads to a structural imbalance at the subnational level between administrative institutions on the one hand and the traditional political institutions (especially state legislatures and city councils) on the other.

To summarize, the administrative side of the politico-administrative system has gained greatly in responsibility and in scope of activity as bureaucratic democracy has developed. In response the traditional institutions of pluralist democracy, especially Congress and state and local governments, have turned to the model of administrative efficiency in an effort to improve their competitive position vis-à-vis the chief executives and the bureaucracy. Ironically, in their effort to restore balance among the various centers of power in governments, the traditional institutions of pluralist democracy democracy themselves contribute to the rise of bureaucratic democracy.

Critiques of the Democracy and Efficiency Models

A basic question that has been in the background throughout this analysis has not yet been answered: Does the democracy model produce "democracy," and does the efficiency model produce "efficiency"? This question can be approached in several different ways. In one sense, it leads to a tautology, for the models create their own self-justifying definitions of democracy and efficiency. If democracy is defined in the pluralist model as group representation and the balancing of power centers, then any increase in group representation must be viewed logically as an increase in democracy. There are other tests of democracy (or efficiency), and in fact critics of American democracy often argue that pluralism fails to advance democracy defined in terms of the advancement of social justice, economic equality, or perhaps even majority rule.[59] We must therefore admit this critique of the democracy model (or equally the efficiency model), but we cannot meet the possible challenge here fully because we have no way of knowing which of many competing definitions of democracies is to be thrown up as a countertest.

A second way to approach the question is to ask whether in practice the models produce the results that they are designed to produce. Do the institutional means employed lead to the political ends sought? This point, I believe, is at the heart of the debate about the democracy and efficiency models. Defenders of pluralism would argue that the American system is indeed very open to interest groups and that there is a healthy competition and balance among rival factions. At one level this defense is powerful, for few would deny that the American system of pluralism does feature intense interest-group activity and widespread political bargaining. Most recent critics of pluralism take a different tack. Rather than denying the facts of multiple power centers and interest-group bargaining, they argue that in practice the pluralist model has created distortions and abuses that undermine its own goals.

Three critiques of this sort come to mind. The first is made by Theodore Lowi, who argues that American government not only is open to interest-group bargaining but has been captured by interest groups. In Lowi's antipluralist portrait of interest-group liberalism, government policymaking and political benefits have been fragmented and parceled out to different subgovernments, each controlled by (or at least defending the interests of) a particular interest group.[60] A second critique of pluralism sees political bargaining being sacrificed to a pattern of single-issue politics, in which interest groups mobilize around one particular issue, such as abortion, and work to force government to respond to their intense interests. In this picture of pluralism gone astray, bargaining and balance are notably absent. The different interests fight separate battles on the single issue that concerns them, and the political system is deeply fragmented and pressured as a consequence. A third critique is offered by C. E. Lindblom. In Lindblom's vision, pluralism does give a hearing to various interest groups, but the problem is that not all interest groups are equal in their political resources. In particular, Lindblom argues that American business corporations occupy a privileged position in economic decisionmaking and exercise a disproportionate influence on the political process.[61]

The question of whether the administrative efficiency model leads, in practice, to substantive efficiency in government sparks an equally sharp debate. Defenders of the model point to the professional, nonpolitical military, the contribution of professionalism and bureaucratic organization to the improvement of urban services, the success of the space program, the lack of corruption among civil servants, the role of experts in organizations like the Council of Economic Advisors and the National Security Council, the coordinating role of the Office of Management and Budget, the role of centralized executive power in policy initiatives during the New Deal and the Great Society (and generally in foreign policy), the organization of research and development in science and medicine, and the development of planning and evaluation capabilities through policy analysis.

Critics of the efficiency model do not lack arguments and examples of their own. Familiar critiques include the views that bureaucratic policymaking is rigid and inefficient, that professionalism has created a barrier between public employees and citizens, that experts have failed to solve pressing problems in, for example, energy and economic policy, that centralized executive power led to the imperial presidency and Watergate, that the isolation of administration from democratic political processes has produced abuses of power in the CIA and the FBI, and that management-improvement systems such as program budgeting have generally been failures.

It is not necessary here to weigh these claims about the workings of the democracy and efficiency models. The point is to highlight the problematic relationship between the *theory* and *practice* of pluralist democracy and administrative efficiency. Then, with this in mind, we will be ready to see how the democracy and efficiency models function (and conflict) in the dominant institution of bureaucratic democracy — the bureaucracy itself.

One final critique of the democracy and efficiency models bears attention. Some have argued that there is no conflict at all between the democracy and efficiency models. This is a two-way argument. On the one hand, Lindblom has argued that a politico-administrative system based on bargaining and mutual adjustment can be both democratic and highly efficient. On the other hand, Norton Long has argued that bureaucracy can both serve the values of administrative efficiency and also provide strong democratic values such as group representation.[62] These arguments constitute an important challenge to the idea that pluralist democracy and administrative efficiency are in conflict. I will evaluate the force of this challenge in my analysis of the role of the bureaucracy in bureaucratic democracy.

3

An Analysis of Public Bureaucracy

THE BUREAUCRACY LIES AT THE CENTER of the politico-administrative system that I call bureaucratic democracy. To answer the questions of whether bureaucratic democracy is democratic and whether it is efficient — whether it serves or fails to serve the values of pluralist democracy and administrative efficiency or both in American government — we need to examine the structure and functioning of the bureaucracy.

In public discourse as well as in more scholarly analysis there is a steady stream of commentary on the "bureaucracy problem." There is no shortage of complaints against bureaucracy, but they often conflict. At the level of daily political conversation, the most common complaint is that the bureaucracy, especially in Washington, has become too big, remote, and inefficient. But there is a contrary chorus that calls for *more* government to deal with problems of teenage unemployment, health care, crime, cancer, energy shortages, consumer protection, national urban policy, and not least, Soviet military power. It is a commonplace that whether government is seen as doing too much or too little depends on what it is doing or not doing for particular individuals and interests.

James Wilson has suggested that complaints against bureaucracy arise because we ask bureaucracy to perform conflicting functions. We demand that it provide accountability, equity, efficiency, responsiveness, and fiscal integrity. Wilson's point is that these demands pull the bureaucracy in opposite directions:

Obviously the more a bureaucracy is responsive to its clients—whether those clients are organized by radicals in Mothers for Adequate Welfare or represented by Congressmen anxious to please constituents—the less it can be accountable to presidential directives. Similarly, the more equity, the less responsiveness. And a preoccupation with fiscal integrity can make the kind of program budgeting required by enthusiasts of efficiency difficult, if not impossible.[1]

Complaints about bureaucracy may also reflect deep-seated differences in political and economic ideology. Those who favor greater economic equality and redistributive social programs may champion a powerful federal bureaucracy. Businessmen who want to get the government out of the marketplace often have a vitriolic view of regulatory bureaucracies. But even here ideology is not a simple or undifferentiated matter. Representatives of the oil and gas industry, the securities industry, and the steel industry do not march together in their attitudes toward government regulation. Ideology and perceived economic interest surely matter, but they cut in different ways.

It should come as little surprise that public perception of the bureaucracy problem is conflicting and confused. This is to be expected in a highly pluralistic society. What we need in our analysis is not a conclusive empirical answer to the question of what is wrong (or believed by the public to be wrong) with bureaucracy. The question here, rather, is whether we can find a coherent theory of bureaucracy that would provide a basis for either defending or criticizing the role of bureaucracy in the American politico-administrative system.

Bureaucracy, Democracy, and Efficiency

As we have seen, bureaucracy has been defended on grounds of both democracy and efficiency. If any of these defenses were to prove persuasive, then we would have a normative theory of public bureaucracy of the sort we are looking for. (There may, of course, be other normative theories of bureaucracy. For example, one possible justification is that a powerful federal bureaucracy is required to redistribute income and produce a more egalitarian society. This is a hard justification to deal with, for it is not obvious that bureaucracy is either a necessary or a sufficient condition of income redistribution, though it is strongly arguable that the absence of a strong central administration would make redistribution very difficult in the context of American federalism).

In Chapter 2 I discussed two versions of the claim that bureaucracy can serve the values of both democracy and efficiency. The first version is Woodrow Wilson's view that administration can be carefully contained within a controlling democratic order. A more plausible version is the one advanced by Charles Lindblom.[2] Building on Robert Dahl's emphasis on a decentralized bargaining process, Lindblom's theory says that various political groups engage in mutual adjustment and interactive problem-solving. Lindblom's vision of the bargaining process in government is both coherent and forceful. The question is whether the actual behavior of public bureaucracies conforms to the theory. This is the question that will be explored in this chapter.

A related justification of bureaucracy as both democratic and efficient is that of Norton Long:

> Through the breadth of the interests represented in its composition, the bureaucracy provides a significant constitutionalizing element of pluralism in our government. Through its structure, permanence, and processes, it provides a medium in which the conditions requisite for the rational interpretation of our experience can develop. Thus it has a substantial part to play in the working constitution as representative organ and as source of rationality.

The argument that bureaucracy can be a significant force for competitive, pluralist democracy is part and parcel of Dahl's view that bureaucracy is a normal part of the pluralist process.[3]

The most interesting and important recent analysis of bureaucracy has been provided by Graham Allison, who underscores the political role of the bureaucracy. Allison develops a model of "bureaucratic politics" based on the notion that bureaucrats behave politically in that they maintain, defend, or enhance institutional roles and positions.[4] Allison's treatment is persuasive as far as it goes, but it does not account for all aspects of the politics of bureaucracy.

Being an important part of governmental operations, bureaucracies naturally engage in political conflicts and develop political strategies to one degree or another. This point has been made by many scholars. Writing in 1949, Paul Appleby termed administration the "eighth political process." More recently, Francis Rourke has written usefully about the political character of bureaucracy, and Peter Woll has underscored the starting point for any political analysis of bureaucracy in the following terms:

> The political nature of bureaucracy is initially revealed in the behavior of administrative agencies acting as interest groups. Administrative agencies operate in a highly charged political environment. They are constantly brought into contact with external groups, both governmental and non-governmental. To retain their power, or to expand, all agencies must maintain a balance of political support over opposition.[5]

There is little argument about the proposition that bureaucracies behave politically. The analytical task is to specify the political behavior of bureaucracy in greater depth and detail.

The task of this chapter is to provide a political analysis of bureaucracy. By testing the positive theories of bureaucracy against the observable behavior of bureaucratic actors, I will construct a political model that systematically relates the many facets of public bureaucracies. In building a political model of bureaucracy, I will present three elements of bureaucratic structure and five elements of bureaucratic functioning and support each point by propositions drawn either from empirical research or from theories about organizations in general or public bureaucracies in particular. At the second level of analysis, I will show what the elements of the model add up to by introducing a number of generalizations and implications that grow out of the logic and interplay of the eight elements. This analysis of the anatomy of public bureaucracy will be concerned more with the similarities than with the differences among bureaucracies. Public bureaucracies differ along many different dimensions, but for the moment I will stress commonalities. This means that the political model of bureaucracy I present is a simplified picture designed to show bureaucracy's basic and pervasive features across a wide institutional spectrum. In the next chapter, I will begin to draw distinctions among different kinds of bureaucracies.

Elements of Bureaucratic Structure

The elements of bureaucratic structure to be examined are (1) political interest-group behavior, (2) fragmentation, and (3) conflict and competition. These three elements interact and overlap, and they underlie the elements of bureaucratic functioning to be discussed later.

1. Bureaucracies as Political Interest Groups

The first element of bureaucratic structure is the familiar notion that public bureaucracies operate as self-conscious political interest groups. A bureaucracy is no less self-regarding as an interest group than a party organization, or a congressional committee, or an association of mayors, or the political arm of a labor or business organization. This does not imply that bureaucratic interests are necessarily narrowly self-serving; it merely means that bureaucracies devote themselves to the advancement of their own political objectives, however defined. At first glance, this analysis seems to make bureaucracies just another part of the pluralist bargaining system, as Dahl has argued. But, as it turns out, we must inspect this argument far more carefully before endorsing Dahl's pluralist view of bureaucracy.

To say that bureaucracies operate as organized interest groups is to say that they constantly calculate the political costs and benefits to themselves of policies being developed or changed in the larger governmental arena; that they design strategies to increase the benefits accruing to them; that they lobby the Congress and the president in pursuit of these strategies; that they seek to develop constituency support wherever possible and use other available political resources—such as the press—to argue and advance their case. The propositions that follow allow a closer analysis of these political characteristics of bureaucracy.

Miles's Law Bureaucrats will seek to advance the interests of the department or subdepartment or bureau for which they work. This proposition is at the core of what Allison calls "bureaucratic politics." Allison articulates this concept in terms of Miles's Law: "Where you stand depends on where you sit":

the diverse demands upon each player shape his priorities, perceptions and issues. For large classes of issues—e.g., budgets and procurement decisions—the stance of a particular player can be predicted with high reliability from information about his seat.[6]

This means not only that bureaucracies advance their own political interests and strategies but also that individual "players" within bureaucracies do the same. This proposition gives the most fundamental meaning to the idea of the political behavior of bureaucracies and bureaucrats.

Mobilizing Constituencies   Public bureaucracies will work to mobilize their constituencies and clients in support of their policies. This means that bureaucracies will seek political partnership with those interest groups which work most closely with them and which are most directly affected by their decisions. For example, as Mark Nadel and Francis Rourke note, the Department of Agriculture played a principal role in the development of the American Farm Bureau Federation, "the largest and most powerful of agricultural interest group organizations." Similarly, in its early history the Department of Labor worked to nurture the development of trade unions. According to Nadel and Rourke, even the State Department, which is not supposed to have a natural constituency, has repeatedly sought to mobilize a political constituency:

> the department has often had to resort to organizing outside group support itself. The organization by the department of a blue-ribbon committee of distinguished citizens to lead a campaign in behalf of the Marshall Plan in 1947 is an illustration of the department's success in establishing its own public support. A similar group was formed in 1967 to win support for the government's Vietnam policy.[7]

Benefits and Costs   The political interaction between bureaucracies and interest groups will be particularly intense when bureaucracies allocate tangible, concentrated benefits and/or costs to a relatively small number of constituents or interest groups. Social Security is an example of a program with widely dispersed benefits and costs; by comparison, the policy decisions made by the Federal Aviation Administration impose costs on or award benefits to only a small group of organizations. James Wilson has described bureaucratic programs with concentrated benefits and dispersed costs:

Programs of this kind facilitate the emergence of voluntary associations that enter into a symbiotic relationship with the agency administering the program. There are any number of familiar examples—the National Rivers and Harbors Congress and the Army Corps of Engineers, the American Farm Bureau Federation and the Department of Agriculture and veterans' organizations and the Veterans Administration.

In cases where bureaucratic programs impose both concentrated benefits and concentrated costs, the bureaucracy faces sharp political pressure from potential winners and losers of government benefits: "where both benefits and costs are concentrated, policy changes will generally only occur as the result of negotiating bargains among preexisting associations or of changing the political balance of power among them."[8] In addition whenever bureaucracy tries to impose a concentrated cost on a particular interest group, it will find itself in a protracted political struggle: witness the auto industry's response to the government's auto emission standards.

The point is that when bureaucracies impose either concentrated benefits or concentrated costs they are drawn into interest-group politics. Whether they are seeking to build their constituency among interest groups or trying to fend off attacks from interest groups. In sum, my proposition is that in the great majority of cases bureaucracies impose either concentrated benefits or concentrated costs on some group or interest, and, as a consequence, they will become deeply involved in the political arts of coalition-building, bargaining, and negotiation with interest groups.

Allies and Enemies Bureaucracies will work to maximize their number of allies among their constituents and in Congress and to minimize their number of enemies among interest groups, on congressional committees, on the White House staff, and elsewhere. This proposition follows from the fact that the rational bureaucrat knows that the bureaucracy's programs are likely to produce both allies and enemies and, moreover, that current allies cannot always be counted on to continue their support. The danger always exists that the old political attitude "what have you done for me *lately*" will lead to a loss of constituency support.

Geographical Benefits Bureaucracies will direct expenditures to particular geographical areas to maintain or win support among congressmen on committees that play an important role in the operations of the relevant bureaucracy. As Douglas Arnold's research has shown:

> Bureaucrats appear to allocate benefits strategically in an effort both to maintain and to expand their supporting coalitions. When it furthers their purpose, they broaden their program's geographic scope and increase the number of shares of benefits so that more congressmen can be brought into their supporting coalitions. When necessary they allocate extra shares of benefits to leaders and to those who are crucial coalition members.[9]

Iron Triangles   Bureaucracies will seek to maintain a stable and harmonious relationship between their interest groups and their congressional oversight committees. This often involves a balancing or juggling of political interests. When a bureaucracy, its supportive interest groups, and the relevant congressional committees working together occupy a strong position of control in a particular segment of public policymaking, their relationship is known as an "iron triangle."[10]

The Role of the Press   Bureaucracies endeavor to use the press to advance their policy positions, sometimes by leaking news to reporters. Leon Sigal has explored this phenomenon:

> News in Washington can be seen as the product of the interaction of two bureaucracies—one composed of newsmen and the other of officials . . . Officials . . . disclose information in an effort to muster and maintain support, both in and out of government, for a particular course of action. The reporter and the official use each other to advantage in their own organizations: the former exploits his contacts in the government to obtain exclusives, the latter exploits the need for news to deliver messages to key audiences.[11]

Friends and Neighbors   A final proposition that draws on many of the above propositions is that bureaucracies will work within other bureaucracies—Congress, the interest groups, the Office of Management and Budget, the president's staff, and the press—in order to develop a host of allies who can be counted on to aid the bureaucracies either to advance their goals or to repel attacks from the outside. These "friends and neighbors" also include former employees of the agency, so-called ins-and-outers, academic specialists, Washington lawyers, and consultants. Together they provide a widespread web of political support for a given agency. Hugh Heclo refers to this process as developing a network across other agencies. Political executives, in Heclo's terms, develop "circles of confidence, lines of trust." Samuel Huntington has described the political role of friends and neighbors in the military services:

> The allies and supporters of a service are at times more royalist than the king. They do not necessarily identify more intensely with service interests than do members of the service, but they do have a greater freedom to articulate those interests and to promote them through a wider variety of political means.[12]

2. Fragmentation

The second element of the bureaucratic structure is its fragmentation. The dictionary defines "fragment" as "a part broken away from a whole; a detached, isolated, or incomplete part." In the case of government bureaucracies, there are large and significant breaks in many of their political and administrative relationships. Fragmentation may be either horizontal (involving separate groups at the same level of government) or vertical (involving a lack of communication and integration among different levels of government). The implication of bureaucratic fragmentation is that government is literally broken apart; it is composed of many distinct, relatively independent, and sometimes uncontrolled pieces. The following propositions amplify the claim that government is fragmented in these ways.

Separate Interests Bureaucracies will pursue their own separate interests. When agencies seek their own political advantage in this way, they create a strong centrifugal pressure on government. Within any given bureaucracy, moreover, there tend to be many substantial administrative fragments, which seek autonomy in their respective realms. As Harold Seidman puts it:

> The plain truth is that such powerful subordinate organizations as the Bureau of Public Roads, Army Corps of Engineers, Public Health Service, National Park Service, and Forest Service constitute the departmental power centers and are quite capable of making it on their own without secretarial help, except when challenged by strong hostile external forces.[13]

The apparently simple point is that the greater the number of relatively autonomous pieces of bureaucracy, the greater the structural fragmentation. The fact that, for example, the Department of Health and Human Services alone runs several hundred separate programs suggests that there are many such pieces in the national government. The point may not in fact be so simple, however: if many or all of the fragments of government were found to participate in the pluralist process of bargaining and mutual adjustment, the result would not be fragmentation in the sense of broken, separate pieces.

Standard Operating Procedures   In the policymaking process, bureaucracies will follow their own routines and standard operating procedures; therefore, when called upon to act, each bureaucracy will march in its own established direction. The problem for national policymaking is one of eliciting some consistency and coherence from the separate standard operating procedures of different bureaucracies. As Graham Allison and Peter Szanton have written about the making of foreign policy:

> In a complex and changing world, where the nation's objectives are many and partially conflicting, consistency, and the subordination of all actions to some grand and rewarding plan cannot be expected. But the ability of separate agencies and particular interests to determine pieces of policy independently, and autonomously to start (or stop) its implementation must be subjected to at least partial control.[14]

Narrow Perspectives   Bureaucrats will tend to take a narrow view of policy and programs, concentrating very much on their own administrative backyards. This proposition reinforces the one on standard operating procedures. It means that for government as a whole, bureaucratic policymaking is composed of a welter of fragments. Hugh Heclo has shown that bureaucrats tend to spend their entire careers in one agency. As a consequence, they can be expected to develop long time-horizons, but also quite narrow outlooks, since all they have known bureaucratically and all they expect to know is confined to a limited administrative space.[15]

The Role of Professionals   The policymaking process becomes increasingly fragmented as groups of professionals and experts develop control in particular segments of policy. Professionals gain authority because they are relied on to provide technical and trained skills, which laymen do not possess. Samuel Beer has written of this professional role in government in terms of a "professional-bureaucratic complex":

> The recent sharp rise of the influence of professionalism in government has been widely recognized . . . Thanks to the growth of specialized sciences and fields of technology and their application to public policy, "professional specialists" gained a new role in policy making . . . The main element in such a complex of political power is a core of officials with scientific and professional training. This bureaucratic core also normally works in close cooperation with two other components: certain interested legislators . . . and the spokesman for the group that benefits from the program initially brought into existence by bureaucrats and politicians.[16]

The rise of professionalism tends to fragment government policymaking in several ways. First, the logic of professional specialization is inherently fragmenting. As Beer puts it, "As science itself grows by the creation of new fields of specialized knowledge, so professionalism in government seems to expand by the creation of specialized programs administered by vertical hierarchies."[17] This specialization makes it increasingly difficult for laymen and for specialists from different areas of expertise to speak one another's language. Inability to communicate creates a barrier to entry into policy discourse and thus has an inherently fragmenting effect.

Another source of fragmentation lies in the politics of professionalism. Professional groups are likely to develop tendencies toward "guild professionalism": the attitude that a particular profession has a proprietary position in a given sphere of policy, that professionals know best about that policy sphere, and that only members of the profession should be allowed to "practice" in the policy sphere. Guild professionalism is familiar among military men, doctors, and nuclear scientists. But it also exists among teachers, policemen, and highway engineers. The effect is further to separate the segments of policymaking and to isolate citizens and politicians from an understanding of policy decisions.[18]

Policy Subgovernments There is also an intergovernmental version of the professional-bureaucratic complex. Professional bureaucrats at all levels of government who work in the same policy arena will form tight and relatively closed coalitions in the administration of their programs. These coalitions are sometimes called policy sub-governments. This pattern of behavior is what Terry Sanford termed "picket-fence federalism."[19] He used this term because from a local perspective the policymaking system assumes the shape of long, narrow, self-contained policy fragments.

Political Executives and Civil Servants　Another break in the fabric of government exists between the interests, habits, and loyalties of political executives and those of career civil servants. Classical administrative theory suggests that a smooth hierarchy ought to link different levels of the bureaucracy. But Heclo's research supports the proposition that political executives and civil servants inhabit two separate and often opposing worlds.[20] This dichotomy adds to the fragmentation of government. Equally, the rise of public-sector unionism produces a division between levels of administration, especially in state and local governments. Authority over the operations of public agencies thus comes to be shared, in varying degrees, between administrators and union officials, and the line of command is fragmented.

Pluralization　When governments feel a need to demonstrate that they are taking action on a problem they often will create a special bureaucratic unit to spearhead their activities. This pattern is easily observable in the cases of energy, antipoverty, and crime-prevention units. These new administrative creations add to the crowd of agencies attending to interrelated problems and thus contribute to the fragmentation of bureaucratic organization. James David Barber calls this process "pluralization" in government, and he suggests that the process of pluralization is self-reinforcing:

> In the first place, pluralization becomes a precedent: the establishment of a new unit serves as an example for all others in the system, especially for those operating in the same general problem area. Pluralization enters the list of political strategies as a legitimate gambit for pursuing the stakes of government . . . Arguments against using this strategy are weakened every time a new example appears.[21]

Ironically, pluralization, which adds to bureaucratic fragmentation, often comes about as a response to existing patterns of fragmentation. Faced with an atomized structure of existing agencies dealing with pieces of a policy problem, a political executive or high-level bureaucrat will often create a new analytic unit or task force in the hope of producing a fresh, concentrated attack on a problem. In the short run, this strategy may work. In the long run, the special task force is likely to become just one more piece in the jigsaw puzzle of government organizations.

Complexity of Joint Action   The horizontal and vertical fragmentation of bureaucratic units makes the implementation of public programs a complex process. This proposition synthesizes many of the earlier ones. (Horizontal fragmentation exists between the authority and jurisdiction of different bureaucratic units at the same level of government; vertical fragmentation exists between the authority and jurisdiction of bureaucracies at different levels of government). This final proposition is drawn from the empirical and conceptual work of Jeffrey Pressman and Aaron Wildavsky, who introduce the notion of the "complexity of joint action":

> In order to get by all the decision points, the program required dozens of clearance actions by a wide range of participants. In situations of high controversy and mutual antagonism, the probability that those actions would be favorable or taken in a reasonable time might be quite small . . . We conclude that the probability of agreement by every participant on each decision point must be exceedingly high for there to be any chance at all that a program will be brought to completion. On the assumption that the probability is 80 per cent . . . the chances of completion are a little over one in a million after seventy agreements have been reached, and fall below the half-way mark after just four [agreements].[22]

3. Conflict and Competition

The third basic structural element of bureaucracy is a pattern of conflict and competition in relationships among organizations. Bureaucracies try to avoid this situation by creating a domain in which they have as much autonomy as possible and thus are free of jurisdictional disputes with other agencies and levels of government. Martha Derthick has studied the way administrators of the Social Security program maneuvered over decades to eliminate bureaucratic rivalries. Public Assistance, a likely rival of funding, was kept under wraps in the Social Security Administration until 1963. Attempts at outside auditing by the Treasury Department were also parried and undermined. At the same time, Social Security administrators mobilized support among constituent interest groups, including organized labor. As a result, according to Derthick, expenditures for Social Security old age and survivors' pensions grew from $1 billion in 1950 to $104 billion in 1979 with a remarkable absence of political conflict and controversy.[23]

Derthick's study is useful in the task of constructing a political model of public bureaucracy. She presents an extreme case that points the way to a simple logic of political economizing in bureaucratic settings. Imagine a departmental head or bureau chief and assume that he wants to maximize the political and economic power of his organization. Building on the analysis that has gone before and on Derthick's study, we might reasonably suppose that the bureaucratic policymaker will seek to maximize the autonomy of his unit and its control over its own policy processes and agenda. At the same time, he will seek to minimize conflicts and entanglements with other bureaucratic organizations. This makes strong intuitive sense, and it also fits Graham Allison and Morton Halperin's analysis of how bureaucratic politics works. According to Allison and Halprin,

> Organizational interests are often dominated by the desire to maintain the autonomy of the organization in pursuing what its members view as the essence of the organization's activity, e.g., flying for the Air Force.
> Organizations rarely take stands that require elaborate coordination with other organizations.[24]

This picture of rational bureaucratic behavior is linked to the proposition about allies and enemies presented earlier, which states that a bureaucracy will try to maximize constituent allies and friendly alliances and to minimize interest-group and other enemies. Given success in both of these maximization efforts, a bureaucracy could hope to achieve the charmed existence of Social Security, as described by Derthick: a kind of bureaucratic self-government. In reality, however, bureaucrats, though seeking autonomy and control, live in a world of conflict, competition, and interdependence. Their immediate problem is how to deal with conflict and competition with other bureaucracies. Conflict and competition arise from various sources, many of which can be traced to the two structural features of bureaucracy already analyzed.

Bureaucratic Self-Advancement If bureaucracies behave as political interest groups and seek to advance their own political positions in a fragmented structure of bureaucratic interests, it makes sense that bureaucracies conflict and compete when they come in contact with one another over policy decisions. This is the essence of Allison's bureaucratic politics:

> The "maker" of government policy is not one calculating decision-maker, but rather a conglomerate of large organizations and political actors who differ substantially about what their government should do on any particular issue and who compete in attempting to affect both governmental decisions and the actions of their government.[25]

Conflicts among Experts The role of experts (inside and outside of government) will often be to defend the policy positions of their respective bureaucracies. In particular, this political role is played — though sometimes unwillingly — by many of the growing corps of policy analysts in government. As Arnold Meltsner has written:

> Like the bureaucrat, the policy analyst is a political actor . . . it is not surprising that analysts succumb to bureaucratic forces, folkways, and incentives . . . The irony is that the analyst starts off expecting to influence the bureaucracy, but it is the bureaucracy that influences him. By working in it he takes on a particular identity.[26]

Bureaucracies will seek to use their experts and their policy evaluations as political weapons in bureaucratic conflict. This leads to the now-familiar pattern of policy debate characterized by a clash of expert testimony. Congressional committee hearings often follow this pattern, as do expert prescriptions to cure inflation or street crime or the energy problem. Many examples can be given of this bureaucratic politics of analysis. Secretary of Defense Robert McNamara's introduction of systems analysts into the Defense Department in the 1960s provides one such example. At first, the analyst "whiz kids" who were installed on the staff of the Secretary of Defense gave the civilian managers an analytical advantage over the military professionals, who were not used to or capable of conducting policy debate in the language of systems analysis and cost-benefit studies. In order not to remain at a disadvantage in analytical disputes, each military service assembled its own corps of systems analysts. Policy debates soon came to be struggles between opposing assumptions, projections, and analyses in the new language of systems analysis. Another example is the process that led to the creation of the Congressional Budget Office: the Congress sought to acquire the analytical capability to do battle with the president's Office of Management and Budget.

In underlining this point about conflict and competition among analysts, I do not mean to imply that analysts typically distort their findings to support their own bureaucratic interests. I do wish to stress, following Meltsner, that the politics of analysis comes to mirror and extend bureaucratic conflict for the simple reason that analysts and experts play bureaucratic roles that carry with them particular institutional interests and objectives.

White House-Departmental Conflict   There will be persistent conflict between government departments and the White House, especially the White House staff. This conflict arises because of differences in perspective: the departments are concerned with their own departmental interests and those of related interest groups; the White House staff is concerned with problems often extending beyond the scope of a single department, and with the president's political interests. Thomas Cronin has noted the pervasive pattern of "White House frustration with department unresponsiveness and parochialism and of cabinet and department distress at the overtly political and abrasive behavior of the White House Staff."[27] Certainly, some department heads do maintain good relationships with the president and his staff. Nevertheless, conflict between the departments and the White House are predictable and persistent.

Political Executives and Civil Servants   As noted earlier, the different administrative perspectives of political executives and civil servants lead to widespread bureaucratic conflict. As Heclo has demonstrated, political executives typically have short time-horizons, want to mount new programs very quickly, and are responsive to presidential priorities. By contrast, civil servants, because of their longer tenure, have long time-horizons, take a gradualist view of policymaking, and often are resistant to the president's political and policy concerns.[28] In these respects, the executives and civil servants are matched opposites.

Higher-Level and Lower-Level Bureaucrats   There will often, but not always, be a basic conflict between higher-level and lower-level bureaucrats. In some bureaucracies, such as the Forest Service, strong centralized training serves to diminish this vertical conflict.[29] But more often than not the differing perspectives of higher-level and lower-level bureaucrats lead to bureaucratic conflict. This is especially true when the lower-level bureaucrats are in the field and the higher-level bureaucrats are stationed in "headquarters." In such cases, higher-level bureaucrats typically feel that their policy directives are not being adhered to, that they do not know what is going on in the field, and that local agents are favoring their own particular constituents. At the same time, lower-level employees express frustration at the arbitrariness of central policy directives, and complain about lack of concern at headquarters for the needs of their particular programs in local communities.

I found this pattern of conflict in my research on urban policymaking. In the police, fire, and welfare departments and in the school system, lower-level bureaucrats, who might be termed "street-level bureaucrats,"[30] frequently expressed anger against their administrative superiors and asserted that they found themselves in constant conflict with departmental rules and directives. Their anger stemmed from their belief that they understood the concerns of their clients and that the department seemed unaware of and even hostile to those concerns. Meanwhile, higher-level administrators complained that lower-level bureaucrats were unwilling to follow and implement *their* policies and programs. They complained that their subordinates seemed committed to their own narrow agendas and lacked a suitably broad perspective.

Interagency Planning   When different departments participate in joint planning, each department will compete with others to make sure that its own programs are represented in the final policy package. This competitive pattern was strongly manifest in the task of planning for the War on Poverty and, more recently, in the development of President Carter's national urban policy.

Jurisdictional Conflicts The more a policy problem impinges on the jurisdictions of different departments, the greater will be the level of bureaucratic competition and conflict. A simpler world may once have existed in which the jurisdictions of cabinet departments were relatively distinct, but today any major policy problem affects various bureaucracies. Problems like inflation, energy, international economic policy, urban development, and environmental policy all call on the imagined prerogatives and the programs of many different agencies. It follows that the level of interbureaucratic conflict over jurisdictions is likely to be increasing.

Guild Professionalism Another source of conflict and competition lies in the rivalry between professional groups within the bureaucracy. This competition is obvious in the interservice rivalries among the Army, Navy, Air Force, and Marine Corps. But it is also manifest in conflicts between different schools of economists and between professionals in higher and lower education and between doctors and hospital managers. At the urban level, planning for neighborhood governmental institutions is marked by sharp conflict among the teaching, social work, and police professions. In all these cases, each professional group believes that it has a special expertise in its domain and resists the encroachment of other professional perspectives. This commitment to particular professional values increases the amount of conflict in interagency planning and over jurisdictional prerogatives. Samuel Huntington has illustrated the intensity of professional conflict in his analysis of interservice competition in the military:

> The intensity and passion of the debates were unprecedented. An Air Force general could publicly refer to the Marines as a "small bitched-up army talking Navy lingo." "Power-hungry men in uniform," could reply a Marine general. For two years the Marine Commandant declared the leaders of the Corps spent most of their time defending it against attacks. Navy officials charged the Air Force with irregularities in plane buying. Air Force officials gloated over the prospective decline in naval power. The Secretaries of the Navy and

the Air Force resigned; the Chief of Naval Operations was fired . . .
"The country is being flooded with speeches, articles, and talks by
admirals on the potency of the submarine and the omnipotence of
large carriers," General H. H. Arnold wrote in October, 1949: "by
ground generals proclaiming how the next war must be won by the
doughboy plodding through the mud; by air generals telling the
power of the large bombers . . ."[31]

Pluralization of Units   As seen earlier, the tendency to create new
bureaucratic units to deal with new crises or to provide new mechanisms for coordination—the tendency toward pluralization—leads to
fragmentation in administrative structure. The proliferation of
bureaucratic units will also contribute to patterns of conflict and
competition. The addition of new units will further crowd the field
of play and cause new jurisdictional disputes. The new units will
have their own particularized bureaucratic interests, which they will
work to advance. As Barber writes:

> Each new pluralistic relationship involves communication at a dis-
> tance, enhancing opportunities for misreading messages . . . Conflict
> incidence is also increased by the inevitable overlapping of jurisdic-
> tions, which accompanies unit proliferation . . . In the course of
> attacking "its" problem, the new unit finds itself more and more in-
> volved with connected problems, finds it more and more difficult to
> avoid trespassing on the jurisdictions of others.[32]

Buckpassing Federalism   A synthesizing proposition which is analytical in character is that public officials and bureaucrats at different levels of government will naturally be in conflict with one another. This point is obvious in some horizontal relationships, for
example where a gain of industrial relocations to State X beggars
neighboring State Y to the same degree. More interesting is the logic
of vertical intergovernmental competition. Let us assume that any
given mayor or governor is a rational economic and administrative
actor with respect to the benefits and costs of doing governmental
business. We assume that such officials will try to increase their expenditures and their administrative autonomy and decrease their
taxes and their supervision by higher levels of government. An intergovernmental system run on this logic should show a fairly simple
pattern of behavior. Governors and mayors will seek to increase

their service expenditures and maintain or lower their taxes. This can only be done by getting increased aid from higher-level governments (unless, in untypical examples, local jurisdictions have a rapidly growing tax base of their own). The highly competitive dynamic that is produced by this behavior is one I call "buckpassing federalism." In relatively good times, when federal spending is high, cities will compete at the state level and cities and states will compete at the federal level to increase their shares of public resources. In less good times, when additional grants are not available, local governments will blame each government higher up for their inability to increase their service expenditures without raising taxes. This produces the pattern of buckpassing: the mayor blames the governor for not producing requested funds, and the governor in turn blames the federal government.

Besides seeking higher expenditures, lower-level governments will always attempt to maintain or increase their autonomy from higher-level supervision or regulation. Any official or bureaucrat will seek more flexibility and discretion and more control over his own affairs. As Jeffrey Pressman has shown, the drive for autonomy produces severe conflict among different levels of government. It is in the interests of local governments to attract loosely tied grants, but it is in the interest of higher-level government (since they occupy a supervisory role), to control funds more tightly.[33]

These twin patterns of conflict between higher-level and lower-level governments are so deep-rooted that they persist regardless of whether the federal government adopts highly specific grant programs or apparently more flexible revenue sharing policies. Even with revenue sharing, local governments complain about the proliferation of federal regulations, which they believe either restrict or complicate state and urban policymaking.[34]

Elements of Bureaucratic Functioning

Five elements of the behavioral functioning of bureaucracy can be isolated: (1) valuative decisions, (2) silent politics, (3) power conservation, (4) loose administrative control, and (5) expansion and proliferation of policymaking. As with the structural elements, many connections exist among the different elements of functioning. In addition, many aspects of the elements of functioning grow out of the structural elements of political interest-group behavior, fragmentation, and conflict and competition.

4. Valuative Decision

One of the significant justifications given for the existence of bureaucracy is that it produces rational, objective, value-free decisions and in so doing fulfills the criterion of efficiency, as defined by Herbert Simon: "choice which produces the largest result from the given application of resources."[35] Various analysts, however, have questioned the applicability of an efficiency standard in a politico-administrative setting. A look at Simon's views on efficiency as presented in his book *Administrative Behavior* will illustrate a number of the main problems involved in the application of the efficiency goal to public management. Simon begins by persuasively challenging an older view in public administration that linked Luther Gulick's influential "principles of administration" with efficiency in organizations. But he by no means dismisses the idea of efficiency; rather he attempts to construct it on a rigorous analytical basis as the foundation of "administrative science."

Simon begins this undertaking by acknowledging that all decisions rest on both factual and value premises. The proper approach, in his view, is to rely on the factual premises and to analyze them as systematically as possible. His implicit proposal is rigorously to distinguish facts from values in public decisions. The problem then becomes, as for early theorists of administration, how to apply this analytical distinction to decisionmaking in actual organizational settings. Here Simon slips back into the improbable strategy of separating politics and administration so as to separate facts and values. He proposes that policymaking would be strengthened by "procedural devices permitting a more effective separation of the factual and ethical elements in decisions" and that "the allocation of a question to legislature or administration for decision should depend on the relative importance of the factual and ethical issues involved, and the degree to which the former are controversial" (meaning that more ethical the issue and the more controversial the facts, the more the issue should be left to the determination of the legislature).[36]

Significantly, Simon himself has trouble believing in this Heavenly City of separated facts and values:

It would be naive to suggest that the division of work between legislature and administration in any actual public agency will ever follow very closely the lines just suggested. In the first place the legislative body will often wish, for political reasons, to avoid making clear-cut policy decisions, and to pass those on to an administrative agency. In the second place the administrator may be very different from the neutral, compliant individual pictured here. He may (and usually will) have his own very definite set of personal values that he would like to see implemented by his administrative organization, and he may resist attempts by the legislature to assume completely the function of policy determination, or he may sabotage their decisions by his manner of executing them.

In later writings, Simon backed further away from his enunciation of an efficiency standard based on a fact-value distinction. In his introduction to the second edition of *Administrative Behavior*, he reflected that he had "yielded too much ground to the omniscient rationality of economic man," and he concluded that his stated criterion of efficiency was "applicable largely to rather low-level decisions."[37]

Simon's analysis was the most notable attempt in a generation to construct a viable value-free concept of efficiency for public decisionmaking. His difficulty in doing so and his partial retreat from the effort provide a starting point for the proposition of this section, namely, that bureaucratic decisions are deeply value-laden.

More direct support for this proposition comes from the work of Reinhard Bendix. For Bendix, the pervasiveness of values in decisionmaking is clear-cut. He argues against "the belief that it is possible to adhere to a rule without the intrusion of general social and political values."[38] Bendix finds the bureaucrat caught in a dilemma:

Too great a compliance with statutory rules is popularly denounced as bureaucratic. Too great a reliance on initiative, in order to realize the spirit, if not the letter, of the law is popularly denounced as an abuse of power, as interfering with legislative prerogative.[39]

Assuming a continuum between these extremes, and assuming that bureaucrats seek to avoid either extreme, it follows that they will occupy a space on the continuum where values are likely to infuse bureaucratic decisionmaking to a significant degree.

An even stronger refutation of an efficiency-oriented fact-value dichotomy is presented by Charles Lindblom, who argues that decisionmakers will uncover many of their values and priorities only in the course of choosing among actual policies:

> Another precept of extraordinarily broad usefulness is: Do not separate the analysis of values or objectives from the empirical analysis of means or policies! This precept flies, of course, in the face of the common scientific admonition to keep value and fact separate. It is a useful stratagem for various reasons, some of which I can suggest. One is that values considered abstractly rather than embodied in specific policy alternatives are difficult to grasp. Most of us cannot claim to know, even for ourselves, very much about how greatly one values full employment, or price level stability, or the reduction of international tensions unless we can evaluate specific policies with implications for these values. Secondly, public discussion of abstract value is intolerably imprecise when the values are bandied about as abstractions. If I tell you that I am for more income equality or for price level stability or for peace or for racial integration, you know almost nothing about what I believe in.[40]

The proposition that bureaucratic policymaking is deeply pervaded by values also follows from the structural elements of bureaucracy discussed above. To the extent that bureaucracies act as political interest groups, they will seek to advance their own values and priorities concerning policy decisions. To the extent that the structure of bureaucracy is fragmented, different bureaucracies will advance different interests. And to the extent that bureaucracies conflict and compete, they will struggle against one another for their own subjective interests. None of these tendencies is likely to enhance the objectivity of bureaucratic decisions. The element of valuative decision is also manifest in other features of bureaucratic behavior, to be described below.

Elusive Goals   To the extent that public bureaucracies have difficulty defining precise goals and measures of performance, policymakers in bureaucratic units are left relatively free to make valuative decisions. In the absence of clear goals, there is at least a partial vacuum that must be filled by somebody's valuative decision. Bureaucracies are often contrasted to private enterprise, which has a measurable, financial, "bottom line" method of measuring performance. Leaving aside the question of how reliable or precise the "bottom line" in business actually is, there does seem to be good reason to contrast the financial goals and measures of business firms with the usual missions of public agencies. Government sometimes has clearly expressed goals — as when it provides rural electrification through the TVA, seeks to reduce the welfare rolls, or makes a benefit-cost comparison between two weapons designed to perform the same fundamental function. More often, programs and agencies have imprecise objectives like "improving health," "decreasing crime," "redeveloping the city," or "protecting the environment." Here the problem of setting goals is quite different from what it might be in business, and leaves considerable room for valuative decisions.

Loose Mandates   A major reason for the difficulty of defining precise goals for public bureaucracies is that Congress often supplies only vague legislative instructions. This loose statutory mandate allows — or even forces — bureaucrats to make valuative decisions as they devise and implement policy. In her analysis of the social services grants program, Martha Derthick portrays an extreme case in which vague congressional legislation left the door open to wholly unexpected results in expenditure and policy design.[41] This extreme example stands for a general class of policies in which the bureaucracy is left to interpret the meaning of affirmative action, aid to dependent children, community development grants, and so forth. One of the most persistent debates in public policy is over whether the bureaucracy is or is not carrying out the legislative intent. The point here is that there is normally room for reasonable debate on the matter.

Circularity of Bureaucratic Policymaking   Not only do bureaucrats typically have some significant discretion in interpreting legislation; it is often true that the same bureaucrats or others nearby designed the legislation in the first place. This circular process, with the bureaucracy located at both ends, gives bureaucratic policymakers a double opportunity to inject their values and goals into the shape of policy.

A classic example of this circularity is portrayed by Richard Blumenthal in his study of the development of the War on Poverty.[42]

The original designers of the program were members of a presidential task force under Sargent Shriver. Many of those same actors were then placed in charge of the War on Poverty programs in the Office of Economic Opportunity. These first antipoverty "warriors" were given the considerable task of translating an idea about social action — the concept of "community action" — into a program. The key phrase in the legislation concerning community action was that there be "maximum feasible participation" by the poor. Some members of the task force had come up with the phrase in the first place, but no one was sure just what it meant. Congress performed only a perfunctory scrutiny of the idea of maximum feasible participation, which, once passed into law, became the guiding concept of the program. The Congress left it to the administrators to work out their own vague idea according to their own vision and values.

Delegation and Discretion The delegation of decisionmaking authority in a bureaucracy gives lower-level administrators significant discretion to make their own valuative decisions. In the Wilsonian theory of bureaucracy and also in management appraisals such as that of the President's Committee on Administrative Management, delegation and discretion of this type are seen to undermine the efficiency and accountability of bureaucracy. The evidence is strong that such discretion is a pervasive characteristic of bureaucracy. According to Nadel and Rourke, "The scope of bureaucratic discretion in all societies is vast with respect to both the everyday routine decisions of government agencies and the major innovative or trend-setting decisions of public policy."[43] We are readily familiar with the scope of valuative decisions made by such organizations as the Federal Reserve Board and the Federal Communications Commission. Research has also revealed a large amount of room for individual valuative decision in the realm of what might appear to be programmed decisions. To give just one example, James Q. Wilson's research on police behavior shows that the surface structure of routinized rules and regulations disguises considerable discretion exercised by individual police officers.[44] In my own research on urban governance I found a strong pattern of value-oriented decisions by the city's footsoldiers (policemen, teachers, and so forth) despite administrative efforts to impose centralized control.[45]

Conflict among Experts   The advocacy role of experts was discussed in section 3, under conflict and competition. To the extent that experts and policy analysts work to advance the perspectives and goals of their own bureaucratic units, they will increase the number of individual valuative inputs into the policymaking process.

5. Silent Politics

Bureaucratic policymaking usually takes place in a setting that is sheltered from political debate and citizen scrutiny, at least as compared with policymaking processes involving elected officials. Presidents, governors, and mayors are heavily scrutinized and questioned by the press, the legislatures, and interest groups. Congressmen typically are eager to make public pronouncements about issues or policy disputes. On a major political issue, the legislative process will produce many voluble opinions and criticisms. On a highly controversial issue such as Watergate, energy, inflation, or the Soviet combat brigade in Cuba, the legislative process (along with the media) will produce a veritable din of public discourse and debate.

By contrast, the world of bureaucratic functioning is often completely unknown to the ordinary citizen or even to organized interest groups. The rising concern about congressional oversight of bureaucracy reflects the fact that legislators often have difficulty keeping track of what the bureaucracy is doing. Because of the fragmentation of the legislative oversight committees, any given representative will typically view only a very narrow segment of bureaucratic functioning and will lack any detailed understanding of the great part of bureaucratic activity. When a legislative subcommittee is in alliance with a bureaucratic subunit, as is the case with iron triangles, the open discussion of bureaucratic policymaking is likely to be even more silent. Recent presidents have also found it difficult to learn what is going on in their own bureaucracies. And as we saw in the last chapter, the growth of the White House staff came about in large part as a means of increasing presidential awareness and oversight of bureaucratic functioning. A careful student of the matter, Francis Rourke, believes that secrecy is a central feature of bureaucratic governance:

> The environment of bureaucracy is a cloistered sanctuary as compared with the limelight of publicity in which a legislative assembly normally

operates. Though an executive agency may hold public hearings, or conduct press conferences, or release news bulletins of one kind or another, it controls to a far greater extent than does the legislature the information available to the public on its internal deliberations and decisions . . . the growth of bureaucracy in American government has certainly brought about an enormous expansion in the secretiveness with which public policy is made.[46]

Some of the reasons for the silence of bureaucratic politics have already been foreshadowed in this analysis. For example, the fragmentation of bureaucratic structures makes it difficult to piece together the various components of policy discourse—even if someone is talking. Fragmentation has also allowed some agencies, like the Social Security Administration, the FBI, and the CIA, at times in their history to achieve a remarkable degree of policymaking autonomy. Once in this position of autonomy, the bureaucratic unit has no need to talk publicly about its activities; it can carry out its business in undisturbed silence. (Obviously, in the cases of the CIA and the FBI, a major additional reason for the existence of silent politics is that their administrative operations are cloaked in secrecy. It is a truism but not a trivial one that the more need for secrecy that is accorded a bureaucracy's decisionmaking, the more silent will be the politics surrounding it.)

The patterns of bureaucratic fragmentation presented above provide other sources of silent politics. The cleavage between political executives and civil servants, as Heclo shows, often creates a context in which the latter possess knowledge that the former need—a context in which it is very easy for the permanent civil servants to withhold relevant information. And the same is true of relationships between higher- and lower-level administrators when the lower levels possess important field or operating knowledge. In my own earlier research I found that many mayors, police chiefs, and school superintendents are ignorant about their city's services because their urban footsoldiers do not talk to their superiors about street-level conditions.

Several other features of bureaucracy's silent politics merit consideration. Most of these features have already come to light in our analysis; here we see a second aspect of their functioning. Because these features are already familiar to us, I will present them and their immediate implications only briefly.

Guild Professionalism   To the extent that a policy arena is dominated by a particular professional group, the group will attempt to
enforce its own norms, values, and professional language and will
seek to confine participation in the policymaking process to fellow
professionals. And the tendency of professionals to talk only to each
other creates another form of silent politics: the deliberate exclusion
of outsiders—both nonprofessionals and rival professionals—from
policy discourse.

Policy Subgovernments   In intergovernmental policymaking, the
existence of a strong vertical alliance between professional administrators at different levels of government will insulate policy discourse from involvement by citizens and officials who are not members of the policy subgovernment.

Circularity of Bureaucratic Policymaking   To the extent that the
bureaucracy designs a policy and then implements it, there is a circular process in which policy discourse is strongly influenced by and
largely confined to the bureaucracy. This does not mean that other
political actors have no say at all in the process. It does mean that
when circularity exists the bureaucracy will have a strong advantage
in policy debate and that its own internal debate will be relatively
silent to others.

Sporadic Press Coverage   In the section on bureaucracies as political interest groups, I offered the proposition that bureaucracies seek
to influence press coverage of their affairs, primarily through the
strategic use of leaks and exclusive stories and the development of
symbiotic relations with reporters. One effect of this endeavor is to
silence public debate about the bureaucracy's performance. An
additional proposition is that the press pays only sporadic attention
to bureaucratic operations *in any case*. Most bureaucratic decisionmaking unfolds over a long period of time, is presented in a technical or highly detailed form, and is not particularly dramatic. This
means that the bureaucracy typically does not provide good copy for
reporters. Consider the journalistic problem of how to report on
urban economic development, the food stamps program, or even
the effects of environmental or safety regulation in the customary
style of print and television reporting. What is needed is a crisis or a

scandal or a dramatic failure in policy to make an arresting story. Any attentive observer will see that the press does not cover ordinary bureaucratic operations in any substantial breadth or depth. Devoted students of the bureaucracy must turn to a publication like the *National Journal* for such information, a publication that is read largely by bureaucrats and lobbyists. In the absence of sustained press coverage, bureaucracies are left to engage in silent politics.

6. Power Conservation

In popular discourse we are confronted with two very different portraits of bureaucratic behavior. It is often claimed that bureaucrats routinely seek to expand their programs and policies as much as possible. The contrasting view is that bureaucrats are rigid, hidebound, and conservative and rarely act aggressively in any way at all. The notion of the rapacious bureaucrat has been dominant in recent scholarly analysis. Anthony Downs, for example, suggests that bureaucrats constantly attempt to increase the resources of their units. In an even stronger claim, William Niskanen asserts that bureaus typically seek to maximize their budgets.[47]

In what follows, I will present a view of bureaucratic behavior that falls between budget maximization and hidebound inaction. I will call that middle position "power conservation." By power conservation, I mean that bureaucratic behavior is characterized by attempts to protect turf, maintain existing programs, and avoid controversial jurisdictional disputes. Bureaucracies also doubtless seek to increase their budgets, but they do this in a limited and guarded fashion. They will be guarded because, above all, bureaucracies fear budget reductions, which would make them look like clear losers in the competitive game of budgetary politics. So strong is this fear that it constitutes an ever present threat to organizational survival and what Louis Bragaw has termed a "hidden stimulus" to bureaucratic vigilance and, more positively, to bureaucratic activism and innovation. On the basis of his experience with the Coast Guard bureaucracy, Bragaw writes as follows about the threat to an agency's survival posed by budgetary reductions:

> Such a threat can take several forms. In mild form it is manifested by fiscal starvation, brought about by the lack of capital funds, or oper-

ating funds, or both. Simply put, the agency's budget is cut or is held constant in an inflationary climate. In strong form the threat is of partial takeover of one or more programs or functions of the agency by another agency.[48]

I believe that this general pattern power conservation is a rational response to a bureaucratic environment characterized by political interest-group behavior, fragmentation, and competition and conflict. I will first present some of the empirical features and sources of power conservation, then fit the bureaucratic impulse to conserve power into a more synthetic account of bureaucratic politics.

Standard Operating Procedures   The concept of standard operating procedures has come up before, in the section on bureaucratic fragmentation. Its implications in the context of power conservation should be obvious. Bureaucracies will adhere strongly to their traditional practices and programs, and will defend their historical ways of doing business against all attackers and challenges. For example, if the Air Force has always had a manned bomber, it will fight hard to retain one — as it did, in fact, in pressing for the development of the Skybolt missile system in the early 1960s. More generally, standard operating procedures tend to wed a bureaucracy to a particular historical set of interests. Thus bureaucracies will attempt to conserve their existing package of programs, that is, to conserve the power they have known in the past.

Mission   Bureaucracies will define a mission for their agency of which they are proud. This proposition is closely related to the one about standard operating procedures. Once a preferred mission has been staked out, the bureaucracy will energetically defend that mission against any external attempts to alter or diminish it. James Q. Wilson has described this tendency:

> Strong organizations are typically those in which the sense of mission is widely shared and successfully adapted to the requirements of organizational survival and enhancement. We describe such organizations as having a high esprit de corps, but we sometimes fail to note that this implies more than mere high morale or good feelings, it refers to an attachment to a distinctive way of doing things.[49]

Clinging to and defending a distinctive historical mission is thus another form of organizational power conservation.

Bureaucratic Time-Horizons   One implication of the tendency of civil servants to develop long time-horizons is that bureaucrats will act to preserve their traditional policies and will move only gingerly in building on that traditional base. This is another aspect of power conservation in bureaucracy. It is important to note, however, that this relatively conservative, gradualist strategy can produce large changes over time. Heclo makes this key point about bureaucratic gradualism:

> What appears to be bureaucratic torpor is in many instances the function of a different, albeit lengthy, time scale within governments. In the life span of political executives a change of 5 percent a year may count for little, but to the civil servants whose clocks are set for ten or fifteen years in influential positions, 5 percent a year can cumulate into comprehensive change . . . Normally . . . the gradualist inclination is likely to prevail: small changes frequently and large changes rarely . . . Gradualism counsels that what can be done serially or integrated into an already accepted activity is to be preferred as a means of reducing the agonies of change.[50]

Boundary Issues   Whenever a bureaucratic unit attempts to influence policy at or beyond the boundaries of its historically established domain, it is likely to encounter strong opposition. Therefore, as part of their power-conserving strategy, bureaucracies will avoid boundary issues and confine themselves to business that falls clearly within their domains.

Derthick has demonstrated this tendency in her study of Social Security. The Social Security Administration was able to expand and consolidate its power greatly within its own preestablished field of influence, but when it tried to implement policies at the boundaries of that field of influence it ran into organized opposition:

> Boundary issues pitted large formal organizations against one another — the Social Security Administration, in alliance with organized labor, against the business federations and the insurance companies, which happened to have little zest for the fight, and against the AMA, which had an enormous zest.[51]

Thus it is in a bureaucracy's interest not to trespass on other organizations' territory but to stay at home and protect its own jurisdictional boundaries from encroachment by outsiders.

Veto Groups   The fragmented character of American policymaking provides both a multiplicity of points of access and also a multiplicity of groups with the power to veto any given policy proposal. Whenever a bureaucracy ventures very far outside its established territory, it is likely to run into one veto group or another. The existence of such groups gives bureaucracies yet another reason to avoid making new enemies and to conserve their power in the policymaking terrain they already dominate.

Reinforcing Old Alliances   Bureaucracies will seek to reinforce their alliances with old constituents and clienteles as a way of conserving their existing power relationships. In a competitive bureaucratic world, it may be hard to find reliable new allies, and it may be rather easy, by comparison, to create new enemies. Thus the rational bureaucrat will be careful to preserve strong relations with old, known friends. This feature also constitutes a power-conserving tendency in that a bureaucracy will tend to favor its old allies and the policies and programs that its old alliances entail. In the extreme case, a bureaucracy may become so rigidly attached to the interests of old clients and constituents that it grows out of touch with the evolution of major new interests. As Samuel Huntington has shown, this form of rigidification appears to have afflicted the Interstate Commerce Commission as a result of its long relationship with the railroad industry.[52] The long-standing alliance between the Federal Trade Commission and the fur and textiles industry is another case in point.

7. Loose Administrative Control

Another element of bureaucratic functioning is loose administrative control of ostensibly subordinate organizations by hierarchically superior ones. By loose control I mean simply that public managers at various levels of government have difficulty monitoring, regulating, and evaluating their lower-level administrators. This element of functioning derives largely from the structural features of bureaucratic fragmentation analyzed above. Since we have encountered these features of bureaucratic governance before, I will present them only briefly in the context of loose control.

The President and the Departments   The president often possesses only loose control of his cabinet secretaries.

Loose Mandates   To the extent that Congress gives the bureaucracy weak and vague mandates, it will be difficult to control bureaucratic implementation of legislative mandates.

Political Executives and Civil Servants   The cabinet secretary and other political executives possess loose control of professional civil servants.

High-Level and Lower-Level Bureaucracies   Higher-level bureaucrats have relatively loose control over lower-level bureaucrats. Herbert Kaufman has shown that managers do possess a large amount of information about what is going on in their organizations; their problem is to find the appropriate source of feedback, out of many possible sources, and then to ask the right questions about subordinates' behavior. In any case, Kaufman's inference is that higher-level bureaucrats have difficulty in selecting and applying their feedback in the process of program and personnel evaluation.[53]

Delegation and Discretion   The discretion given to lower-level administrators compounds the control problem, since higher-level administrators often do not know what discretionary decisions are made at lower levels and for what reasons.

Guild Professionalism   The various professional guilds will be difficult to control by administrative superiors for reasons given above.

Policy Subgovernments   The relative autonomy of intergovernmental policy subgovernments will also present a problem of control for political executives at all levels.

8. Expansion of Bureaucratic Policymaking

A recurrent complaint against bureaucracies is that they constantly seek to increase their expenditures and their authority. This view of "creeping" or even "marching" bureaucratic activity envisions a progressive domination of other sectors by a calculating and ever more autonomous "bureaucratic state." I have already addressed the question of whether bureaucrats maximize their budgets and have offered an alternative pattern of behavior in power conservation. Nevertheless, it is necessary to take on the broader question of bureaucratic expansionism directly. I will present an analysis of the proliferation of bureaucratic policymaking that, in a general way, supports ordinary notions of bureaucratic expansionism. Several key points should be made about this analysis. First, it is important to understand that bureaucracies expand their activities in many different ways and for various reasons, rather than on the basis of a self-conscious, imperialistic agenda. Second, bureaucracy expands for both offensive and defensive reasons. This is in keeping with the concept of power conservation, which depicts bureaucracies as defending their jurisdictions and inching ahead more often than setting out on bold new initiatives. Third, bureaucracies expand their policymaking activities in response to both internal and external pressures. Beer has suggested that bureaucracies themselves provide most of the energy and momentum behind their own activities.[54] I will pay careful attention to these internal forces but will argue that an account of bureaucratic behavior that ignores external pressures tells only part of the story.

Given the analysis so far, it should be no surprise that bureaucracies tend gradually to enlarge their roles over a wide spectrum of policymaking functions — spending money, designing new programs and bureaucratic units, developing new regulations, expanding their evaluation of lower-level governments, and increasing their control of the flow of information. If bureaucracies act as political interest groups, operate in a fragmented environment, and compete with one another, it makes sense that the bureaucratic landscape should be populated by many different actors fighting to expand their own spheres of action. The interest groups that are the clients and constituents of the bureaucracies create another pressure for expansion in the myriad claims they press on government. In what follows, I will list some of the major features of the expansion and proliferation of policymaking among bureaucracies. Once again some of these features are quite familiar by now, and I will discuss them as briefly as possible.

Professionals as Innovators   Professionals within government have initiated many recent government policies. As Daniel Moynihan has pointed out, professionals in the social services field played a primary role in the development of the War on Poverty and especially its community action program. Beer generalizes the point to suggest that wherever professionals hold a strong grip within a bureaucracy, they will seek to expand their domains so as more fully to implement their professional strategies and techniques.[55]

This tendency toward program expansion is strongest when professionals have developed new technologies that they wish to introduce in their policy initiatives. Medicine provides a familiar example of this consequence of new technology as publicly supported hospitals are continually pressed to provide new and more sophisticated techniques and instruments (such as the CAT scanner). This pattern exists elsewhere as well: in education, for example, professionals in the field seem to be constantly developing new technologies, such as the new math, programmed instruction, teaching machines, and so forth. The pattern also obtains for new weapons systems in the military. The general proposition is that professionals will consistently seek to increase program expenditures for their methodologies and new technologies.

Micromanagement of Public Policy As discussed earlier bureaucracies often have difficulty specifying clear objectives and hence measuring performance. In the absence of clear ends, bureaucracies will often choose a strategy that emphasizes detailed, tangible means as a surrogate measure of performance. For example, as Paul MacAvoy has shown, a regulatory bureaucracy like the Occupational Safety and Health Administration (OSHA) may lack any clear sense of how to improve occupational safety.[56] What it can do is to develop detailed standards for factory equipment and procedures — even, in the extreme case, establishing precise regulations for the size and structure of ladders. Although OSHA may not know which of its efforts will improve safety (a means-end problem) or even how to define safety adequately (the ends problem), it can measure compliance with its regulations and thus show tangible results of its programs. Medicine is another field in which such patterns often obtain: elaborate means measures, such as number of patient-visits or length of stay in the hospital, are used as surrogates for measures of "health care." A similar example occurs in the case of federal grants-in-aid. Federal bureaucrats may not be able to prove that they have awarded grants to the best renewal or social service applications. But they can prove that eligibility requirements were strict and that many aspects of the proposal were examined — if they develop a highly detailed application form.

Thus bureaucracies will tend to develop highly detailed measures and regulations that demonstrates tangible results of some sort. As bureaucracies follow this tendency, they will increasingly be drawn into the micromanagement of their programs; that is, they will devote attention and energy to devising ever more microscopic regulations. And micromanagement manifestly entails the proliferation of bureaucratic policymaking.

The Camel's Nose Syndrome For at least three reasons, public programs will often be begun on a small, even experimental basis and then over time will grow far beyond their initial dimensions. I call this the camel's nose syndrome, after what happens when you decide to let *just* the nose of the camel under the tent. One reason for this pattern is that bureaucratic policymakers and legislators often feel genuine uncertainty about how a proposed program will work in practice. In this situation it is a rational strategy to try out a program on a limited basis. Once a program is running, its professional administrators will usually favor its expansion. They will have a bureaucratic stake in the program, and they will have begun to operate as another political interest group within the bureaucracy.

A second more strategic reason for the camel's nose approach is that what appears to be only a short-term pilot program is likely to encounter less criticism from the Office of Management and Budget and the Congress. Congressmen will scrutinize the merits of a program less rigorously if the price tag is low and if it appears that the program can be eliminated later. Once a program has been enacted, it is easier to expand it gradually without encountering intense opposition. Also, if a program simply turns out to be more expensive than expected (as happens with many military projects), it is harder to stop it after time and money have already been invested. So the camel's nose strategy succeeds both coming and going.

A third reason for the camel's nose syndrome is that once a program is implemented, even on a small scale, it will attract its own particular clients and constituents, who will exert pressure for program expansion.

Trickle-Down Effects   Expansion of policy at the federal level will cause a chain reaction leading to similar expansion at the local level. As I noted in Chapter 2, local governments often serve as the operating agencies to carry out federal policies. In this case, local bureaucracies obviously must expand their own activities to meet new responsibilities imposed from above. It is not unusual for state and local governments to create new bureaucracies in direct response to developments in the federal structure. The growth of local environmental protection agencies is one case in point. Whether or not new bureaucratic units are created, any new policy initiative undertaken at the federal level is likely to impose information and transaction costs on the governmental system below it. This will cause the policy subgovernments to expand their administrative activities, and the same will be true for the governors' and mayors' central bureaucracies.

Citizen Participation   Since the early 1960s, the level of citizen participation throughout government has greatly increased. Minorities and women in particular have increased their involvement as a consequence of the civil rights and women's movements. As I have shown elsewhere, the rise of citizen participation has been especially significant at the urban level, and specifically in terms of the involvement of neighborhood groups.[57] Two observers have termed this development the "community revolution."[58] Increased citizen participation has two main implications for bureaucratic policymaking. First, the simple fact of participation requires bureaucracies to develop new procedures to deal with citizen involvement. Typically these procedures add steps to the policy process, and for that reason expand the length and complexity of government deliberations. Second, citizen participation is likely to generate a new set of problems, issues, and complaints for bureaucracies to deal with, thus expanding the agenda on which bureaucracies are to work. Both of these effects encourage the bureaucracy's tendency to expand.

Responsiveness and Red Tape   When bureaucracies take new initiatives to respond to new needs and problems, they will tend to create additional regulations, guidelines, administrative structures, and policymaking routines. In the extreme case, the government may create a new agency or department to tackle a new problem. To a critical observer, this proliferation of policymaking may seem to be just another example of bureaucracy's instinct for red tape. But, as Herbert Kaufman has suggested, much red tape may be a function of responsiveness to demands for governmental action. If the government is to "do something" about environmental protection, welfare fraud, highway and occupational safety, civil rights and affirmative action, it needs to design policymaking routines, information-gathering mechanisms, standards, and added institutional capacities, all of which add up to more bureaucracy. In Kaufman's view, "Every restraint and requirement originates in somebody's demand for it . . . each constraint is the product of a fairly small number of claimants. But there are so many of us, and such a diversity of interests among us, that modest individual demands result in great stacks of official paper and bewildering procedural mazes."[59] Whether or not one agrees with Kaufman's strong statement of the point, it is hard to deny the general relationship between responsiveness and the proliferation of bureaucratic policymaking.

The Doctrine of Equality   An idea that has been prominent in recent public discourse, the ideal of equality, also contributes to the proliferation of bureaucracy. Equality means very different things to different people, but however one defines it, it bears on this analysis in two important ways. First, it encourages public policymakers to become more inclusive in defining the groups they are attempting to aid. In recent years, for example, bureaucracies have attempted to make sure that all people whose incomes fall below a government-defined poverty line receive assistance from public programs, and similar efforts have been made for the handicapped and the elderly. This impulse toward inclusiveness naturally tends to expand bureaucratic activity. Second, not only does the idea of equality lead to greater inclusiveness within the groups aided by public programs; it also lengthens the list of groups that should be given aid. This expanding definition of those who deserve help traces a course from a concern with blacks in the civil rights movement, to other minorities such as Hispanics, to women, to the elderly, to the homosexual community. The flexibility of the concept of equality is demonstrated when residents of ethnic neighborhoods begin to assert that they too are suffering from inequality, in part as a result of previous egalitarian strategies like busing and the War on Poverty. The concern for equality expands the agenda for bureaucratic policymaking and creates a dynamic in which additional groups come forward to press their particular claims for equal treatment.

In summary, in this chapter I have broken down bureaucracy into its major components in order to develop a detailed political model of bureaucratic behavior. I have listed eight basic features of bureaucracy and supported and amplified each feature with a number of empirical propositions. As demonstrated here, the structure of public bureaucracies is characterized by interest-group behavior, fragmentation, and conflict and competition, and the functioning of public bureaucracies is distinguished by valuative decision, silent politics, power conservation, loose administrative control, and the expansion of policymaking activities.

4

The Politics of Bureaucracy

Now that we have a detailed political analysis of bureaucratic behavior, the next task is to present a more schematic
and unified view of the politics of bureaucracy. It is necessary to
look at bureaucratic politics from both a "micro" and a "macro"
point of view.

From the micro point of view, the question is whether the political
model of bureaucracy I have presented can provide a persuasive explanation of the behavior of the individual bureaucrat or head of an
administrative unit. The notion of the bureaucrat as a rational economic actor will be useful here. In particular, William Niskanen's
analysis of bureaucratic behavior, reinforced by the work of Anthony
Downs, treats the rational bureaucrat as a maximizer of budget out-
lays. For Niskanen, this budget maximization is a close analogy to
the idea of profit maximization in the theory of the private firm.
The analogy is not exact, however, because bureaucrats operate in
an environment that constrains simple budget maximization. As
Niskanen puts it:

> The constraint that ultimately limits the size of bureaus is that a
> bureau, on the average, must supply that output expected by the
> sponsor on its approval of the bureau's budget. A bureau that con-
> sistently promises more than it can deliver will be penalized by the dis-
> counting of future promises and lower budgets.[1]

The concept of the bureaucrat as rational maximizer fits well with
certain characteristics of the bureaucracy presented earlier. I have

suggested, for example, that bureaucracies will seek to maximize the number of allies they can claim among their constituents and elsewhere, and that they will attempt to increase their autonomy, authority, and control as much as possible.

On this view, we have a rational bureaucratic maximizer who strives single-mindedly for more funds, autonomy, and control. The next question is what kind of government would exist if all or most bureaucrats really acted as rational maximizers. A simple response is that the bureaucratic maximizer, if left to his own aspirations and devices, would establish a world of separate bureaucratic monopolies. In such a world, each bureaucratic unit would hold complete, or virtually complete, sway over a particular area of policy. Each bureaucracy would attract its corps of constituent allies, congressional subcommittee members, outside experts, denizens of the White House staff and OMB, as well as friendly press reporters. Each bureaucracy would also work out stable treaties and boundaries with neighboring bureaucracies and so would not have to worry about bureaucratic conflict and jurisdictional disputes. This picture of administrative life would delight the bureaucratic maximizer.

The question for us here is to what extent the maximizer's aspirations in fact explain typical bureaucratic behavior. In the first place, it is true that a small number of government agencies may have come close to achieving the status of a bureaucratic monopoly in which the strategy of the budget maximizer would have a good chance of success. The category of strong public monopolies includes the CIA and FBI at the peak of their power and autonomy, and the Social Security Administration, which has so successfully defended its share of the market of public business.[2] The TVA, local police departments, and state departments of corrections also occupy relatively monopolistic positions in the markets for their services. These examples notwithstanding, few public bureaucracies hold at any time a clear monopolistic position like that of the FBI. Any bureaucratic maximizer knows that there are other bureaus, interest groups, congressional committees, and presidential assistants who are likely to contest his control of his domain.

Another relatively attractive strategy for a budget maximizer would be the creation of stable bureaucratic oligopolies. If an area of public policymaking were controlled by two or three bureaucracies and each had a stake in keeping other "public firms" from influencing that policy sector, then the budget maximizer could follow his inclination to increase his agency's expenditures and authority. It may be that there are some examples of actual government oligopolies, such as the Army, Navy, Air Force, and Marines in military policy. But even in military matters, other political forces in the White House, in the Congress, and among the interest groups come into play depending on the circumstances. Involvement in military policy will have a very different complexion depending on whether the issue is a new troop carrier, SALT II, or relations with Iran. If the service branches do constitute an oligopoly, it is an unstable one.

To take a quite different case, the bureaucratic budget maximizer might face a highly competitive bureaucratic market for goods and services. If there were many different units in direct competition to supply the same services, this would surely influence our maximizer's strategy. But it takes little reflection to realize that bureaucracies do not operate in an open market with many competing suppliers of services. Most bureaucracies enjoy a relatively exclusive position in a special area of policymaking, and the barriers to entry are high for other institutions wishing to get into the public business. Even the Social Security Administration found it difficult to penetrate other public (and private) markets.

What does this add up to in terms of bureaucratic behavior? The bureaucratic maximizer knows that he is unlikely to establish a full monopoly of his business. But neither does he operate in a fully competitive market environment. He cannot act at will, but he does have some definite leverage in his policy arena. In other words, the maximizer is a constrained maximizer. He would like to increase expenditures and autonomy but recognizes that there are many actual or potential contestants in his environment. The constrained maximizer realizes that if he pushes too far he will run into intense conflict with other agencies as well as with the Congress, the OMB, and opposing interest groups. Given the fragmentation of government, he also knows that he has a strong advantage in maintaining control of and working to advance his own particular piece of policy.

These characteristics generate a picture of a bureaucratic policy-maker who, in the language of game theory, follows a *minimax* strategy. In the face of hostile forces, he pursues the course that will advance his interest as much as possible while also being least likely to generate intense conflict. To go one step further, a minimaxer will cautiously and defensively inch ahead, being highly protective of his domain at the same time as he tests the possibilities of extending the limits of his expenditures and authority. Posing the minimax strategy in this way shows how the structural elements of fragmentation and conflict bear on the behavior of rational bureaucratic actors, viewed in micro terms. Significantly, this explanation supports the idea of power conservation developed in Chapter 3. It means that bureaucrats will seek to advance their own policies and enhance their power but that they will do so in a limited and guarded fashion.

The conception of the minimaxer also fits well with other elements of bureaucratic behavior presented in Chapter 3. For one thing a careful minimaxer can never be sure that existing alliances are stable. Issues may arise in which previous allies suddenly become antagonists. This insight constitutes a counsel for caution, because if the minimaxer moves carefully he will be less likely to disrupt existing alliances. A minimaxer also knows that there are many interest groups, not active at present in his arena, who might come into play as opposing forces if his bureaucracy were to push too far or too fast. As in the case of the Social Security Administration, it is particularly difficult to cross the preestablished boundaries of policymaking activity without arousing opposition from those who have a previous stake on the other side of the boundary. Inching ahead within one's own policy domain is a far safer strategy than incurring the risks of moving into a new field.

The notion of silent politics also fits with the minimax strategy in that one bureaucracy will have relatively little knowledge of what is going on in a rival bureaucracy. Given this situation, a rational bureaucrat knows that he ventures out of his own domain only with a great deal of uncertainty about what to expect.

The minimax strategy also fits well with the observed tendency toward the expansion and proliferation of policymaking activity. We saw earlier that there are many pressures for expansion. But they are fully consistent with the inching ahead strategy of the bureaucrat who calculates possible advances in the face of actual or potential opposition.

There is a final point to be made about the minimaxer's strategy.

In game theory, an actor faced with opposing forces will seek to form coalitions with friendly forces in order to solidify his position. Indeed, we find much coalition building by bureaucracies. It is particularly manifest in a bureaucracy's efforts to create iron triangles among the bureaucracy, constituent groups, and congressional committees. The attempt to create this triangular relationship is a specific instance of the minimaxer's effort to gain secure control of a small part of the policy process. If iron triangles were pervasive and fully successful, then the minimaxer could be less cautious. But while iron triangles are clearly an important feature in national policymaking, they usually do not end the competitive game of bureaucratic politics. Even if the services, for example, have strong allies in Congress who will protect the Defense Department against antimilitary sentiment, these allies do not provide complete protection. Criticisms of military spending have prospered in spite of the iron triangle. Also, even if external forces were entirely muted, which is highly unlikely, the competition among the services for new weapons systems and force buildups would continue. So even in the case of the military and with the supporting connection of iron triangles, the minimaxer would still be inclined to pursue his limited, defensive strategy of inching ahead.

There are at least two other reasons why coalition building does not solve the bureaucrat's problem of dealing with hostile forces in the environment. First, issue contexts change and in changing create new configurations of allies and enemies. Second, the way that funding is handed out in government budgets does not provide an incentive for cooperative behavior among agencies. Bureaucrats know that fruitful partnerships with other agencies do not translate easily into gains for one's own unit.

Segmented Pluralism

The question from a macro point of view is, if the rational bureaucrat behaves as a minimaxer because of the forces present in his environment, especially the combination of fragmentation and conflict, what does this mean for the political structure of bureaucracy? One implication is that a minimaxer working in the bureaucratic environment I have depicted should produce a system that might best be termed *segmented pluralism*. In general, in any given policy arena, there will be multiple influences—from the bureaucracy, interest groups, Congress, lower-level officials, and other players in pluralist politics. But the bureaucratic impetus will be to segment policymaking, to try to control a particular portion of policy and hold it tight against assault. Fragmentation permits a strategy of maintaining control over relatively small segments of policy, but conflict and competition make this strategy likely to be a somewhat insecure and potentially contested one.

This conception of segmented pluralism departs significantly from two recent characterizations of bureaucratic policymaking. One line of argument is presented by Theodore Lowi, in his notion of "interest group liberalism." According to Lowi, the idea of the public interest and the older philosophy of liberalism have been abandoned for a new public philosophy, which gives interest groups a disproportionate influence over government.[3] In some cases, Lowi asserts, authority has been directly delegated to the interest groups. In other cases, government agencies have become the handmaidens of powerful interest groups. Lowi also asserts that this apparent capitulation to interest-group power is a consequence of the very pluralist doctrine that emphasizes the importance of interest-group activity and portrays government as a source of multiple points of access. This characterization is highly arguable, but the important point here is that the bureaucratic actor (and thus bureaucracy as an independent force) is a phantom in Lowi's analysis. I believe that the motivation and typical behavior behind the supply of bureaucratic services are as important as the demand for those services by interest groups. Specifically, it is easy to see how the development of segmented pluralism could be sought and influenced by interest groups. But my point here is that segmented pluralism is a logical consequence of the minimaxing behavior of bureaucrats in the environment of fragmentation and conflict and the other features detailed in Chapter 3.

Another line of argument, offered by Anthony King, suggests that American government has in recent years become "atomized" —split into tiny elements, disintegrated.[4] I believe the idea of atomization is too strong a characterization for the behavior of bureaucracy. I have chosen the term segmented pluralism because it implies a large number of policymaking centers, but it does not entail a state of anarchy or near anarchy in bureaucratic political and policymaking relations. As we have seen, bureaucratic fragmentation and conflict operate against a backdrop of often stable and persistent interactions—those of constituency relations, professional guilds, policy subgovernments, issue networks, and even iron triangles.

A second macro implication of a rational minimax strategy in bureaucracy is that government, as a whole, will come to pursue a kind of *something-for-everyone politics.* This follows from the central idea of a minimaxer inching ahead in a bureaucratic context of segmented pluralism—where many different minimaxers can play the same game. Something-for-everyone politics also reflects a bureaucratic world in which there are more interest groups pressing their demands, more devices for citizen participation, more activity by policy subgovernments and by organizations of local officials, and more issues and problems placed on the public agenda. In such a world, increases in government spending and in bureaucratic activity do not require dramatic shifts in decisionmaking, nor do they require that individual bureaucrats be greedy maximizers. Nor do they require, as Lowi asserts, that interest groups capture particular agencies of government. All that is required to create something-for-everyone politics is that the minimaxer be inching ahead in a segmented bureaucratic world.

This is not the time to assess the policy consequences of this analysis. But it should be obvious that the controversial problem of controlling government is complicated if what must be controlled is hundreds of segmented bureaucracies attempting to inch ahead in a climate of something-for-everyone politics.

Bureaucracy and Pluralist Democracy

The political system of bureaucracy depicted above is obviously not entirely compatible with the doctrines of pluralist democracy and administrative efficiency. The next task is to understand what kinds of problems this behavioral portrait of bureaucracy presents for these two models of how government ought to operate.

Let us take the model of pluralist democracy first. In appraising the politics of bureaucracy against the ideal of pluralist democracy, the important issues are the need to avoid excessive concentrations of power and the roles of multiple centers of power in checking one another, creating access to government, and accommodating and balancing interest-group demands.

To take the matter of excessive concentrations of power, our analysis of bureaucracy, with its emphasis on fragmentation and conflict, suggests that the bureaucratic system is surely not a monolith. This monolithic view of bureaucratic power is almost certainly not an accurate one. A more plausible problem that might be posed by bureaucracy for democratic theory is that instead of one great monopoly, the bureaucratic system comprises a great many small monopolies, operating separately. I appraised this conception in Chapter 3 and concluded that while monopolies may have existed from time to time, for example the CIA and the FBI, the picture of pervasive small-scale monopoly does not accurately characterize the structure of bureaucratic politics. This conclusion was largely based on the argument that there are substantial conflict and competition among bureaucracies.

So far, one might conclude that since no extensive monopoly of power and few small-scale monopolies exist, and since there is observable conflict and competition, bureaucracy is in fact a microcosm of the hoped-for pluralist system of multiple centers of power and checks and balances. Whether this interpretation provides gratifying evidence for believers in pluralist democracy will depend on how strictly one constructs tests for pluralist democracy. Any appraisal will depend on the amount of competition and conflict required, on what degree of access one insists on for interest groups, and on what kind of balance and accommodation are required in the pluralist bargaining process. These are questions that have not been fully answered in the theory of pluralist democracy either by the Founding Fathers or by more recent writers. For example, Dahl speaks in *Who Governs* of five patterns of leadership, two of which are "independent sovereignties with spheres of influence" and "rival sovereignties fighting it out."[5] Both of these characterizations seem to fit my description of segmented pluralism in bureaucracy particularly well. But again the questions are: How democratic are the patterns of "independent sovereignties" or "rival sovereignties"? And how strict are these tests for pluralist democracy?

Let us consider the implications of segmented pluralism for democracy from three different vantage points: (1) relationships within a bureaucratic segment, (2) relationships among segments, and

(3) relationships between bureaucracy and neighboring institutions like the Congress and state and local governments.

1. Behavior within a Segment

Even within a policy segment, decisions are influenced by a variety of bureaucratic, congressional, and interest-group actors, so the process is not entirely closed to outsiders. But inside a segment is also where competition is likely to be at a minimum. It is precisely within policy segments that the minimaxer is likely to be most successful in stabilizing and controlling his turf and that policymaking is most likely to be shielded from public view. Thus bureaucratic behavior within a policy segment appears to be at odds with the norms of pluralist democracy.

Several reinforcing points can be made about the undemocratic nature of behavior within policy segments. Where guild professionalism operates in bureaucracy, professionals will naturally have their strongest impact within their own particular policy segment. The same should be true of policy subgovernments in the intergovernmental system and for lower-level bureaucrats who have developed narrow areas of expertise: their impact will be greatest within their own segment. Bureaucracies are also most likely to have developed favored relationships with old clients within their own segments; this tendency to reinforce old alliances may create a barrier to access and participation by newer interest groups (as Huntington has shown it did in the case of the ICC).[6] Bureaucrats also have the most freedom to make valuative decisions without strong opposition in their own small policy segments. Furthermore, bureaucratic policymaking is most likely to be silent inside a policy segment that is heavily influenced by professionals, policy subgovernments, and old allies.

If bureaucratic conflict and competition increase as one moves away from one's own policy segment, the minimaxer has a powerful incentive to spend his time fortifying his particular segment against encroachment. He will seek to limit the number of actors in his sphere, to restrict competition, and to regulate the access of new interest groups. None of these activities squares with the doctrine of pluralist democracy, unless one sets very low standards for competition and access.

A fundamental implication of this description of the workings of bureaucratic segments is that bureaucratic preferences and initiatives count heavily in the policymaking process as compared to the preferences of citizens and elected officials. This situation is not troublesome from the point of view of the administrative efficiency model, but giving this much importance to bureaucratic preferences is certainly at war with the pluralist doctrines of participation and control by citizens and their elected representatives.

2. Relationships among Segments

If the political process within policy segments seems to work against pluralist democratic values, perhaps the relationships among policy segments are more favorable to the overall system of pluralist democracy. Support for this view is found in the observation that conflict and competition exist among bureaucracies. In a highly segmented bureaucratic structure, there are apt to be many different points of access for interest groups pressing their claims. With all the different policy segments looking for allies, something like an open market for bureaucratic services emerges in government. Formal procedures such as affirmative action have been established to ensure the representation of various minorities among the employees of government bureaucracies. A number of bureaucracies also have procedures for public hearings, community involvement, and other forms of citizen participation that work to increase the access to government of groups previously unrepresented.

These aspects of bureaucratic politics do appear to fit with the goals of pluralist democracy. It will be easier, however, to appraise the democratic character of interbureaucratic relationships if we make some assumptions about the structure of those relationships. Let us briefly map some possible structures of bureaucratic interaction and consider their implications for pluralist democracy.

One possibility is that the bureaucratic system of politics contains a small number of large segments that operate pretty much in isolation from one another (see figure 4.1). This structure implies that each of the major segments is a monopoly. Such a structure prevents an absolute concentration of power but does little to promote the competitive checking and balancing process of pluralist democracy.

A second possible structure is one in which bureaucracy has a small number of large segments that do interact and check and bal-

Figure 4.1 Interbureaucratic relations I.

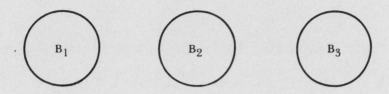

ance each other. ("Balance" is used in the limited sense that no one section is so powerful that it can overcome other bureaucratic interests at will.) This structure is depicted in figure 4.2, with the arrows indicating lines of interaction and competition. This structure resembles figure 2.2, the map of the Congress, the presidency, and state and local governments. It might very well provide a strong expression of the norms of pluralist democracy, but it is an unrealistic map. Bureaucracy of course is not divided into a few neat policy segments, and there is considerable reason to believe, following the behavior of the bureaucratic minimaxer, that bureaucracies do not seek to interact as openly and symmetrically as the diagram suggests. Rather, they try to maintain or strengthen control over their own segment and to limit competition as much as possible in the interests of their own autonomy.

A third possible structure of interbureaucratic relations involves a multiplicity of policy segments with little or no mutual interaction, as indicated by the broken lines in figure 4.3. Such a structure

Figure 4.2 Interbureaucratic relations II.

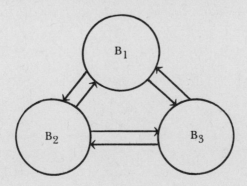

Figure 4.3 Interbureaucratic relations III.

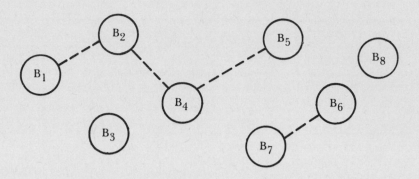

would represent a triumph for the minimaxer seeking autonomy and control in his own segment. It would allay the pluralist democrat's fear of absolute concentrations of power, but it would not eliminate smaller concentrations. Nor would there be any process of checking and balancing among bureaucracies, since each bureaucracy would be left alone to work on its own affairs. This depiction of conflict-free bureaucratic relationships is unrealistic, however.

A fourth possible structure of relationships among bureaucracies is one that has a large number of policy segments, some of which interact, check, and balance (figure 4.4). This map clearly corresponds to my account of segmented pluralism. At first glance, this structure seems to fulfill several of the norms of pluralist democracy. Its segmentation is likely to prevent intersectoral concentrations of power, and it does provide for a certain amount of competition and checking of opposing forces. What it does not prevent is a progres-

Figure 4.4 Interbureaucratic relations IV.

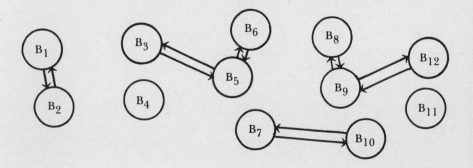

sive accretion of power *within* particular policy segments, since the competitive forces are strongest at the boundaries of different bureaucratic jurisdictions. Nor does it insure that citizens involvement or congressional control will be very strong or decisive. Indeed, the fundamental problem that segmented pluralism presents for pluralist democratic theory is that bureaucrats have substantial power to set the government's agenda, make valuative decisions, interpret the decisions of other bodies such as the Congress, and operate in an environment of relatively silent politics. Segmented pluralism in bureaucracy deserves one cheer from advocates of pluralist democratic theory, but it also raises grave problems about citizen control of public policymaking.

The rough map in figure 4.4 does not amount to a precise measurement of the structure of the bureaucratic system. It merely indicates that there are many relatively small segments which experience some degree of conflict and competition; it gives no information about how small and insular they are or how much competition they experience. It seems to me that how well these segments fit the pluralist democratic model depends critically on these two variables. At one extreme, segments might be very insular and experience only weak competition from other agencies. Such a situation would not provide outsiders with access to a given segment's decisionmaking, and would leave the segment free to act without being checked or balanced by other bureaucratic units. At the other extreme, if segments were highly inclusive of diverse interest groups and experienced widespread, strong competition, the bureaucratic system would be far more justifiable according to the criteria of pluralist democracy.

This matter cannot be resolved conclusively because no emprical evidence exists that would allow a precise mapping of bureaucratic relations. In the absence of such evidence, I offer a simple theoretical proposition: the more inclusive the participation in bureaucratic segments, and the more competitive their environment, the more closely the bureaucracy will conform to the norms of pluralist democracy.

3. Bureaucracy and Neighboring Institutions

Let us now fully incorporate the bureaucratic world into the larger system of American policymaking and ask how well that system as a whole fits the requirements of pluralist democracy. Public policy is made in a complex interactive world composed not just of bureaucrats but also of presidents, congressmen, interest groups, state and local governments, and the like. The question is how the bureaucratic political order is related to the larger political order. Again, this question hinges on how strict a test for pluralist democracy is applied. A weak test leads to the conclusion that bureaucracy does indeed contribute to the pluralist bargaining system. Certainly, bureaucracy's segmented pluralism, with its fragmentation and conflict and competition, adds to the simple number of competing power centers in American public policymaking, and the bureaucracy's interaction with congressional committees and interest groups and state and local governments helps to decentralize the process of bargaining in the system. But even under this weak test there are troubling aspects of the role of bureaucracy. For one thing, to the extent that a bureaucracy succeeds in controlling some small segment of policymaking, it at least partially removes an issue or decision from the arena of pluralist bargaining. Further, when bureaucracies practice silent politics they undermine the vitality of the larger bargaining process, and when they make valuative decisions they introduce preferences that have no direct democratic origins (except insofar as the bureaucracies reflect interest-group preferences). The fundamental point here is that bureaucrats are not under the same kind of democratic control by citizens as are elected officials.

Even if the politico-administrative system of bureaucratic democracy does include open bargaining and balancing of institutions, there are strong reasons for concern about the role of bureaucracy in American democracy. This is because bureaucracies do possess special resources in their competition with other elements of the political system. Bureaucracies, unlike most interest groups and even many congressional staffs, command professional expertise and technical capacity that give them an advantage over other contestants. In addition, bureaucracies, with their career civil servants, are apt to have a better historical understanding of policies than other political actors. The circularity of bureaucratic policymaking also tends to give bureaucracies a grip on the detail of the development and implementation of policies that surpasses that of other actors. These advantages allow bureaucracies to occupy a privileged position in the pluralist bargaining process, and thus the ideal of open, balanced bargaining is undermined.

In sum, we have seen that bureaucracies do engage in public policymaking and make some contributions to the pluralist bargaining process; and, if we adopt weak criteria for pluralist democracy, we might let the matter rest at that. But we have also seen that bureaucracy poses a number of very serious problems for numerous reasons, constitutes a threat to the basic norms of the pluralist model.

There is one final point to make at this juncture. In the classical theory of checks and balances, the starting point for establishing a balance of power was the existence of multiple centers of power. but there was another feature: different centers of power would perform different functions, and the division of functions itself would help to check and balance political power. As any schoolchild knows, the different governmental functions are called legislative, executive, and judicial. Today it would be difficult to argue that a strict separation of power by function exists in American government. The president certainly affects the legislative process, and many would say the judiciary does as well. To the extent that we take the doctrine of separation of power by function at all seriously, modern bureaucratic policymaking poses a special problem for democratic theory. Bureaucracies assume a legislative role when they interpet weak congressional mandates and become the major force behind new legislative proposals. They play an executive role as they make substantive decisions about the innovation and implementation of public policies. They play a judicial role, especially in the regulatory sphere, when they try appeals of their own decisions and hold hearings to resolve conflicts about administrative law. There may be nothing intrinsically sinister about the multidimensional roles of bureaucracy, but if one function is supposed to balance another, the balancing device is weakened when bureaucracy is at once legislator, administrator, and judge.

Bureaucracy and Administrative Efficiency

The political behavior of public bureaucracies seems to be wholly at variance with the norms of the administrative efficiency model. The portrait of bureaucratic behavior drawn in Chapter 3 violates virtually every principle of administrative efficiency. Instead of strong hierarchy, we find pervasive fragmentation among different levels and segments of administration. Instead of Wilson's hoped-for professionalism, we find guild professionalism, vested interests in policy subgovernments, and political uses of expertise. Instead of dispassionate, rational decisionmaking, we find a widespread pattern of valuative decisionmaking. Instead of a highly centralized chain of command under the chief executive, we find a broken chain, fragmentation of authority, and a pattern of loose control. Instead of performing a neutral administrative role, bureaucracies are themselves important sources of innovation and makers of substantive policy.

Faced with this discrepancy between the administrative efficiency model and the actual behavior of bureaucracies, the advocates of efficiency might respond in various ways. For example, they might decide that what bureaucracy needs is a larger dose of efficiency principles to correct its deficiencies and make it fit the initial doctrine. Or they might revise the efficiency model to take account of some of the features of the political behavior of bureaucracy. I will not attempt to work out the implications of these possible responses now, but will return to the concerns of advocates of administrative efficiency in Chapter 7.

Bureaucracy, Democracy, and Efficiency

Recall from Chapter 2 that two doctrines of public policymaking suggest that bureaucracy may combine the norms of pluralist democracy and administrative efficiency. One such view is offered by Norton Long, who writes that bureaucracy may provide widespread democratic representation as well as effective, rational administration. The second view, presented by Charles Lindblom, is that a bureaucratic process of bargaining and mutual adjustment will serve the value of both pluralist democracy and efficient decisionmaking.[7]

Long's position is significant in that it provides a justification of bureaucracy that might transcend the nondemocratic features of bureaucracy. In Long's view, even if bureaucrats practice silent politics and make valuative decisions, and even if many policy decisions are made within the bureaucracy, the bureaucracy might still be justified on the grounds that it is internally democratic, that is, it is representative of many different interests. There is some immediate plausibility in this view, for if bureaucracies forge widespread alliances with different interest groups, as they do, then it follows that there should be a widespread representation of different interests in the bureaucracy. Long's view is buttressed by the various strategies of citizen participation, minority recruitment, and affirmative action that have to some degree opened up the bureaucracy to participation by diverse groups. There are, however, several serious difficulties with Long's analysis. First, even if we assume some substantial level of democratic representation within bureaucracy, we have no assurance that competing interests will be equally represented or that there will be a rough balance among interest groups. We cannot be sure that older interest groups will not dominate newer ones, that larger groups will not dominate smaller ones, that organized business and labor groups will not dominate other citizens' groups of various kinds. There is no process by which the amount of power accorded to different groups is publicly voted, influenced, inspected, evaluated.

Another problem with Long's view is that even to the extent that bureaucracy is democratic and representative the process of representation is largely hidden from public view and controlled by the bureaucracy. That is, the bureaucracy often sets the terms of citizen participation; it declares what categories of citizens are to be represented. For example, the bureaucracies have created a complex formula for deciding to what extent different groups should participate in health service agencies. The same was true in the community action and model cities programs. The results of these bureaucratic decisions might appear to be highly representative and democratic, but the representatives themselves do not control the rules of bureaucratic representation, and it often turns out that those rules can be changed without their consent.

Another problem with the idea of representative bureaucracy is that the direct employment of people from different backgrounds, including minority backgrounds, while it may be a necessary condition for an internally representative bureaucracy, is by no means a sufficient one. It would be a sufficient condition only if new government employees were guaranteed to act consistently in their public roles as representatives of their appointed groups. If they began, instead, to work to advance the interest of their bureaucratic unit, as my analysis of bureaucratic politics implies that they would, then the significance of their backgrounds would be greatly diminished. In sum, Long's doctrine of bureaucracy as internally democratic is plausible up to a point, but it runs into several major objections and falls short of being persuasive.

Lindblom's depiction of the pluralist bargaining process is a more interesting attempt to show that the policymaking process, including the role of bureaucracy, is democratic and efficient. Many points that bear on this analysis have already been made: we have seen the ways in which bureaucracy is nondemocratic and in which it possesses special advantages over other participants in policymaking. We have seen that the pattern of segmented pluralism entails a highly constrained and even defensive bargaining process.

It is necessary to be more precise about the range of bargaining and mutual adjustment that must exist for Lindblom's theory to work. There is no denying that bargaining and mutual adjustment take place among bureaucracies and between bureaucracies and the larger political order; the question is how strict to make Lindblom's test. To the extent that a minimaxer succeeds in walling off his policy domain, bargaining is reduced and confined, and Lindblom's idea of coordination among various actors is undermined. The bureaucratic minimaxer will coordinate with others if he has to, but his motivation is to reduce the necessity of coordination by establishing control over his own domain.

The kind of inching ahead, something-for-everyone politics that characterizes bureaucracy presents a curious mirror-image view of Lindblom's notion of incrementalism as a crucial element of the "intelligence of democracy." For Lindblom, incrementalism is a largely benign process—partly because, by making policy in small, reversible "increments," it recognizes the limitations of comprehensive once-and-for-all decisionmaking, and partly because it promises to register and reward the views of many different groups, at least at the margin. But the interpretation of incrementalism that has emerged from my analysis—the protectionist strategy of inching ahead and the systemic self-interest of something-for-everyone politics—does not look so benign. The picture I have drawn of bureaucratic behavior may well be much the same pattern as Lindblom's incrementalism. But the interpretations and appraisals of bureaucratic motivations and their policy consequences are quite different.

A final point relevant to Lindblom's argument is that it seems obvious that the pattern of segmented pluralism would be greatly deficient for certain kinds of policymaking. Policymaking that concerns energy, the environment, the economy, or urban policy requires the cooperative involvement of many different bureaucratic units. It is hard to see how policies to deal with such collective national problems can be effectively developed in a setting of widespread segmentation. This problem seems significantly to undermine Lindblom's aspirations for the strategy of incrementalism.

In sum, the political model of bureaucracy developed in Chapter 3 has mixed implications for pluralist democracy, but plainly there are many ways in which bureaucratic behavior works against pluralist democratic norms. The implications for the efficiency model are even bleaker: here theory and practice seem to be totally at odds. Finally Long's and Lindblom's accounts fail to provide a justification of bureaucracy that can answer and overcome the problems bureaucratic behavior poses for both pluralist democracy and administrative efficiency.

5

Institutional Differences

IN PREVIOUS CHAPTERS, we examined a number of structural elements common to public bureaucracies. The identification of these elements, such as fragmentation, conflict, and power conservation, permitted the development of a schematic view of bureaucratic behavior, a view in which minimaxers operate in and shape an environment of segmented pluralism. We saw too that this pattern of bureaucratic politics has important implications for the normative models of pluralist democracy and administrative efficiency. It is appropriate now to recognize that although bureaucracies share many fundamental characteristics, there are also significant institutional differences among bureaucracies.

The task of this chapter is to enumerate significant institutional differences and to give the implications of these differences for the normative doctrines of democracy and efficiency. Because ultimately we will be considering the problem of how to control bureaucracies, we must understand what distinctive problems of control are presented by different kinds of bureaucracies.

Characteristics of Bureaucracies

There are many institutional features that might plausibly be offered as constituting important differences among bureaucracies. The following eleven institutional characteristics provide a useful framework on which to build an examination of the ways bureaucracies differ.

1. Function or Task
2. Nature of the Problem
3. Natural History or Evolution
4. Constituencies
5. Hierarchy
6. Technology
7. Professionalism and Expertise
8. Standard Operating Procedures
9. Open or Closed Structure
10. Centralization and Decentralization
11. Dominance and Competition

1. Function or Task

Different bureaucracies often perform very different functions and tasks. Curiously, political analysts have devoted little attention to the question of what bureaucracies actually do; more typically, the structural characteristics of bureaucracy have been studied. One recent book, James Q. Wilson's analysis of the FBI and the Drug Enforcement Administration, does take a task-oriented approach.[1] In general, however, detailing all the distinctive tasks found in public bureaucracies would require an enormous amount of up-close empirical research—research that simply has not been done. Acknowledging that we have relatively little empirical evidence to draw on, let us attempt to outline a few straightforward distinctions among bureaucratic functions and tasks.

As Edward Hamilton has written, there is a basic distinction, especially in intergovernmental policymaking, between agencies or units that perform a "banking" function and those that perform a direct "service delivery" function. By the banking function, Hamilton means the grant-in-aid process and the financing, regulatory, and evaluation procedures that surround it. By service delivery, he means the relationship between public officials and citizens ("the servers and the served"), a relationship in which bureaucrats attempt to deal with highly varied and conflicting local needs, often have a personal relationship with their citizen-consumers, and, as a consequence of both features, are often drawn into competitive local politics. The two functions require very different skills and procedures for successful performance and raise quite different kinds of policymaking and administrative problems. They also differ significantly in terms of democracy and efficiency. In the banking function, the bureaucratic objective is likely to be to centralize control. But to the extent that the bankers achieve this objective through strict auditing and distribution formulas, they may find that it is difficult to respond to diverse local interests.[2] Conversely, the service deliverers may become highly responsive to local needs and may tailor their services accordingly. Here the values of democratic interest-group representation appear to be well emphasized, and the administrative problem is the opposite from that presented by the bankers. If the service deliverers create a variegated, decentralized service system, it is likely to be difficult to establish coherent central control.

Another distinction is that some bureaucratic functions are relatively easy to control from the center — often because they are highly routinized. The writing of checks by social security bureaucrats or the tasks of motor vehicle department clerks are relatively easy to specify and monitor. So is the functioning of fire departments. By contrast, the functioning of teachers, policemen, or welfare caseworkers is far harder to control because their jobs contain greater room for individual judgment and are conducted largely beyond the direct scrutiny of central administrators.

Some tasks are so hard to monitor directly that they pose obvious problems for both democracy and efficiency. Three dramatic examples are the police, federal narcotics agents, and field operatives in the CIA. In these cases, the public bureaucrats are to an important extent on their own in their particular "beats." Central control — ensuring a reliable and consistent implementation of higher-level policies — is a perpetual problem. There is a problem of pluralist democracy here too: since these bureaucrats function with considerable discretion and often in secret, it is very hard for outsiders — citizens, interest groups, and other public officials — to scrutinize, evaluate, or influence bureaucratic behavior. When controversies break out in these areas — a case of police brutality, a drug raid in an innocent household, a CIA plot that backfires visibly — democratic oversight and appraisal become more feasible. But these are special cases as contrasted with public scrutiny of performance of daily bureaucratic tasks.

Thus bureaucratic functions and tasks differ widely, with varying implications for the normative models of pluralist democracy and administrative efficiency. We cannot know what kind of bureaucratic problem we face and what remedies might be advocated unless we understand what a bureaucracy's functions and tasks actually are.

2. Nature of the Problem

Different bureaucracies face very different kinds of policy problems, problems having different internal structures and calling for different kinds of solutions. In the late 1960s, at the high-water mark of Great Society initiatives, the prevailing view was that social problems (and especially urban problems) could best be tackled by new public expenditures for additional government programs. Most urban problems were defined as "resource" problems. Given this definition, a chief analytical task for policymaking was to use cost-benefit analysis to determine the most efficient program expenditure. And this analytical task, in turn, led to the development of centralized, expert policy analysis such as program budgeting following closely the principles of the administrative efficiency model.

There can be no denying that many policy problems are at heart resource problems. The development of new weapons systems obviously requires capital expenditures, as does the construction of highways, parks, and public housing projects. But resource problems are by no means the only type of policy problem. Four other types of problems that bureaucracies routinely face and which imply different emphases on the values of pluralist democracy and administrative efficiency are responsiveness, trust, control, and restructuring.[3]

Responsiveness. Sometimes public services and policies do not respond to the felt needs of citizens. For example, a city may deploy its police officers in a way that ignores a certain neighborhood's concerns about crime and safety. Or an interest group, such as the elderly or the handicapped, may believe that its needs have been ignored by policymakers. Increasing the government's responsiveness may well involve increasing expenditures, but the main issue is that of refining the fit between the supply of and the demand for services. Faced with complaints about responsiveness, governments will often create new avenues for interest-group representation and participation in order to improve the relationship between the servers and the served. Thus they will be led to emphasize the values of the pluralist democracy model. But note that here democracy and efficiency are intended to be mutually supportive. Democratic instruments such as citizen participation are chosen not entirely for their own sake (although making the process of decision more democratic may be valued in itself) but partly as a means to greater efficiency in the delivery of services.

Trust. Especially in urban government, the service relationship depends on the existence of mutual trust between public employees and citizens. For example, is crucial for urban street-level bureaucrats such as policemen and teachers. It is also important for public officials in the medical field, broadly defined. When there is a breakdown of trust in service delivery, citizens express anger at and alienation from government, as has frequently occurred in recent years in minority communities. Once the trust relationship has broken down, public employees find it more difficult to perform their tasks. Police, for example, find that they do not receive cooperation from community residents. To deal with problems of trust, public employees often turn to democratic, participatory devices to improve their relationship with citizens.[4] They may create new police community boards or school councils to bring parents and teachers into closer contact. The point is that emphasizing pluralist democratic values appears to be the appropriate response to trust problems. An emphasis on the efficiency model's concern for centralization and professional control would appear logically to move in exactly the wrong direction. Simply, one cannot decide how to improve performance in a given bureaucracy unless one can identify the distinctive character of the problems it faces.

Control. Frequently, the complaint is made that a governmental program is out of control, that no one knows what impact it is having or whether it is functioning at all. These fears proved justified in my own observation of efforts to set up methadone clinics in New York City. As Arthur Levin has shown, the control problem also existed widely in the implementation of the Great Society's experimental social programs.[5] When this kind of problem exists, the obvious recourse is to emphasize the efficiency model's concern for central planning, regulation, and evaluation in the hope of creating a measure of order out of perceived chaos.

Restructuring. Bureaucratic policymakers often find that a major obstacle to improved performance in their programs lies in the fragmentation, competition, and lack of coordination among bureaucratic units. This diagnosis has been made in the areas of energy, housing and urban development, and economic policy, and the problem probably exists in other areas as well. The most frequent response to this type of problem has been to follow the efficiency model's emphasis on centralization and long-range planning. Bureaucratic reorganizations have been a favorite attempted remedy; hence the creation of the Departments of Energy and Housing and Urban Development and the consolidation of small agencies into "superdepartments" at the state and local level. It is also possible to respond to a restructuring problem by emphasizing pluralist democratic values, as in the various decentralization experiments of the last two decades. The question becomes: What precise kind of restructuring problem does a bureaucracy face? Is it fragmentation and a lack of coordination, or is it a lack of interest-group and citizen involvement in decisionmaking? Only when one knows the answer to this question can one begin to make sensible prescriptions for solving a particular bureaucracy's structural problems.

In this classification of bureaucracy's problems, I am not arguing that the various types of problems exist only one at a time or in isolation from one another. A bureaucracy is likely to face more than one problem at a time or to find that different problems arise at different times. Still, understanding the different types of problems should improve our ability to make distinctions among the administrative difficulties facing different bureaucracies and to choose appropriate remedies for different bureaucratic problems.

3. Natural History or Evolution

Different bureaucracies also have very different natural histories. Some, like State and Treasury, are in American terms ancient institutions. Others, such as the Energy Department, the Environmental Protection Agency, and the Department of Housing and Urban Development, are relative newcomers. Some bureaucracies, such as the Army Corps of Engineers, the Forest Service, and local fire departments, have assumed relatively narrow well-specified missions over long periods of time. Others, such as HHS, HUD, and local social services departments, are recently created "holding companies" for a wide range of different programs and functions. Some bureaucracies have greatly expanded their functions and tasks, while others have not, at least not to the same degree. In what follows I will emphasize three types of historical differences: differences in age, in unity or diversity of mission, and in proliferation of policies and programs.

Age. The chronological age of bureaucracies has been given substantial attention by many political analysts. A commonly held view is that the older the bureaucracy the more tightly controlled and rigid it becomes. This notion reflects an anthropomorphic life-cycle metaphor in which more mature bureaucracies are less flexible, more set in their ways. Anthony Downs, for one, has argued that the older the bureaucracy is the more likely it is to be dominated by conservers — bureaucrats who cling tightly to their historical functions and prerogatives.[6] Conversely, younger bureaucracies are seen by Downs and others to be more innovative, risk-taking, and open to influences from their environment. The age thesis is highly suggestive. It seems logical that a bureaucracy that has survived for a long time will have established a relatively secure niche in the bureaucratic environment. Conversely, it is logical that a younger bureaucracy will be more fluid as it seeks a stable adaptation to its environment. To the extent that these propositions are true, older bureaucracies will have established relatively firm structures of internal control. They may indeed take on many of the characteristics favored by the administrative efficiency model. The State Department and the Department of the Treasury, for example, have many of these characteristics. These old bureaucracies may also be relatively unwilling to accommodate new interest groups and new policy problems. Conversely, very young bureaucracies like HUD, Environmental Protection, and Energy may have less stable patterns of internal control and, perhaps for that reason, may remain open to a wide variety of constituencies.

If it takes a bureaucratic organization substantial time to become strongly institutionalized, then it is likely that over time bureaucracies will evolve toward greater institutionalization of their policymaking procedures. Nelson Polsby has shown that the Congress gradually developed a differentiated committee structure and elaborate rules;[7] we might expect bureaucracies to follow an analogous course. For example, the young Department of Energy is likely to be weakly institutionalized as compared with a venerable bureaucracy like the Department of State.

Bureaucracies sometimes try to rapidly accelerate the process of institutionalization as a reaction against earlier disorganization. This has been the case in urban service bureaucracies. As I showed in *The Ungovernable City*, urban services were highly disorganized in the nineteenth century. Police were untrained and undisciplined; fire protection was typically provided by volunteer social clubs; sanitation was frequently provided by scavengers and other irregulars. The reaction to these extremely loose administrative practices was a strong emphasis on institutionalization: detailed regulations, organization charts, accounting procedures, specialized licensing and training efforts, and so forth. Simply put, the "search for order," as Robert Wiebe writes, will be particularly strong in organizations that had ramshackle beginnings.[8]

Mission. Bureaucracies also vary in the unity or diversity of their mission. It is easier to control and implement policy in a bureaucracy with a relatively unified mission. By contrast, the task of organizing and managing a "holding company" or conglomerate type of bureaucracy is far more difficult. But again, the norms of pluralist democracy and administrative efficiency do not always run together. Whatever its problems in maintaining external control, a holding company bureaucracy is likely to exhibit more internal competition and to allow the representation of a wider variety of interests than a more unified bureaucracy.

Program proliferation. Some bureaucracies, over time, multiply the number and range of their policies and programs far more than others. The greater the amount of proliferation, the harder it is likely to be to manage and control a bureaucracy. But, like diversity of mission, proliferation of programs and policies serves the pluralist democratic value of increasing the range of interests and constituencies involved in the bureaucratic decisionmaking process.

4. Constituencies

In earlier chapters I argued that most bureaucracies have a range of constituencies — both supportive and not, both actual and potential

—and that all bureaucracies will seek to develop allies among their constituents. But the structure of constituency support will differ considerably from one bureaucracy to another. Let us consider three possible constituency structures and their implications.

First, a bureaucracy may have few if any well-organized groups of constituents pressing claims on it. It is hard to imagine a bureaucracy that faces no pressure from its constituency at all. Bureaucracies like the State Department, the CIA, the Social Security Administration (because of its diffuse clientele), and the Defense Department (albeit acknowledging the unusual constituent/client role of defense contractors) experience low constituent-group activity. The absence of intense constituency pressure may well make it easier to organize and manage the work of an agency and to pursue the norms of the efficiency model. At the same time, a lack of constituent-group activity implies a low level of competition for bureaucratic benefits and services and suggests also that there may be little external public scrutiny and evaluation.

Second, a bureaucracy may be strongly allied with a single interest group. Recall from the concept of a bureaucracy's natural history, that some bureaucracies, such as the Departments of Agriculture, Labor, and Commerce, were created to represent the interests of a particular client. Even bureaucracies not explicitly designed to be client agencies may face a single dominant constituency group; examples are boards that license and regulate occupational groups such as doctors, liquor store owners, and morticians. Or over time a bureaucracy may develop a strong attachment to an "old friend" constituent group even though other interest groups exist. This, as Samuel Huntington has shown, was the case with the ICC and the railroad industry.[9] Such cases are worrisome in terms of the values of both pluralist democracy and administrative efficiency. In the first place, if a bureaucracy is dominated by a single interest group, the efficiency model's conception of detached, rational benefit-cost analysis will be undermined as the bureaucracy accommodates the privileged constituency. The ICC's historical tendency to emphasize the needs of the railroads at the expense of demands for a more balanced transportation policy is a good example of the inefficiency that a dominant interest group may produce in bureaucracy. At the same time, the single dominant constituent group works against the norms of pluralist democracy, since dominance implies weak competition among interest groups and therefore weak interest-group bargaining and accommodation.

Third, a bureaucracy may have numerous interest groups involved in a tug-of-war over its policymaking. In this situation there is likely to be widespread competition and bargaining among the interest groups and between interest groups and the bureaucracy. Such competition supports the values of pluralist democracy, but the efficiency model's values of centralized control and rational decisionmaking may be undermined when policymakers are pulled in many different and conflicting directions. An institution like HHS has often been viewed as unmanageable in part because of the range and intensity of the demands its constituents place upon it.

The existence of multiple constituent groups does not always necessarily lead to widespread competition and bargaining. Instead, constituent groups may follow the same strategy of segmented pluralism that the bureaucracies themselves pursue. If groups of constituents act as cautious minimaxers, they will stake out some relatively narrow segment of policy and then work to protect that turf from the advances of other groups. To the extent that this kind of segmentation does exist among constituent groups, the policymaking process will be too fragmented to please advocates of the administrative efficiency model. It will also be too uncompetitive from the point of view of the pluralist democracy model—even if, in aggregate, numerous constituent groups are operating in the bureaucracy's immediate environment. If segmentation of constituent groups were pervasive and deeply rooted, the result would be a micro version of the pattern of single-group dominance discussed above. In fact, we lack sufficient evidence to tell just how segmented interest groups really are. But it is plain that the pattern is more than just an analytical possibility. In HHS, and in many state and local social service agencies, constituent groups typically form around small segments of policy. Although there are surely many groups on the political map, a large number are concerned with their particular program—be it a service for the deaf, the blind, the elderly, the handicapped, or the mentally retarded. When Connecticut decided to create a consolidated Department of Social Services, it ran into strong opposition from narrowly defined constituent groups wanting to retain the independence of the agency or subunit that directly served their particular interests.

5. Hierarchy

According to the administrative efficiency model, a strong hierarchical structure is a necessary condition of good administration, and for many analysts, including Woodrow Wilson and Max Weber, hierarchy lies at the very heart of the concept of bureaucracy. In practice some bureaucracies are significantly more hierarchical than others. Certain bureaucracies, especially those with a military or paramilitary chain of command, place a special emphasis on maintaining a strict hierarchical structure. It is certainly likely that such bureaucracies are more hierarchical than less command-oriented bureaucracies like HHS, HUD, local school systems, and welfare agencies.

Even a military structure like the Defense Department or a paramilitary structure like a police or fire department does not guarantee strict hierarchy. At least in the case of police departments, the appearance of a strict hierarchy may disguise the fact that the central administration has difficulty controlling its agents in the field. This is true in the police because of the opportunities for exercising discretion that are inherent in the jobs of policemen and other street-level bureaucrats.[10]

The greater the degree of hierarchy, the greater the likelihood that the values of the administrative efficiency model will obtain. At the same time, the more hierarchical the organization, the more difficult it may be for external pressure groups to make a dent in the bureaucracy, since a hierarchical bureaucracy is apt to offer fewer points of access to interest groups than a loosely structured one.

6. Technology

Bureaucracies also differ in the level and precision of the technology that they possess. I use the word "technology" to refer to the repertoire of means or practices through which a public agency seeks to achieve its ends. For example, fire departments have a clearly established technology for responding to a fire—a technology that includes not only fire trucks and other equipment but also clear procedures that firemen follow when they arrive at the scene of a fire. Similarly, forest rangers have a well-established technology for managing forest growth, sanitationmen have at least a basic technology for collecting garbage, the navy has an established technology for launching a blockade, and surgeons have a range of established techniques for performing operations. By contrast, many public bureaucracies possess relatively weak technologies. School administrators fluctuate in their estimation of the best way to teach students how to read. Administrators of drug treatment programs display the same uncertainty about the effectiveness of different approaches. Policemen face considerable uncertainty about which of their technologies — decoys, plainclothes patrol, car patrol — work best to combat street crime.

The nature and strength of a bureaucracy's technology has important implications for the organization's structure and performance. As with hierarchy, bureaucracies with strong technologies are more apt to follow the principles of the administrative efficiency model than those with weak technologies. Agencies with strong technologies are more likely to have clear policies and procedures and to implement these procedures consistently through their bureaucratic structures. Agencies that are uncertain about their basic technology and that tend to experiment with a multiplicity of new technologies are likely to lack consistent and reliable operating procedures and therefore to be difficult to manage. Also as with hierarchy, what works well for the administrative efficiency model may not work as well for the pluralist democracy model. The stronger an agency's technology, the more resistant it is likely to be to demands from citizens that it alter its habits or develop new responses. Agencies with weak technologies are more likely to be open to new approaches and willing to experiment.

7. Professionalism and Expertise

It is tempting to say that there are obvious intuitive differences in the level of professionalism and expertise in bureaucracies, such as the difference, say, between scientists and school teachers. But the concepts of professionalism and expertise can stand for many things, and we need to anchor this institutional difference in more specific analytical distinctions. Let us begin by assuming that all groups of professionals tend to practice guild professionalism — to protect their own established norms of procedure and training and to defend their occupational turf against incursions by outsiders. This is the commonality, stressed in the last chapter, that conceptually links the behavior of professional groups of all kinds, from forest rangers to doctors to military officers to public health nurses to social workers to teachers. So the pattern of guild professionalism does not distinguish; it joins together. There are, however, four distinctions that can be drawn among professions. These are (1) the level and precision of technology in a profession, (2) the amount of training required to become a professional, (3) the extent of the gap between professional expertise and ordinary laymen's knowledge, and (4) the degree to which a professional group dominates and restricts employment in its bureaucratic arena. At the high end of the spectrum of professional attributes are groups like doctors in public hospitals, career military officers, research scientists at the National Institutes of Health, economists at the Council of Economic Advisors, highway engineers, nuclear physicists in the Atomic Energy Commission, and foreign area specialists in the CIA. In each of these cases, the professionals work with a strong and well-defined technology; they are highly trained; their knowledge is relatively technical; and, as a professional group, they have established significant control over employment in their area. Without a "professional union card," so to speak, one is unlikely to get a job.

Many bureaucracies do not have this high degree of professional control. Sanitationmen have a clear technology but rank much lower on the other dimensions of professionalism. Professional groups of school teachers and policemen do restrict employment opportunities in their fields, although the fact that the training required to become a teacher or a policeman is not onerous diminishes somewhat this professional barrier to employment. At the federal level, the criteria of professionalism are weakly manifest in many social service programs in HHS, in HUD's urban development programs, and in departments like Commerce, Labor, and the nontechnical areas of Agriculture.

In other bureaucracies, the force of professionalism is diminished by conflict among various professional groups over the shape and substance of policy. Such conflict is most likely to occur in bureaucracies that rely on experts from various disciplines, as, for example, in the Department of Energy and the Department of Environmental Protection. Or it may exist among economists and financial analysts within the government's economic policymaking bureaucracies.

The implications of strong professionalism are similar to those of hierarchy and technology. Bureaucracies dominated by strong professional groups are able to fulfill many aspects of the administrative efficiency model. They have strong operating procedures and they strongly defend their established professional policies. Highly professionalized bureaucracies perform in a relatively consistent fashion and carry out central administrative policies with some reliability. But the stronger the degree of professional control, the harder it may be for citizens and interest groups to gain access to bureaucratic decisionmaking or to persuade professionals to depart from their usual procedures.

In a bureaucratic environment characterized by weak professionalism or by professional conflict, exercising central administrative control is more difficult, because the administrator cannot rely to the same degree on the coherence and regularity of embedded professional behavior. In such a bureaucracy it is likely to be easier to stimulate debate or to inject new views and interests into the policymaking process. Thus, a bureaucracy without strong professionalism and expertise may pose problems of administrative control, but it may also be more open to the competition and bargaining emphasized by the doctrine of pluralist democracy.

8. Standard Operating Procedures

Certain bureaucracies possess far stronger standard operating procedures (SOP's) than others. The strength of SOP's is likely to reflect, in aggregate, the earlier distinctions concerning an organization's hierarchy, technology, and professionalism. When these features are strongly manifest, a bureaucracy's behavior will be strongly institutionalized. Where these features are weakly manifest, operating procedures will be far less structured. Bureaucracies such as Defense, the State Department, the FBI, and local fire departments display these attributes and also have powerful SOP's. In the forest service, as Herbert Kaufman has shown,[11] the combination of hierarchy, technology, and strong professional training enables the service to perform with a remarkable degree of regularity and consistency: central policies are implemented with striking reliability in the field. An organization with weak SOP's, by contrast, is likely to be hard to manage effectively; but, as a compensation, it may be relatively flexible, particularly if it is a young bureaucracy, and relatively open to new strategies and new interest-group demands.

9. Open or Closed Structure

Bureaucracies differ in their degree of openness to scrutiny and involvement by citizens and elected public officials. Bureaucracies like the Defense Department, the State Department, the CIA, and local police departments, in which secrecy is an element of normal functioning, are relatively closed by virtue of the nature of their organizational task. Highly technical bureaucratic institutions, such as the Atomic Energy Commission and various research institutes, also operate at a substantial remove from public debate and from the daily political process. The latter type of bureaucracy is also closed partly because of the professionalism and expertise inherent in the organization.

In contrast, some bureaucracies are typically quite open to involvement by citizens, interest groups, and interested public officials. Client agencies, like Agriculture, Commerce, and Labor, come to mind, as well as social service agencies with their particular constituencies, such as the handicapped or the elderly, and local school systems, which often pride themselves on their openness to parental and community concerns.

The more closed a bureaucracy is, the more difficult it will be for the normal processes of pluralist democracy, especially interest-group competition, to work within it. By contrast, the lack of openness, by diminishing competition among interest groups, aids in the establishment of a strong hierarchy, in the maintenance of professional spirit, and in the centralization of decisionmaking.

By contrast, in a relatively open bureaucracy, many different interest groups participate in bureaucratic decisionmaking at various levels, ranging from mere consultation to stronger forms of participation.[12] In an open system, involvement by many interest groups foster substantial conflict and competition. These features reinforce the values of pluralist democracy, except in cases where "participation" turns out to mean domination by a single interest group.

It is possible for a public bureaucracy to be relatively open at one level of the organization and relatively closed at another. In particular, experiments in decentralization of government have sometimes had the effect of opening up channels of participation at lower levels of administration while maintaining relatively closed decisionmaking at higher levels. In my work on urban neighborhoods I found this to be particularly true of various experiments in increasing participation in schools, policy community relations boards, and health councils.[13] The danger of this split-level structure of open and closed features is that it is likely to lead to serious intrabureaucratic conflicts. An extreme case of such conflict occurred in the community control experiment in New York's Ocean Hill-Brownsville school district. In that experiment, citizens believed that they had been given substantial power and control over educational decisionmaking in their community. Citizen participants at the local level, however, quickly discovered that their sense of discretion and autonomy collided directly with the closed, centralized decisionmaking habits of the Board of Education "downtown." The result was uncertainty about power relationships, alternations between open and closed styles of decisionmaking, and, ultimately, bitter conflict and personal antagonism between central bureaucrats and community-level participants.[14] The same pattern of conflict has been played out in health consumer councils over the proper role of citizens' preferences and priorities as against professional authority. In the police context, citizens often complain that the grievances of community participants at the precinct level are lost or ignored at higher levels in the administrative structure.

Conflicts can also arise between open and closed features of a bureaucratic system when efforts are made to increase participation at the top but when plans made jointly by citizens and bureaucrats at the top have to be implemented through a more closed system at lower levels. In such a case, efforts at openness at the top are likely to be choked off or ignored at lower levels. This situation often arises with presidential advisory commissions and other advisory boards working with governors, mayors, school superintendents, or police chiefs. New policy initiatives or reorganization schemes will be offered by these high-level commissions but then will be shelved or "studied" at great length at lower levels where the bureaucracy is less open.

10. Centralization and Decentralization

Bureaucracies also differ in the extent of centralization or decentralization in their structure. A bureaucracy with a centralized structure, as I use the term, is one whose locus of activity and authority is essentially in the federal government. Examples are the Departments of State Defense, and the Treasury, the CIA, and the regulatory agencies. Such bureaucracies may have field offices, but their decisionmaking power is centralized in Washington. By contrast, various other bureaucracies are in the position, by virtue of federalism, of having to share decisionmaking responsibility with many different state and local governments. This decentralized form is particularly manifest in many areas of HHS, HUD, the Department of Environmental Protection, the Justice Department (in its relationships with local police departments), the Department of Energy, the Economic Development Administration, and certainly the Department of Education (in its relationships with local school systems).

The implications of these forms of centralization and decentralization parallel our earlier discussions. Highly centralized bureaucracies tend to foster the conditions called for by the administrative efficiency model: centralized decisions, hierarchy, and professionalism. By contrast, in decentralized bureaucratic structures there are likely to be many different governmental groups competing for power and policy outcomes. The diversity of and competition among many different bureaucracies in this case will reinforce the values of the pluralist democracy model.

11. Dominance and Competition

Some bureaucracies occupy a relative monopoly in their fields; others participate in an oligopoly structure; still others are characterized to one degree or another by competition in their areas of operations. This institutional difference draws on and synthesizes some of the differences discussed earlier.

I have argued that there are few if any pure monopolies among public bureaucracies. Perhaps only the FBI and the CIA at the height of their power could be called monopolies. I have also argued that even superficially apparent oligopolies like the service branches in the Defense Department are unstable at best. Still, some bureaucracies dominate their policy areas far more than others. The organizations already mentioned are relatively dominant bureaucracies. So are the State Department (in its role in diplomatic communications), many but not all regulatory agencies (for example, the Federal Communications Commission is more dominant than the Interstate Commerce Commission, whose decisions intersect with the policies of the Department of Transportation), public authorities like the TVA and Port Authorities, and independent licensing and regulatory commissions. Bureaucracies that are relatively dominant in their policy arenas are likely to achieve a centralized, coordinated, and hierarchical style of administration—in other words, to meet the conditions called for by the administration efficiency model.

In contrast to the situation of the relatively dominant bureaucracy, many bureaucracies face strong competition. Bureaucratic competition may be horizontal or vertical. Horizontal competition exists among different institutions in the federal bureaucracy. Vertical competition exists among bureaucracies at different levels of government. The two categories are not mutually exclusive; in some cases the prevailing pattern of competition is both horizontal and vertical in character.

Horizontal competition can be found in the recurrent competition over foreign policy between the State Department and the National Security Council. Another example occurred in the Skybolt affair, when the Departments of State and Defense came into conflict over whether to offer Great Britain the Skybolt missile or the Polaris missile as a substitute. State, Treasury, the Federal Reserve Board, and the Agency for International Development compete over international economic policy. Various social service agencies often disagree with HHS over the design and delivery of social programs. The Department of Energy, the Environmental Protection Agency, and the Atomic Energy Commission, as well as foreign-policy-oriented bureaucracies and the Council of Economic Advisors, all try to have their say in shaping national energy policy. An impressive case of horizontal competition arose over President Carter's attempt to formulate a national urban policy. HUD was originally given the responsibility of gathering proposals for urban policy and creating a comprehensive package. But many different bureaucracies including HHS, Commerce, Labor, and Transportation quickly began to press for the inclusion of their own programs in the urban policy package. This was bureaucratic politics in the classic sense of competition over overlapping policy turf. The resulting policy statement was such a hodgepodge of disparate and competing bureaucratic proposals that President Carter was forced to start over from scratch, centralizing control over urban planning in the hands of the head of his domestic policy staff. It is difficult to establish precise measures of bureaucratic infighting, but I believe that competition, ranging from mild to ferocious, is the dominant pattern of bureaucratic interaction at the national level.

Vertical competition is closely related to centralization and decentralization in bureaucracies. The central proposition is that the more a national bureaucracy has to work with and through state and local governments, the more vertical competition will exist. Conversely, the lack of vertical competition works to reinforce the dominance of organizations like State, Defense, and Treasury that are not drawn, by their tasks and by governmental architecture, into persistent conflict with subnational governments.

Vertical competition is pervasive among the various educational bureaucracies at different levels, among social service organizations of the federal, state, and urban governments, and in housing and economic development programs where mayors and governors and their bureaucracies are prominent actors in the policymaking process. The tendency toward vertical competition in such organizations may be offset by the existence of bureaucratic policy subgovernments, but even where these subgovernments exist, competition and conflict arise from the different perspectives and interests of federal, state, and local policy actors.

Many policy arenas show patterns of both horizontal and vertical competition. Various federal bureaucracies or subunits are involved in the particular arena, and various political and bureaucratic actors at the state and local level also play significant roles in the policymaking process. Again an impressive example is the attempt to formulate a national urban policy. Not only were a large number of federal bureaucracies competing over the design of the programs, but mayors and governors and county executives were also drawn into the conflict. Competition among subnational groups was partly a function of regional interests (Sunbelt vs. Frostbelt) and partly a function of the differing interests of large cities, small cities, counties, towns, and so forth.

The greater the number and diversity of competing groups, the more representative the policymaking process is likely to be and the more bargaining is likely to occur. At the same time, the greater the amount of interest-group competition and bargaining—horizontally, vertically, or both—the harder it will be for any central policymaker to hammer out a policy that is comprehensive, consistent, or even coherent. Thus the two normative models of governance once again conflict. In the case of national urban policy, extensive group pluralism made a mockery of the White House's attempt at central, nationwide planning. The White House responded by replacing a pluralist strategy with an executive-centered strategy, the logic of which followed directly from the administrative efficiency model.

Institutional Differences: A Composite Analysis

I have identified eleven institutional differences among bureaucracies that I believe have significant implications for the ordinary functioning of bureaucracies as well as for the normative models of pluralist democracy and administrative efficiency. It is time to recognize a danger of offering too many distinctions: the analysis itself may produce a fragmented and disjointed portrait of the politics of bureaucratic organizations.

A step toward a more integrated view of bureaucratic politics can be taken by examining some relationships among institutional differences. We have seen that some institutional characteristics are linked to others. For example, the nature of the problem faced by a bureaucracy obviously relates to its own definition of task or function. The natural history of a bureaucracy, as can be seen in the reasons for the creation of the Departments of Labor and Agriculture, obviously is related to the kind of constituencies it serves. The fact that a bureaucracy has evolved into a conglomerate also affects the structure of its constituency pressures (a conglomerate is likely to face a large number of diverse constituency groups). Furthermore, the strength of hierarchy in a bureaucracy is often related to its dominant function or task, as for example in police departments, where the discretionary, street-level role of individual policemen limits the hierarchical tendency of the bureaucracy.

Many other simple institutional relationships also emerge from the foregoing analysis. A clear and strong technology often aids in the establishment of hierarchy, as in public hospitals where a relatively clear understanding of a given technology (such as surgery) reinforces authority relationships within the hospital staff. The level of technology is also related to the influence of professionals and experts in a bureaucracy. Furthermore, the stronger the hierarchy, technology, and professionalism, the better established and stronger a bureaucracy's standard operating procedures are likely to be.

A bureaucracy's tendency to be open or closed is affected by the strength of professionalism, hierarchy, and standard operating procedures. As suggested earlier, these factors work in favor of a relatively closed bureaucratic environment. The amount of centralization or decentralization in an organization also has obvious implications for how open or closed it is likely to be. For example, it is difficult to maintain a closed environment in the face of significant involvement by diverse subnational governments. The degree of intergovernmental decentralization also bears a straightforward relationship to the degree of dominance or competition existing in any given bureaucratic environment. Finally, the nature of a bureaucracy's task (is it a "secret" one), its natural history (is there a single dominant mission), the structure of its constituency (is it monolithic or diverse), as well as its degree of hierarchy, technology, professionalism, and closedness are almost certain to have an impact on the amount of dominance it achieves or competition it faces.

Type A and Type B Bureaucracies

Piecing together the relationships among institutional differences is a step toward establishing a coherent composite view of these differences and their implications. We can go one step further by schematically depicting the way the various institutional differences cluster or cohere. To do this, we will need to oversimplify and to recognize that the clusters of differences and oppositions may not add up to a perfect characterization of any given bureaucracy. With these caveats in mind, I will present a simple, aggregate portrait of two sharply opposed types of bureaucratic structures (see table 5.1).

The stark differentiation between Type A and Type B bureaucracies has strong implications for the two normative models of bureaucracy. Type A offers most of the structural preconditions for the administrative efficiency model: it emphasizes a dominant, established mission, hierarchy, technology, professionalism, strong oper-

Table 5.1 Institutional differences in aggregate: Two types of bureaucracies.

Type A Bureaucracies	Type B Bureaucracies

1. Natural history
    Single dominant mission
    Old, established bureaucracy
    (influenced by task)*
	1. Natural history
	    Conglomerate
	    Newly created bureaucracy

2. Constituencies
    Virtually none or monolithic
    (influenced by 1)
	2. Constituencies
	    Diverse, conflicting

3. Relatively strong hierarchy
    (influenced by task and
    2, 4, 5, 6, 7, 8)
	3. Relatively weak hierarchy

4. Strong technology (influenced by task and 5)	4. Weak technology
5. High professionalism (influenced by task and 4)	5. Low professionalism

6. Relatively strong operating procedures
    (influenced by task and
    3, 4, 5, 7, 8)
	6. Relatively weak operating procedures

7. Relatively closed
    (influenced by task
    and 2, 3, 4, 5, 6, 8)
	7. Relatively open

8. Centralized—
    in intergovernmental terms
    (influenced by task, natural history,
    and to some extent 3)
	8. Decentralized—
	    in intergovernmental terms

9. Relative dominance
    (influenced by task, natural history,
    and 2, 3, 4, 5, 6, 7, 8)
	9. Relative competition

*Influence relations are noted only under Type A. The relationships are parallel for Type B.

ating procedures, and centralized decisionmaking. At the same time, Type A bureaucracies pose obvious problems for the normative model of pluralist democracy. The features of hierarchy, professionalism, expertise, closedness, centralization, and relative dominance in a particular policy field all work to undermine the competitive, participatory aspects of pluralist democracy. In addition, the workings of a Type A bureaucracy are likely to be relatively inaccessible to ordinary citizens and interest groups; the emphasis is likely to be on professional, expert decision-making rather than on citizen participation and oversight.

Type B bureaucracies present the reverse problems for the pluralist democracy and administrative efficiency models. Bureaucracies that are conglomerates, are recently created, have diverse constituencies, have weak hierarchies, and are relatively open, decentralized, and competitive provide many of the structural preconditions for the participatory, representative, competitive, and bargaining features of pluralist democracy. But Type B clearly presents enormous obstacles to the design of the administrative efficiency model. Open, loosely structured, competitive Type B bureaucracies are likely to be hard to manage in the professional and hierarchical way that Woodrow Wilson and his successors imagined for their ideal politico-administrative system.

How closely do these analytical depictions of institutional structure resemble the functioning of actual bureaucracies? I do not claim that any perfect Type A or Type B bureaucracies exist—perfect in that they reflect every dimension of one of the two types. Yet there are certainly many bureaucracies that possess many of the structural attributes of either Type A or Type B.

Bureaucracies that display many or most of the characteristics of Type A include the Departments of Defense, State, and the Treasury, the CIA, the Atomic Energy Commission, the National Security Council, scientific research institutes, public authorities, independent boards and commissions, most regulatory agencies, the FBI, local fire departments, and public hospitals. I will not attempt here to judge how successfully these bureaucracies actually achieve the hoped-for virtues of the efficiency model. It is enough to say that the prospects for centralized, hierarchical, professional administration are likely to be brightest in these institutional settings.

Let us now take a remedial look at Type A bureaucracies, following Lindblom's advice to identify and attempt to remedy policy problems.[15] If the analysis so far is correct, Type A bureaucracies are likely to be defective in providing the competitive, participatory, open bargaining features prized by pluralist democracy. In these bureaucracies, citizens and public officials will be at a disadvantage vis-à-vis professionals and hierarchical superiors in influencing the policymaking process. From the point of view of pluralist democracy, then, the problem to be remedied in such bureaucracies is how to democratize them to conform better to the ideal picture of governance in a democratic society.

Bureaucracies that approximate the analytical portrait of Type B include many of HHS's social service programs, HUD programs (especially under revenue sharing legislation), educational programs, economic development programs, drug prevention programs, neighborhood government experiments, the inflation-fighting bureaucracy, and even the Department of Commerce (with all its different business constituencies). A Department of Consumer Protection, if one were created, would also certainly fall into this category. In these cases, the preconditions for participatory, competitive bargaining exist, although they may not be completely fulfilled. Taking a remedial approach again, the problem of Type B bureaucracies is how to organize and manage them—how to infuse enough of the efficiency values into them to prevent them from being ungovernable.

Many bureaucracies present elements of both Type A and Type B bureaucracies. Such mixed types include institutions like the Department of Energy, the Department of Environmental Protection, and local police departments. These are agencies that may be centralized but not strongly hierarchical; they may be conglomerates but still rely heavily on expert decisionmaking; they may be relatively closed to public scrutiny but still have relatively weak technologies and standard operating procedures. In mixed cases, the task for the bureaucratic analyst, especially one taking a remedial view, is to decide which aspects or clusters of institutional difference seem to be most salient and problematic and then consider the design or redesign of the relevant bureaucracy in that light—and particularly in terms of democracy and administrative efficiency norms.

Institutional Differences in Urban Bureaucracies

Different urban issues wind up on the doorstep of particular urban institutions. Some are directed at the police department, some at the school system, some at independent boards and commissions, some at City Hall itself. The character of urban policymaking thus depends on the character of the principal urban institution involved. As noted above, some, such as police departments or redevelopment agencies, are relatively closed to citizen involvement. Others, such as the school system, have a tradition of providing far greater access to citizens. Some urban institutions exercise relatively strong hierarchical control over their internal administrative processes, while others are perpetually searching for effective mechanisms of hierarchical control.

In theory, a rational central policymaker would doubtless wish to foster both pluralist democracy and administrative efficiency: to create a bureaucratic structure that was both open to citizen involvement and strongly in control of its internal operations. Such a combination would presumably provide responsiveness to citizens' demands as well as confidence that central decisions would be carried out at the street level. In fact, this combination is rarely found in urban bureaucracies; the pattern is more likely to be one of weak or unstable citizen involvement in policymaking and weak hierarchical control of internal operations. The point is that the different structural features of urban bureaucracies lead to markedly different operating characteristics and policy outcomes.

Here my proposition is that urban bureaucracies vary along three basic dimensions: (1) the institution's degree of openness or closedness to citizen participation; (2) the degree of hierarchical control within the bureaucracy; and (3) the degree to which the institution has a well-established technology for carrying out its functions. These three variables determine the way a particular urban bureaucracy makes policy and delivers its services. This analysis is a simplified version of the analysis above because it focuses on only three institutional differences. By combining the three variables we can describe two very different kinds of possible urban bureaucracies, both of which have clear strengths and weaknesses.

The first type is closed to citizen access and has both strong hierarchical control and a well-established technology. Such a bureaucracy would possess the structural conditions for administrative and managerial competence: it would be able to put out fires or clean the streets. On the other hand, such a bureaucracy would not be responsive to the nuances of citizens' demands (since it would have little contact with citizens); it might not be particularly innovative or experimental; and it might be slow to adapt its techniques and procedures to changing conditions. In particular, such a bureaucracy would cling to the regularity and mechanical precision of its techniques and avoid any features of its service function that could not be easily managed and transformed into clear administrative routines. It would take pride in its proven ability to get the job done and would be unwilling to depart from its basic techniques and processes. Fire, sanitation, and health departments come close to this type.

The second type of urban bureaucracy is open to public access and has both weak hierarchical control and weak technology. Such a bureaucracy would find it difficult to formulate consistent policy over time, implement programs, and monitor the delivery of basic services. In fact, service delivery would be irregular; services would be delivered in different ways by different people in different places. To a large extent, "policy" would be made by street-level bureaucrats whose discretion would be enhanced by the lack of hierarchical control and clear technology. At the same time, such a loosely structured, fragmented bureaucracy would arguably be more responsive to citizens' needs, not only because it would have a closer relationship with citizens but also because its lack of regular procedures and a binding technology would permit flexibility. Such a bureaucracy might therefore be highly adaptive to local pressures, and it might be willing to change its policies quickly because, in Huntington's terms, it is weakly "institutionalized," that is, its institutional structures and programs are neither deeply rooted nor widely agreed upon.[16] Finally, such a bureaucracy would be apt to innovate and experiment extensively—even frantically—in a search for new techniques and technologies that would work.

I suggest that the major urban bureaucracies fall on a continuum between the two ideal types as shown in table 5.2. This analysis per-

Table 5.2 An institutional classification of urban bureaucracies.

	Fire	Sanitation	Health	Police	Welfare	Education
Closed	high (3)	high (3)	medium (2)	high (3)	low (1)	low (1)
Control	high (3)	medium (2)	medium (2)	low (1)	medium (2)	low (1)
Technology	high (3)	medium (2)	high (3)	low (1)	low (1)	low (1)
Score	9	7	6	5	4	3

mits us to make several inferences about the way different urban bureaucracies will typically formulate policy, respond to problems, and innovate and implement programs. A highly structured bureaucracy like the fire department is strongly committed to existing procedures and relatively unresponsive to citizens' demands and new problems. A fire department will be willing to refine its technology (for example, to improve its equipment) but resistant to attempts to change its basic organizational format (such as by reducing the number of pieces of equipment sent to each fire or by adopting new procedures for dealing with small garbage fires or suspected false alarms). Equally, because fire departments have a closed relationship with citizens, they will be slow to adjust to new problems such as arson, racial tension in the community, harassment, and malicious false alarms that fall outside their mission understood in narrower technological terms.

At the other end of the continuum is the urban school system. Issues in the schools are highly politicized, since neighborhood residents are typically familiar with the way the schools work and have a long tradition of participation in school affairs (as in PTA's). Thus citizen participation is strong in schools; ironically, the servers and the served have the closest relationship in schools but also generate the most conflict over the authority and prerogatives of citizens and public employees. This is borne out by the fierce battles over school decentralization and busing and by the high incidence of teacher strikes which lead to further conflicts between street-level bureaucrats and neighborhood residents. More important, the school system is weakly institutionalized: policies, programs, and standards vary from classroom to classroom, from school to school. This means that there is little careful accounting of teaching performance and little assurance that new programs will be implemented reliably. Finally, because they have no well-established technology, school systems are constantly trying new educational techniques. Innovations (teaching machines, open classrooms, decentralization) are tested and then replaced with bewildering rapidity. In short, school systems tend to be in a state of flux, always attempting to control their operations but always subject to visible political conflicts and to rapid changes in educational technology and fashion.

Police departments offer an interesting mixed case, involving elements of both tight and loose structure. Like fire departments, police departments are relatively closed to public involvement, and they would prefer to stay that way: to continue to exercise their authority without consultation and review by citizens. For this reason, police departments strongly resist attempts to increase citizen involvement (as in plans for civilian review boards and various kinds of decentralization and community control). At the same time, the amount of discretion exercised by patrolmen on the street and the inherent subjectivity of deciding when, for example, a person is disorderly or a public nuisance keep police departments from establishing strong hierarchical control over the delivery of police services at the street level. Despite uniforms and quasimilitary ranks, the existence of a strong formal hierarchy in the bureaucracy does not in this case produce a strong functional hierarchy. The consequences of weak internal control in police administration are well known: corruption, policy brutality and harassment, variable enforcement of criminal law and procedures. This lack of strong centralized control means that even if police bureaucracies were opened to community involvement in policymaking, new community-oriented policies might not actually be carried out on the beat. It would be difficult for community participants to know what impact, if any, a new policy was having on day-to-day police conduct at the street level.

As noted above, police departments not only lack strong hierarchical control, they also lack a well-established technology. Like school systems, police departments continuously move from one technique to another, sometimes using different but equally uncertain techniques at the same time. These techniques include electronic surveillance, stakeouts, plainclothes patrols, and the use of decoys. Sometimes patrolmen are taken out of patrol cars and put on walking beats as a new way of reducing crime in an area. At other times the opposite policy is employed. Central policymakers simply do not know what works and what does not work in police protection. Thus any effort to improve police policymaking and performance is likely to produce a flurry of uncertain initiatives, most of which will never be fully or consistently implemented at the street-level.

Whatever the structural characteristics of a particular institution, urban service bureaucracies now face a number of conflicting pressures, especially pressures for *more* pluralist democracy and *more* administrative efficiency. The widespread demands for citizen participation in the 1960s forced all urban bureaucracies to adopt one strategy or another for increasing citizen access. As Robert Yin and I have shown, the more closed bureaucracies tended to adopt weaker strategies of participation and decentralization.[17] But the institutional structure of every bureaucracy was affected in some measure by the participation movement. At the same time, the efficiency-oriented impetus toward greater professionalism in service bureaucracies pulled in precisely the opposite direction. The growth of public service unions worked to strengthen policymaking by professional bureaucrats rather than neighborhood residents. Taken together, these two opposed forces have worked to intensify the fight between citizens and professional bureaucrats over control of service bureaucracies.

In sum, my analysis of institutional differences enables us to move beyond a general portrait of bureaucratic behavior to illuminate the distinctive policymaking and organizational problems that are likely to arise in particular bureaucracies. With this added analytical equipment, we are able, as political detectives, to bring a more fine-grained understanding of bureaucracy to bear on the basic question of how to improve bureaucratic functioning—a question that I will treat in detail in Chapter 7.

6

The Search for Control of Bureaucracy

I BEGAN THIS BOOK by observing that the bureaucracy is a favorite whipping boy of politicians, businessmen, journalists, and ordinary citizens. The charges leveled against bureaucracy are numerous, but the one I have focused on so far is that bureaucracy is in important respects both undemocratic and inefficient. Another major complaint is that the bureaucracy is "out of control." It is widely agreed — even among those who disagree on most other political issues — that something must be done to get the bureaucracy under control. But what does this talk about control mean? Presidents complain that they cannot get the bureaucracy to respond to their bidding. John Kennedy once lamented that the State Department was a "bowl of jello," meaning presumably that it either resisted his leadership or was incapable of carrying out his policies. On the other hand, certain Presidents, especially Lyndon Johnson and Richard Nixon, have been criticized for seeking to exercise inordinate political control over the bureaucracy.

Congressmen also frequently complain about their inability to get a firm grip on the bureaucracy. Thomas P. O'Neill, the Speaker of the House, said in 1979, "There are so many programs in this government of ours that are obsolete in nature and we have done nothing about them . . . America is crying to put oversight to work." One congressman thought that increased oversight and control might lead to a significant budget cut for the Soil Conservation Service, whose operating performance had been seriously questioned in a General Accounting Office Study. In a quite different vein, another congressman looked forward to greater congressional oversight in the area of federal programs for the handicapped because he was "interested in *expanding* its appropriation and increasing the dialogue among all parties involved to make sure it works" (italics added). This is just one example of the fact that bureaucratic control means very different things to different people.

In the executive branch, cabinet officers are quick to decry the lack of control they feel they possess over their own bureaucracies. Others would say that public bureaucracies are overcontrolled by their own internal procedures. Whatever the problem of control may be, lack of coherence and overcontrol are certainly not the same culprit.

In Congress the argument is made that the nation's representatives exercise virtually no control over particular elements of the bureaucracy. One congressman was "flabbergasted" that Congress had not "examined the General Services Administration for years prior to the recent corruption scandal."[1] At the same time, the complaint is frequently made that some congressional committees have an intimate relationship with certain bureaucratic segments, leading to a high level of mutual support, mutual protection, and the advancement of the allied interests of the relevant congressmen and bureaucrats. The problem of control here might be described as excessive self-interested control by a congressional subcommittee.

Public managers also attempt to assert control over the bureaucracy, and they demonstrate that similar levels of control can be sought for very different purposes. One public manager, for example, wanted to increase his administrative control over the functioning of the Massachusetts Department of Youth Services in order to dismantle its programs. Another set out to establish strict managerial control over a number of drug programs in New York City in order to expand the number of methadone maintenance programs in the city.[2]

The problem of controlling the bureaucracy is also issue among interest groups. Some wish they had more control of bureaucratic decisionmaking, so that their concerns and interests would be given higher priority. Some feel excluded from the bureaucratic policymaking process and complain vigorously that rival interest groups possess disproportionate control of bureaucratic activity in their policy arena.

The conflicting perceptions of the problem of controlling the bureaucracy are also present at the state level and were recently captured in a report of the National Governors' Conference. On the one hand, the governors argued that excessive federal controls hamstring their administrations. On the other hand, they assert with no less force that the "feds" must better control and coordinate their programs to reduce fragmentation and overlap of policies. These two arguments are not necessarily incompatible, but they certainly point in different directions.

Suffice it to say that the definition of the problem of bureaucratic control varies widely and is usually based on the perspective and interests of the perceiver. It appears that Miles's Law applies again: Where you stand depends on where you sit.

The Meaning of Control

Given this variability of perception and definition, what can be said with clarity and rigor about the meaning of control in bureaucratic settings? Dahl and Lindblom provide one strict definition of control: "B is controlled by A to the extent that B's responses are dependent on A's acts in an immediate and direct functional relationship."[3] This kind of strict control relationship in government is attained when a president orders a staff assistant to perform an assignment, or when a general instructs a subordinate to pursue certain training procedures. When a congressional appropriations committee reduces a bureaucracy's budget, it directly controls administrative spending in that particular instance. But in general the problem of bureaucratic control involves looser interpretations of control relationships.

It is unclear in the illustrative sample of complaints cited above whether bureaucracy suffers from too much or too little control or whether the bureaucracy is doing too much or too little in a particular policy arena; the examples given demonstrate both positive and negative conceptions of control. The problem is whether a given president, cabinet secretary, congressional committee, interest group, or administrator possesses too much or too little control in the course of advancing or curbing particular interests. The issue of control, thus, looks like one of standard politics of who gets what, when, how. If this is so, it follows that the discussion of bureaucratic control is essentially a discussion of bureaucratic politics in a different guise.

It may be tempting to view the control problem as merely a question of normal politics. But that is too simple a solution. As soon as one asks questions like for what purpose are you controlling or by what principle of authority are you doing so, to correct what kind of general defect in bureaucracy, or what particular institutional trait, one reaches deeper, substantive issues. Although we cannot ever fully isolate the political complaint that a given actor or group has too much or too little control over bureaucracy, these questions point the way toward issues about the values bureaucracy serves or ought to serve: whether bureaucracies' internal processes are accessible, participative, and open; whether bureaucrats are accountable to superiors, citizens, and elected officials; whether citizens or interest groups have recourse against decisions or processes they object to; whether bureaucracies are capable of implementing their programs or regulations in a reliable way; whether these programs are coordinated within a department or between departments; and whether these programs are effective and responsive to different citizens' needs.

These questions carry substantial normative and evaluative weight. They raise the general issues of accessibility, openness, participation, accountability, reliability, coordination, effectiveness, and responsiveness. Under the rhetoric of the need for control of bureaucracy and alongside the political issue of who gets what in the bureaucratic policy process, these are the concerns that must be addressed.

The pattern of loose bureaucratic control does not mean that the bureaucracy is totally out of hand. Rather, as seen in Chapter 4, bureaucracies are typically hemmed in by turf rivalries and internal competition, and in a world of segmented pluralism, we find cautious bureaucratic minimaxers, inching ahead, not an unchecked, rampaging bureaucracy. Also as noted earlier, some bureaucratic settings show patterns of relatively strong control, whether by a congressional committee, an interest group, a president or a presidential agency like OMB, or by internal mechanisms (whether we call them standard operating procedures, red tape, or pathological bureaucratic rigidity).

The false hope of Woodrow Wilson, that bureaucracy would

prove to be a wondrous efficiency machine in which rational decision would reign and hierarchical authority would be perfectly ordered, also needs correction, as I have said. The view that there can be no problem with bureaucracy, or that if there is a problem it must lie with the bureaucracy's masters in the White House, Congress, the state house, or city hall, is too simple. While it is possible to find examples of what might reasonably be called rational planning and decisionmaking (NASA) or smooth hierarchical authority (the Marine Corps) in bureaucracies, there are more cases of the opposite. Wilson's hopeful argument is often extended by analogy to the thought that the government should be run like IBM or General Motors, or that the American civil service should emulate the professionalism, status, training, and esprit of its English, French, or Japanese counterparts. Here we are trafficking in counterfactuals or at least great cultural differences. As I argued in Chapter 3, bureaucratic politics, in all its manifestations, is deeply embedded in American government, and the central features of bureaucratic politics include fragmentation, competition, valuative decisions, loose administrative control, and silent politics, all of which militate against the model of bureaucracy as a system of highly rational, neutral, hierarchical authority.

An advocate of the Wilsonian vision, even if he accepted this description of current bureaucratic politics, might propose that we destroy the existing structure of bureaucracy, start over again, and impose the kind of highly independent, professional, hierarchical system that Wilson believed functioned elsewhere. This proposal is too radical to consider very seriously. And even if the bureaucracy, viewed as a self-contained unit, could be rebuilt from scratch according to the specifications of the efficiency model, the behavior of other political actors in the American system would also have to be changed radically. Bureaucratic politics arises not only from internal political pressures in the bureaucracy but also from political pressures emanating from the presidency, the White House staff, the Congress, state and local governments, interest groups, and other citizen organizations.

In some discussions of bureaucracy there is a fear that the problem of control could lead to an overreaction—to a proliferation of controls—such that bureaucratic functioning would be greatly fettered, if not crippled. It is true that a persistent tension exists in public management between desirable levels of independent action and constraint. Peter Self makes this point crisply: the "tensions between the requirement of responsibility or 'accountability' and those of effective executive action can reasonably be described as *the* classic dilemma of public administration."[4]

James Fesler poses this dilemma in terms of the costs of control:

> The problem of analysis would be eased if we could assume that maximization of control is a desirable objective. In fact, the costs of pursuit of such an objective would be intolerable. Why is this so? Because an abundance of negative controls creates a pervasive climate of distrust, which can demoralize those on whom we depend for achievement of public programs. Because controls external to administration may displace or undermine internal administrative controls. Because controls multiply requirements for review of proposed decisions, increase red tape and delay action; controls, therefore, may dull administration's responsiveness to its public.[5]

The nightmare vision of overcontrol implicit in Fesler's warning arises when the quest for control multiples widely among various actors in the policymaking process. For example, in the name of strict hierarchy as called for by the efficiency model, superiors might institute elaborate control measures to monitor the every coming and going of their subordinates. Kaufman has found that superiors already possess a vast amount of such "administrative feedback"; far more detailed reporting would strain feedback channels and greatly constrain subordinate behavior. If congressional committees, interagency committees, and the General Accounting Office all stepped up their control activities, the picture drawn by Fesler would seem increasingly accurate. In an extreme version of this situation we could imagine a police detective who spends one hour on the street investigating a case and three hours doing related paperwork.

The search for balance in controlling bureaucracy is also complicated by the effects of increased controls that might be designed to make bureaucracy more democratic. Following the logic of pluralist democracy, bureaucrats might increasingly be called on to create new citizen advisory boards, hold more public hearings, open their meetings and their files, hire ombudsmen, emphasize affirmative action in hiring, hold more news conferences, increase their accessibility to interest groups, and so forth. Such control activities, presented in the name of democratic norms, would add enormously to the burdens and constraints on administrators in the bureaucracy. And a combination of the potential administrative efficiency controls described above with these democratic controls might easily add up to the condition of bureaucratic control that Fesler terms "intolerable."

In fact this nightmare of overcontrol does not currently exist. From the analysis of bureaucratic politics in Chapter 3 and 4 we can see that this level of control is indeed unlikely to exist in the bureaucratic world of segmented pluralism, with its features of silent politics, valuative decision, and loose administrative control. Our task now is to define the problem of controlling bureaucracy in a way that will be analytically useful. Four basic propositions can be made about the control of bureaucracy.

1. Loose Control

The clearest way to pose the problem is to say that from most perspectives and institutional vantage points the bureaucracy is *loosely* controlled. The notion of loose control is intended to mean, in its ordinary usage, slack, not tightly bound. Some of its main features are the difficulty presidents have in controlling their departments, weak congressional mandates, the trouble political executives have in taking charge of career civil servants, slack control relationships between higher- and lower-level bureaucrats (especially street-level bureaucrats), the pervasiveness of delegation and discretion, and the difficulty higher-level managers have in asserting control of professional groups, intergovernmental policy subgovernments, or public unions because of their independence, expertise, entrenched alliances, or, in the case of unions, their adversary posture.

Viewed more broadly, in a bureaucratic structure of segmented pluralism many clusters of bureaucracies, along with their allies, exercise a degree of autonomy or self-control over their policy arenas. Segmented pluralism is a structure in which the bureaucracy as a whole is made up of unconnected or loosely connected fragments. The features of silent politics and power conservation add to the difficulty of tightening control relationships.

The reference above to *most* perspectives and institutional vantage points is important to the clear statement of this first proposition. When we are talking about bureaucratic control, we are usually not talking about a one-dimensional control relationship. The bureaucracy and its control environment might be mapped as shown in figure 6.1. In the pure case of loose control every institutional connection with the bureaucracy would be represented on the map by a broken line to signify a weak control relationship. This might be too simple and symmetrical a depiction, however. The control environment for bureaucracy X portrayed in figure 6.1 is a more complex case. There are certain institutional connections where no control relationship exists at all. There are others, in this case three in number, where there is a relationship of loose control, and one relationship between the bureaucracy and an interest group where the control relationship is significantly stronger (represented

Figure 6.1   A bureaucracy and its control environment.

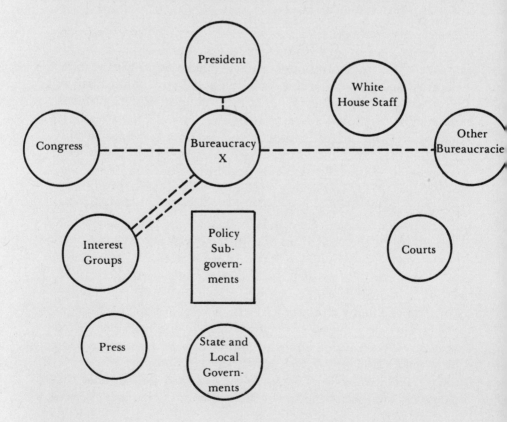

by a double broken line). Viewed in aggregate, bureaucracy X is loosely controlled. But that one instance of significant control (interest group-bureaucracy) may be worrisome for any of a number of reasons. Although the situation depicted, seen in macro terms, is one of loose control, the micro terms we might want to inspect more carefully the nature and implications of the one strong control relationship.

2. Multiple Mechanisms of Control

Despite the general pattern of loose administrative control, many different mechanisms of bureaucratic control and efforts at control can be identified in the American policymaking process. Modern presidents have repeatedly tried to tighten their grip on their departments through the use of political appointments and through the introduction of systems like Management by Objectives, which was introduced during the Nixon administration. The White House staff has repeatedly tried to clamp down on the bureaucracy and better coordinate the policy advice of different agencies. The Office of Management and Budget has intensified its scrutiny of management operations and expenditure patterns. Congress has attempted to increase its oversight capacities in various ways. Legislators have greatly expanded their staffs, have instructed their subcommittees to give more attention to bureaucratic oversight, and have even, at one point, created special-purpose "oversight committees." Congress has also begun to enact more laws than in earlier decades containing provision for a legislative veto of executive actions. The 1974 Congressional Budget Act includes several provisions that mandate "more systematic program evaluation throughout the government." The Congressional Budget Office provides the Congress with enhanced analytical capability to do battle with OMB and the departments over program requests, estimates, and forecasts. Finally, the Congress has frequently passed "sunset" legislation, which puts termination dates of one year, three years, or some other fixed period on new laws. The General Accounting Office has also expanded its range of inquiries.

In addition to the above attempts at bureaucratic control, various older and newer mechanisms have meshed to assist control. Bureaucratic decisions of regulatory agencies may be challenged in the courts. State and local governments have increasingly banded together as lobbies to better monitor and influence federal aid programs, revenue sharing, and related intergovernmental regulations. Various citizen watchdog groups, such as Common Cause and Ralph Nader's conglomerate of organizations, have arisen to appraise and criticize bureaucratic functioning. The press has increased its commitment to investigative reporting, including reporting on the bureaucracy. Affirmative action programs have increased the representation of minorities in the bureaucracy. Finally, if my analysis of the cautious bureaucratic minimaxer operating in an environment of segmented pluralism is correct, a degree of reciprocal control exists among bureaucracies. Bureaucracies move carefully and defensively, either because they confront identifiable bureaucratic competitors, jealous of their own programs and jurisdictions, or because they anticipate that any sudden, substantial changes or initiatives in policy will stir up competition and conflict with other bureaucracies. Thus, the bureaucratic politics of competition and conflict constitutes a control or constraint on bureaucratic behavior.

With so many control mechanisms in operation, why should there be a general pattern of loose control of bureaucracy? One obvious answer is that many of these controls are relatively weak. There is indeed considerable evidence that the apparently formidable control systems are not as potent as they appear. There is some evidence, for example, that presidents can influence the attitudes of bureaucrats, where influence means increasing bureaucratic support of presidential policies. But there is little evidence that the president can systematically impose his objectives in the bureaucracy or that he can "manage" detailed bureaucratic operations from the Oval Office.

Efforts to fortify presidential control by the introduction of Management by Objectives led to little more than an avalanche of paper, much of it containing vague aspirations (such as improved chances for peace in the Middle East), or agency wish lists, or carefully calibrated listings of activities that the bureaucracy had expected to perform anyway.[6] Also, as Robert Wood and others have shown, attempts by the White House staff to control bureaucratic functioning often lead into a trap of administrative overburden: overcontrol can mire administrators in operational detail and thus perhaps give the bureaucracy even greater freedom on broader policy questions.[7]

The control measures that legislatures have managed to institute give a mixed picture. The Congressional Budget Office and the larger congressional staffs have increased legislators' capacity to oversee the bureaucracy. But other congressional control mechanisms allow less oversight than meets the eye, because the responsibility for overseeing bureaucracy is typically fragmented among a number of different legislative subcommittees. This situation arose because after deciding to create specific oversight subcommittees, the Congress then removed the *requirement* that its committees do so; the number of oversight committees was also reduced because of a Senate rule limiting the number of subcommittee chairmanships a senator can hold. The increased range of congressional activity has fragmented the attention Congressmen can give to any particular program or subcommittee. Thus any real increase in congressional oversight capacity that may have occurred is likely to reside to a significant extent in the hands of congressional bureaucrats, that is, the professional staff members of legislative committees.

The legislative veto is often thought to be a significant control weapon. But according to the Congressional Research Service, although hundreds of laws were enacted between 1932 and 1979 "providing for legislative review and hundreds of resolutions filed to require specific reviews," only 81 executive actions have ever been reversed.[8] Sunset laws also sound promising as a control mechanism. But thus far the existence of statutory termination dates has not spurred Congress actually to terminate programs. Fesler comments, "Neither the relevant legislative committees nor Congress as a whole has seized the opportunity to terminate poor programs by simply failing to reenact authorizing legislation; the strongly criticized LEAA [Law Enforcement and Assistance Administration] was renewed in 1970, 1973, and 1976."[9]

More generally, congressional control mechanisms have a built-in weakness. Authorization controls are ex ante; they can only prescribe what a bureaucracy is supposed to do in future (although the increasing practice of requiring annual authorization tightens this leash). At the same time, the oversight role played by appropriations committees is certainly broad as regards bureaucratic expenditures as a whole, but because of the very requirements of broad coverage, is not, in Fesler's appraisal, "deep."

In sum, it is true that Congress has increased its oversight activities; recent research by Joel Aberbach underscores that point.[10] But the word *increase* is a relative one and we must therefore ask: What kind of increase is meant, and what does it cover? As recently as 1977 a Senate committee characterized oversight as "unsystematic, sporadic, episodic, erratic, haphazard, ad hoc, and on a crisis basis only."[11]

If congressional control is inherently weak, what about other mechanisms for control? The issue of whether the judicial remedy works is debatable—but we must remember that it becomes available only after the plaintiff has lost in his bureaucratic proceedings. Then too, most disputes over administrative rulings are settled *out* of court. And research has shown that in cases concerning disputed decisions by federal agencies, the Supreme Court is more likely than not to uphold the agencies' decisions.[12]

What about investigative reporting? It still appears that the press is more attracted to dramatic stories of bureaucratic abuses and corruption than to ordinary bureaucratic functioning or the long-term evolution of bureaucratic policy. A disagreement between the Secretary of State and the National Security Advisor is a good story, as is misuse of CETA funds by localities. But most programs and policies lack the drama to attract news coverage.

To avoid flogging the visible limitations of bureaucratic control mechanisms to death, let us rest with the conclusion that although many mechanisms exist, many are indeed weak. This is one explanation of the pattern of loose control of bureaucracy. This explanation leads to the following question: If bureaucracies are surrounded by weak control mechanisms but if there are many such controls, why call looseness a problem? In such a situation bureaucracy presumably cannot get very far in misconduct, power seizure, nonfeasance, or discrimination before it runs into one kind of control or another. Controls may bend or stretch, but they do not typically break down. Indeed, one observer has referred to a "doctrine of big loose control" to describe this relationship of bureaucracy to its control environment.[13] Portrayed graphically, this doctrine might look something like figure 6.2. As the figure shows, most of the institutional control relationships are weak, but there is more than one instance of a stronger control relationship, and in two instances no control relationships exist at all. Wilson might not be delighted by the situation mapped here, but we would not have to worry that bureaucracy X was going to rob us blind or take over the

Figure 6.2 Big loose control of bureaucracy.

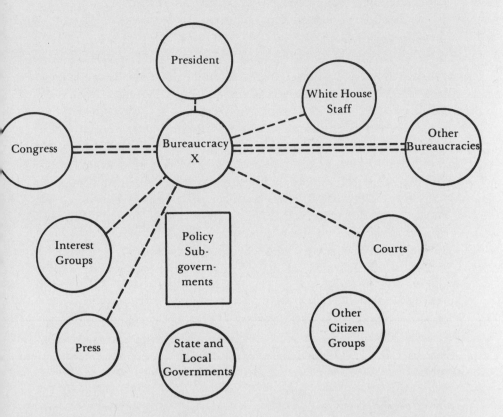

republic. Perhaps the doctrine of big loose control is therefore a viable, practical theory of the "second best." Why consider it a problem?

Answering this question leads into a deeper inquiry into the bureaucratic control problem. One answer is that big loose control presents additional problems and second-order effects that I have not yet attended to. A second answer is that we worry about bureaucratic control because we care, at root, about specific institutional control relationships (see proposition 3 below). For various institutional reasons we believe that certain control relationships should be relatively strong and others relatively weak. A third answer is that we worry about loose control because of what it tells us about the formidable defense mechanisms that bureaucracy possesses against control. And we believe that in a democracy it is *dangerous* for bureaucracy to possess those defense mechanisms. They are after all, an expression of power resources (this issue lies at the heart of proposition 4 below).

The first objection to big loose control is partly policy-oriented and partly related to the normative models of pluralist democracy and administrative efficiency. For one thing, while big loose control may preclude "bull in a china shop" behavior by bureaucracies—witness recent congressional efforts to reign in the aggressive regulatory policies of the Federal Trade Commission—many small bureaucratic actions will go unnoticed. Indeed, citizens or public officials often will not know anything about these small-scale actions. This ignorance is worrisome because, when generalized across bureaucratic behavior, it means that confidence about the reliability and consistency of the bureaucratic policy process is necessarily diminished. To anyone who cares intensely about a particular aspect of bureaucratic policy, the degree of potential unreliability and inconsistency is that much more troubling.

More important, the depiction of the cautious bureaucratic minimaxer, inching ahead, implies that a great deal of bureaucratic activity goes on without being dramatic or unusual enough to activate the control mechanisms provided by the doctrine of big loose control. It might even be true that the vast amount of ordinary bureaucratic activity proceeds undisturbed within the confines of big loose control. If this is so, there is surprisingly little safety in the simple number of the control mechanisms depicted above.

From a more normative perspective, the doctrine of big loose control is problematic on democratic grounds because of the character of at least some of the controllers it depends on. For one thing, reliance on control by the White House staff is worrisome in democratic terms because of the sometimes loose control of that staff by the president. The worst case, where members of the White House staff possess large measures of authority and are weakly accountable, amounts to loose control *squared*. In any case, bureaucratic control by the White House staff entails a long chain of control relationships running from citizens to the president (via an election every four years) to the White House staff to the bureaucracy. Similar democratic concerns arise in the legislative arena, where the controllers themselves are loosely controlled professional staffers in the General Accounting Office or in a legislative subcommittee. Michael Malbin and Michael Scully have outlined the sources of relatively independent staff power in the daily functioning of legislative staff committees. They found an increasingly autonomous legislative bureaucracy, amounting to legislative control, in large part, by what they call "our unelected representatives."[14] This concern diminishes directly as a congressman exercises more control over his own staff. But with the simple growth of the legislative bureaucracy and the familiar scattered (if not overloaded) activity pattern of the present-day senators and representatives, the role of the "unelected representatives," especially when cast as democratic controllers of bureaucracy, cannot be lightly dismissed.

In the same vein, if within a context of big loose control bureaucracy X is controlled by organized interest groups, other bureaucracies, or the press, we are once again confronted with controllers who are themselves only loosely controlled by elected officials or ordinary citizens.

From the point of view of the administrative efficiency model, certain kinds of loose control make a mockery of valued norms concerning executive leadership and hierarchical efficiency. For example, when a president orders "his" CIA to destroy supplies of poisonous shellfish toxins but then discovers (or is told by the press) that the supplies still exist, the whole structure of the efficiency model is made to look ridiculous. The same problem of control is demonstrated when a mayor proudly proclaims that his sanitation workers have cleaned major highway arteries after a snowstorm—he has instructed them to do so and has been told his instructions have been carried out—only to be confronted by contradictory television news clips of actual snow conditions. At one level, this failure to carry out an assignment is a simple matter of administrative incompetence or faulty bureaucratic communication and reporting. At a more important level, this kind of case strips the administrative efficiency model of its normative credibility and authority.

3. Particular Control Relationships

The third proposition about bureaucratic control is that it is necessary to consider particular institutional control relationships, particular problems of bureaucratic behavior, and the character of particular policy problems. The debate over controlling the bureaucracy can be fully understood (and the control problem perhaps remedied) only if we move beyond the aggregate view of control and consider what I call the "micropolitics" of control. This closer look is illustrated in figure 6.3, where the general bureaucratic control environment is depicted once again, but in a significantly different way. Drawing the map this way calls attention to four particular institutional relationships in which issues of bureaucratic control are often especially intense.

Figure 6.3   The micropolitics of bureaucratic control.

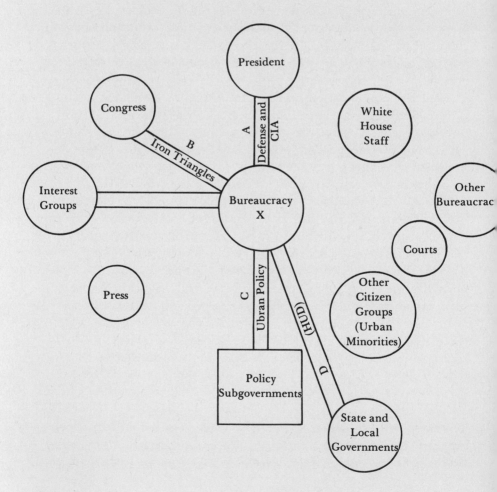

1. Relationship A focuses on the president's control of the Defense Department and the CIA. As citizens we care about the president's management of his bureaucracy in general, but we care especially about his control of the military. This is both because of democratic concerns about civilian control (as in Truman's struggle with MacArthur) and because of the efficiency model's concern that the development of a professional "corps," to use Wilson's term, should reinforce rather than compete with central executive leadership. In the case of the CIA, it is a clear threat to democratic norms to have an agency, on its own, making decisions that have a substantial effect on foreign policy. Such behavior calls, at the least, for strong presidential control. But when the president himself uses the CIA as a private, secret instrument of foreign policy, the control problem is compounded; the ostensible controller becomes part of the control problem. In cases like this countervailing control mechanisms are crucial — and indeed such mechanisms have been developing in the Congress. When control from the usual source — the president — is absent, an important part of foreign policymaking has the potential for completely evading democratic oversight.

2. Relationship B is an iron triangle relationship among bureaucracy X, an interest group, and a congressional subcommittee. Such a three-way alliance represents an extreme form of segmented pluralism, in which a piece of public policy takes on the character of a private government. Iron triangles pose grave problems for both the democracy and efficiency models because (*a*) public scrutiny and involvement are prevented and (*b*) there is little or no central administrative direction of the bureaucracy. The remedy is for either the Congress as a whole or the president to break into the private government and reestablish both democratic and administrative control of bureaucratic policymaking.

3. Relationship C highlights the control relationship among bureaucracy X (in this case HUD), state and local governments, and a citizens' group (in this case urban minorities). It is strongly arguable that HUD has the strongest impact of any bureaucracy on urban policy and, by implication, on the welfare of urban minorities. If local governments and urban minorities believe that HUD policies are ineffective or unresponsive, the democratic character and the administrative efficiency of a major part of domestic policy are undermined. The remedy in this case is to establish a strong positive

control relationship—that is, substantial involvement by local governments and citizens in bureaucratic decisionmaking.

4. Relationship D identifies a general class of control problems in which an administrative supervisor's control over lower-level bureaucrats is at issue. When policy decisions are not carried out or are distorted at lower levels, we encounter a fundamental violation of the norms of administrative efficiency and a classic case of the implementation problem. This type of control problem has implications for democratic norms as well, as Herbert Kaufman has written:

> If leaders exert but little influence on the actions of subordinates, then one of the axioms of democratic government ceases to apply. In general terms, democracy in the modern state presupposes that changing a handful of officials in high places will ultimately change the actions of thousands of employees throughout the system . . . To a greater or lesser extent, virtually all commentators on democracy in the same way take for granted the essential contribution of leadership. Subordinate compliance is thus a pillar of democratic government.[15]

Relationships A and B focused sharply on policy features of particular institutional control relationships. Relationships C and D, however, only specified general classes of control problems—albeit ones of manifest importance. The first two cases illuminate the strategy of thinking selectively about the salience of particular problems in bureaucratic control. The last two cases reveal the control problem as it exists more typically in the world of bureaucracy. In relationship D the number of potential problems for superiors in controlling subordinates is enormous, for public managers direct thousands of employees, not to mention thousands more in local government, where the implementation of social policy requires at least an indirect control relationship.

To put the problem of control in perspective, consider Kaufman's estimate that there are roughly 420 agencies, bureaus, and group bureaus in the federal government.[16] If each of these units is responsible for 20 significant programs or policies (leaving aside the thousands of small decisions made every year), that yields a total of 8400 potential control activities to perform.

The huge number of potential control activities makes a selective strategic approach to control not only administratively shrewd but logistically necessary. My normative proposition here is that controllers pick out specific institutional control relationships, related to particular policy issues, that they wish to emphasize. They should base this selection on the salience of the problems involved for democracy and/or efficiency, as in the examples of the Defense Department, the CIA, and iron triangles. The same logic applies to high-level political executives in a particular department. They face the same strategic choice: they can attempt a comprehensive assault on the problem, reacting to whatever comes over their desk marked *trouble*, or they can consciously select their targets of control.

The vast number of bureaucratic actions to be controlled is not the only reason to adopt a strategic approach to control. A second reason concerns the likely nature of the control problems themselves. Let us adopt a police detective's attitude toward public bureaucracies, assume that they are up to something wrong, and then try to figure out what offenses are to be discovered and prevented. Consider the following list of possible offenses:

1. corruption
2. noncriminal misallocation of funds
3. deliberate defiance of or noncompliance with orders
4. unauthorized reallocation of funds
5. inconsistent interpretation of orders
6. weak high-level coordination of policies and programs
7. miscommunications among levels of the hierarchy
8. valuative decisions in the context of loose mandates
9. lack of responsiveness to clients' needs
10. loose monitoring of program expenditures in the field
11. exercise of discretion by individual bureaucrats
12. conflict among lower-level bureaucrats (including state and local officials) in the implementation of policy
13. weak or ineffective participation by affected groups.

Four main points can be made about this list:
1. Even if the strategic policymaker has focused on a small number of institutional control relations (and their main policy arenas) for particular scrutiny, he still confronts a wide range of potentially troublesome bureaucratic behaviors.

2. The most flagrant offenses, put at the top of the list (numbers 1-3), are the most likely to be detected in the normal functioning of big loose control. There are the kinds of offenses that the OMB, the

General Accounting Office, hierarchical superiors, and the press are most likely to notice. It also may be that these "page one" abuses are relatively rare in occurrence.

3. As we move down the list the relative frequency of offenses committed is likely to increase and the difficulty of detection is greater, because these less conspicuous offenses are embedded in the ordinary structure and functioning of bureaucracy.

4. Following point 3, to get to the heart of bureaucratic control, policymakers must dig deeply into the workings of bureaucracy, where the problems are most pervasive and the detective work is more difficult.

The main implication of this analysis is that a strategic policymaker who wishes to get a firm grip on any bureaucratic control relationship must apply his control activities sharply and systematically. This requirement, in turn, reinforces the importance of choosing a small number of control problems to work on. Another implication of this analysis is that the grosser kinds of bureaucratic offenses may well be caught by the system of big loose control. In strategic terms, one kind of control mechanism may work for offenses at the top of our list, but a far more intensive strategy is required to get at the bedrock control problems toward the bottom of the list.

4. Defense Mechanisms

The fourth proposition about bureaucratic control is that bureaucracies typically possess strong defense mechanisms against both external and internal controls. These defense mechanisms were presented in Chapter 3 as fundamental characteristics of bureaucratic functioning. I will review a number of them now to demonstrate their ability to defend against various control mechanisms.

Bureaucratic fragmentation poses a major structural problem for central controllers like the president and the Congress because it gives them so many different segments to deal with and because the bureaucratic segments are usually well fortified. To the extent that they inch ahead continuously, their actions are often inconspicuous and hard to detect. To the extent that they practice power conservation, they are alert to any outside threats to their functioning — including controls. To the extent that they have deeply embedded operating procedures, control activities aimed at changing their behavior encounter powerful obstacles. To the extent that they make valuative decisions, it is hard for central controllers to determine exactly how policies are being carried out. To the extent that they practice silent politics, central controllers have difficulty knowing what if anything they need to control. To the extent that civil servants possess special knowledge and use it strategically, it is also hard for controllers to gain a full picture of problems they might wish to control. To the extent that bureaucracies are dominated by professionals and experts, it is difficult for would-be controllers to break through professional barriers and establish stronger central control. To the extent that professional power relies on sophisticated technical expertise, controllers encounter barriers of knowledge and language. To the extent that policy subgovernments have created firm intergovernmental alliances between higher and lower officials, it is difficult for controllers to break into the policy systems and do their work as control detectives. Finally, to the extent that delegation and discretion are pervasive in bureaucracy, the control detective's job becomes one of tracking down small-scale and often inconspicuous individual actions—many of which occur at great remove from the White House, or Capitol Hill, or a cabinet secretary's office. All of these defense mechanisms mean that the costs in time and energy of undertaking control activity are likely to be great.

Many of these defense mechanisms reflect the bureaucracy's superior organizational resources and degree of institutionalization relative to controllers in the White House or in the Congress. By institutionalization, I mean that the bureaucracy's organizational resources are likely to be well entrenched, focused, and well prepared to react to control activities viewed as intrusions into the bureaucracy's business. This is a powerful defense mechanism because would-be controllers in the White House, in the Congress, and among appointed political executives often lack these resources. The controllers often are new to their jobs, lack detailed institutional knowledge, and find that their energies are fragmented across a wide range of problems.

There is a need for mobilization and collective action among those who seek to get any given bureaucracy under control. If they could concentrate their energies on control for any sustained period, if we could get congressmen, hurrying in different directions, together, they might exercise control more successfully. This constitutes yet another argument for a highly strategic and intensive approach to control.

The above comments about institutionalization, mobilization, and collective action do not apply without exception. "Old pros" on congressional committees, in the OMB, and in interesting-group lobbies possess resources similar to those of entrenched bureaucracies. It is with these actors, not surprisingly, that the bureaucracy's organizational resources often meet their match.

A Remedial Approach to Control

I have argued for taking a strategic approach to identifying particularly salient institutional control relationships. A further prescription is that control activity be consciously, and again strategically, remedial. This is because there are so many features of bureaucratic functioning that a president or a congressman *might* wish to control. Just as the simple number of potential institutional control problems requires a selective attack, so too the number of behavioral characteristics that might be worrisome requires selectiveness. A would-be controller confronts scores of behavioral characteristics that might be addressed, including professional insularity, jurisdictional conflicts, iron triangles, secrecy, fragmentation, valuative decision, expansion and proliferation of programs, rigid operating procedures, the camel's nose syndrome, and so forth.

No controller can embrace all these possible concerns about characteristic bureaucratic behavior. If he did, his control activity would inevitably be a mile wide and an inch deep. Furthermore, it is not enough simply to call for greater democracy or greater efficiency in bureaucracy. To strengthen these values, we have to cut into the concrete behavioral characteristics that threaten them. The logical strategy is therefore to pick a number of behavioral characteristics in bureaucracy and to seek, through increased control, to remedy them. One's selection of problematic behavioral characteristics will determine whether one reaches for remedies suggested by the pluralist democracy model or for remedies suggested by the administrative efficiency model.

I will present my own views about a remedial strategy for dealing with the bureaucracy in Chapter 7; at present the point is not that a certain behavioral characteristic must be addressed but rather that the task is to select a small list of such behaviors. Reasonable people will doubtless differ on the composition of this list.

Lest this strategic approach appear to involve a frighteningly complex problem of how to design controls, note that the earlier analysis of institutional differences provides substantial clues to the kinds of problems and remedies one is likely to find in a particular bureaucracy. In certain bureaucracies characteristics of closedness and secrecy naturally commend an effort to open up or to democratize bureaucratic functioning. In other bureaucracies fragmentation is so great and coordination so weak that an obvious control remedy is to tighten central administrative control. In other cases, guild professionalism may be so glaring, as in health care, that establishing a countervailing force to professionalism is an obvious remedy. In a final case, an interest group may have such a strong grip on policymaking that the obvious control remedy is to introduce competing interests and wider citizen involvement.

Democracy and Administrative Process Values

Faced with this barrage of complaints and conflicting perceptions of the control problem, a conscientious bureaucrat might well be dismayed. He would point to all the different actual and would-be controllers who prowl around his domain. Most important, in terms of democratic theory, he would defend himself by invoking his allegiance to what I call *administrative process values*. He might cheerfully concede that not every bureaucratic decision is correct or every program well run, but he would insist that citizens and public officials nevertheless have strong protection against bureaucratic misjudgments and other suspect behaviors because bureaucrats are faithful to the administrative process values of accessibility, accountability, responsiveness, participation, and responsibility. The conscientious bureaucrat might add, strengthening his point, that in a world of conflicting interests, where there is often no simple "right" decision, fidelity to these process values is the best insurance policy we can have that bureaucrats are performing both democratically and efficiently. This defense has some plausibility. Words like accessibility, responsiveness, and accountability have a reassuring ring to them. But they may also be misleading, for the various process values may be defined and applied in ways that imply very different results for citizens and elected public officials.

The problem is that there is considerable analytical variation in ordinary use of terms like accessibility, responsiveness, accountability, and participation. Does responsiveness mean being available to hear the complaints of a citizen or congressman, or does it mean recognizing those complaints and satisfying them? Does accountability mean simply that a government official can give a reason for an action or a policy? Or does it mean giving reasons that are "satisfactory" to the citizen or congressman?

Take participation. Does it mean that citizens are heard, or heard and listened to, or heard, listened to, and as a result, given their way? Does the test of participation lie in improved procedures for decisionmaking or in improved results of decisions? Is it possible to have improved procedures without improved results? Further, who is to participate? How widespread must participation be? How many issues or decisions must be governed by participatory procedures for participation to be considered real? What of the nature of the participatory decisions? Is it enough that most minor decisions are participated in, or must citizen participation extend to some major issues, or to all major issues? Who decides what issues are minor or major? We could dissect all of the administrative process values in the same way and show that each apparently simple idea unpacks into a number of more subtle questions.

Each administrative value can be understood from both a procedural and a substantive point of view. In the procedural sense, strengthening administrative process values entails greater communication and interaction between citizens and public officials. Citizens might attend meetings or review boards and speak their minds: participation. Government might establish mechanisms to allow citizens more easily to approach officials: accessibility. Government might bring officials closer to the problems that they must deal with: responsiveness. Bureaucracies might clarify what bureaucrat is in charge of what program and who is to answer for breakdowns and failures: accountability. As against these procedural notions, there is also a substantive construction of each value. The substantive issue is the question of what kinds of decisions are made. The test in this case is whether those affected by the decision feel that the right decision was made.

In addition to the distinction between substantive and procedural concerns, there is a distinction between strong and weak constructions of the process values. The values are weak when they provide only mild forms of redress for citizens and other interested parties and strong when they go further toward changing the nature of proceedings or the resulting policy. The process value of responsiveness, for example, may be defined both substantively and procedurally and in strong and weak senses in each case. In the procedural sense, responsiveness may be weakly defined to mean that bureaucrats will merely listen to citizens who try to press their claims, or it may be defined more strongly to require that bureaucrats restructure their administration so that they can act on citizen complaints more quickly. In the substantive sense, responsiveness may have the weak meaning that public officials will listen to what a citizen has to say and try to find answers that reflect the content of the citizen's concerns. In the stronger substantive sense, public officials may be required to do precisely what the citizen wishes; to respond directly, decisively, and quickly to the citizen's complaint. Since the administrative process values have strong and weak, substantive and procedural meanings, the mere invocation of the process values— responsiveness, participation, accountability—tells us very little about what precisely is being asked for and therefore what bureaucracy should provide.

We often hear the argument that for democratic reasons bureaucracies should be opened up, should both be more visible and involve citizens in their activities to a greater extent. I believe that opening up the bureaucracy is a critical aspect of any useful reform of bureaucracy. There are numerous institutional mechanisms by which bureaucracies might be made more open. They range from citizen advisory and policy review boards, to question periods in the British fashion, to ombudsmen, to joint citizen-bureaucrat decision-making bodies, to stronger forms of community control. In *Street-Level Governments* Robert Yin and I examined a wide range of such arrangements at the local level and found that many of them do increase communication between citizens and bureaucrats and lead to improved delivery of services. It is not our task here to design specific institutional mechanisms for opening up bureaucracies; the appropriate mechanism will differ from one bureaucracy to another and from one kind of policy problem to another.[17] The important task here is to define what is meant by an open bureaucracy. And what I want to say analytically is that greater openness is measured by movement from weak to strong applications of administrative process values, understood in *both* procedural and substantive terms.

The Substantive Values of Bureaucrats

This analysis of administrative process values leads naturally to a consideration of the substantive value decisions that bureaucrats often make. On grounds of both democracy and efficiency, it is worrisome when bureaucrats — and expecially lower-level bureaucrats — make valuative decisions on their own. On democratic grounds, this means that important elements of public decision are made by officials who are not democratically controlled by citizens — or are at best loosely controlled. On efficiency grounds, it undermines the norms of central executive leadership, hierarchical authority, and bureaucratic neutrality. The problem of substantive valuative decisions is embedded in many other problematic bureaucratic behaviors: weak congressional mandates, silent politics (including secrecy and closedness of operations), the self-governing tendency of professional groups, the barriers of technical expertise, elusive goals, the circularity of bureaucratic policymaking (designing and implementing the same policy), and the pervasiveness of delegation and discretion. Because it is related to so many other aspects of bureaucratic functioning, emphasizing valuative decision is an especially powerful way to cut into the "bureaucracy problem."

Taking a remedial approach to bureaucratic control, what might bureaucrats do to correct the worrisome features of valuative decision? One answer is that bureaucrats might provide an open, public accounting of the valuative basis of their decisions on significant policy issues. (We will see in a minute that the word "significant" poses considerable analytical difficulties.) Indeed, accounting for decisions in this way is how I would define *substantive responsibility* in bureaucratic decisionmaking. Without such an accounting, citizens have little way of knowing why bureaucrats decide to act as they do, and without that knowledge, the idea of democratic control of administration is little more than a dangerous fiction.

One public official who attempted to provide a public accounting for a valuative decision was former Secretary of Transportation William Coleman at the time of the controversy over whether the Concorde could land at New York's Kennedy Airport. In his written decision, Coleman performed a careful analysis which involved an explicit concern for legal, environmental, and political values. He sought to give a full accounting of his weighing of relevant values.

> This decision involves environmental, technological, and international considerations that are as complex as they are controversial, and do not lend themselves to easy or graceful evaluation, let alone comparison. I shall nonetheless attempt in some detail to explain my evaluation of the most significant issues . . . and the reasons I have decided as I have. For I firmly believe that public servants have the duty to express in writing their reasons for taking major actions, so that the public can judge the fairness and objectivity of such action. Moreover, explaining our reasons in writing may help us avoid unreasonable actions. A decision that "cannot be explained" is very likely to be an arbitrary decision.[18]

Coleman's concern to spell out value considerations both enabled citizens and other public officials better to understand the Concorde problem and gave citizens an opportunity to see what kind of person, with what kind of concerns and values, was making decisions in the office of the Secretary of Transportation. This kind of public accounting opens up bureaucratic policymaking in precisely the way I recommended earlier. Moreover, it provides the basis for a broader public debate about policy in which competing voices and interests are more readily evoked and expressed.

Calling for a public accounting by bureaucrats may sound like a fine idea. But the rub comes when we ask which decisions should be subject to this careful public scrutiny. I referred to "significant" decisions earlier, knowing full well that this word does not do the required analytical work. One way to deal with this problem is to make it a principal task of would-be strategic controllers, such as presidents and congressmen and cabinet secretaries, to set an agenda of policies and institutional control relationships that in their view require open, competitive public debate. This approach is consistent with the more general strategic approach to control recommended above. The same strategy could be used by other would-be controllers: the press, citizens' watchdog groups, and so forth. It is unlikely that the resulting agenda for public debate would be perfectly symmetrical, but it would be a way of focusing and sharpening control activities.

Even a successful external agenda-setting process would not eliminate the possibility that only a bureaucrat would know the likely significance of a policy decision, given the patterns of silent politics, loose mandates, professional control, and the like. Inevitably, we must turn to the substantive importance of particular decisions and rely to some extent on the bureaucrat's own sense of responsibility to make a public accounting when he deems an issue significant. Without purporting to establish a precise formula for measuring significance, I will advance two criteria as useful guidelines: (1) A policy merits public accounting when it is either a nonroutine new initiative or a marked departure from past practice. (2) A policy merits public accounting when it involves the application of a major social value such as equality, equal opportunity, personal liberty, or the public interest. This second criterion is especially strong when a conflict exists within a value (as in two competing definitions of equal treatment) or when two or more values are in conflict. Clearly, the first and second guidelines will often overlap, and they do not fully dispose of all interesting cases—but they do provide a starting point for a bureaucrat who wants to increase the level of open public accounting.

A possible objection to my call for open accounting is as follows: Partisan argument, as Lindblom asserts, is a virtue in a democracy. Since it is impossible to achieve full neutrality and objectivity about values, it is better to conduct a frankly partisan debate.[19] Asking bureaucrats to decide which decisions should be justified and explained to the public and how the explanations should be made is asking them to be neutral and objective—in short, is asking the impossible. What is more, it is contradictory to cast bureaucrats as the guardians of open accounting, since the purpose of open accounting is to guard the public against bureaucrats. This apparent contradiction does not really present a problem for my proposal, however. What my proposal demands from bureaucrats is not perfect objectivity but simply openness. It is fine for bureaucrats to take sides, to argue for or against substantive value positions—as long as they provide the essential service of arguing openly and explicitly. Given the likely diversity and range of bureaucratic views and interests, a public debate by bureaucrats on substantive values, even a partisan one, would give us a far greater clarification of value conflicts than we presently possess as citizens and supposed choosers of policies and electors of political leaders.

Explicit analysis of the values behind bureaucratic decisions may be seen either as a compensation for possible defects in partisan bargaining or as a useful supplement to the process of bargaining and adjustment. To the extent that the bargaining process blurs or ignores basic value conflicts in the interest of accommodation, an open value accounting would inject an important missing element into policy debate and decisionmaking. From a different vantage point, value analysis might be viewed as a supplement to normal bargaining processes in that it would generate discussion of a broader range of issues at the political bargaining table.

Lindblom advances another argument that bears directly on this analysis, namely, that values and policies are usually so intertwined in the evolution of policymaking that any attempt to isolate and analyze values is apt to be fruitless.[20] I have considerable sympathy with this argument, particularly as it relates to policies that have been hammered out over a long period of time in keeping with the pattern of incrementalism. But as American government has instituted more social programs and transfer payments, values like equality and equal opportunity play increasingly strong and independent roles in the policymaking process. Some major policies, such as affirmative action and busing, are explicitly designed to advance notions of equality or equal opportunity. Therefore to understand and evaluate such policies we need to know what their guiding values are understood to mean. Here is where the need for a careful clarification of values becomes so prominent. As I pointed out earlier, values like equality and equal opportunity are not simple notions but rather unpack into a multitude of different conceptions and interpretations.[21] An open public discourse about the meanings of and conflicts among our stated values is required if we are not to fall into policymaking by slogan and highly subjective definition of public policy.

Summary: A Strategic Madisonian Approach to Control

I resorted above to a policy detective metaphor to depict the problem of designing a strategy for controlling the bureaucracy. No doubt this metaphor will strike many responsible bureaucrats as objectionable, for it carries the implication of bureaucratic wrongdoing. Nevertheless, from the perspective of the would-be controller, the problem of control does take on many aspects of a policing problem, and the metaphor sharpens the issue of strategic investigation and enforcement that is at the heart of my analysis of bureaucratic politics. For the bureaucratic controller, no less than the policeman, must begin with the realization that he cannot completely control all the activities in his domain that he might like to. He must let certain kinds of behavior (and certain segments of the population) go unwatched if he is to have any success in dealing with problems he considers particularly important. Just as devoting police energies to making numerous low-level drug arrests is likely to have little impact on the drug problem, so too, dividing controllers' attention among many scattered bureaucratic control problems wastes control resources and diverts attention away from the most objectionable patterns of bureaucratic behavior.

The main thrust of my argument has been that a would-be controller must adopt a highly selective and strategic approach to control. This is important not only because of the simple number of control problems that might be addressed but also because of the difficulty of digging deeply into the workings of bureaucracy. The idea of a strategic approach carries with it the features of focus and depth — linked to an identification of problems that are especially worrisome on grounds of democracy and efficiency. At the same time, the doctrine of big loose control offers some hope that a larger number of control problems will be caught somewhere in the oversight process.

We have also seen that the process of deciding which problems are most worth attention cannot be performed abstractly. It is important to take a remedial approach and to focus on particular bureaucratic behaviors and particular institutional defects. We can worry about democracy and efficiency until the cows come home, but only when we locate those concerns in specific features of bureaucratic behavior are we likely to make any substantial remedial progress. The analysis of public bureaucracy and of particular institutional differences presented in this book offers some substantial clues about where to look in the bureaucracy in taking a remedial approach.

I have noted that bureaucrats will typically defend themselves against efforts at control by invoking administrative process values. But we have seen that there are analytical defects in the definition of these values, and any effort to open up the bureaucracy requires a stronger application of those process values in both procedural and substantive terms. Finally, we saw that the making of substantive valuative decisions by bureaucrats occupies a central place in the analytical structure of the control problem.

If controllers behave strategically, if process values were strengthened, if bureaucrats gave an open accounting of "significant" decisions, and if controllers shaped the agenda of that accounting, we might achieve a competitive public debate about bureaucratic policymaking that would overcome many of the obstacles to control discussed above. The result might be termed a strategic Madisonian approach to control: various controllers and bureaucrats would openly fight out major administrative issues and, in so doing, enhance the checking and balancing process envisioned by Madison. Such a competitive public debate would of itself open up bureaucratic functioning and enhance the citizen's ability to understand and appraise the performance of government. This emphasis on open public debate draws, in part, on the legal tradition of adversary, verbal disputation. The word "verbal" is important here because the Madisonian approach, in its pure institutional form, is highly mechanistic. It requires a complicated linkage and weighting of opposed institutional forces that, when applied to governmental organizations, resembles an elaborate Rube Goldberg contraption that is unwieldy if not unworkable. The emphasis I place on a selective and strategic public debate is intended to avoid the costs of building complex structural counterweights or of imposing control systems like Management by Objectives that produce administrative paperwork morasses of their own. A Madisonian approach to checks and balances through open public debate offers the advantages of focus, competition, and, in Martin Landau's term, "redundancy" (given multiple participants)[22] without risking the danger that Fesler alerts us to of fettering the bureaucracy with ever more rigid formal controls.

7

Strategies for Democracy and Efficiency

IN AN ANGRY INDICTMENT of American government, two law professors, Charles Reich and Burke Marshall, have summarized the inadequacies of the way we have been governed. They make the following assertions:

> We can no longer afford a government that does not engage in long-range planning and have the courage openly to persuade through law or otherwise, the necessary sectors of our society to follow its plans . . .

> We can no longer afford a democratic system in which basic choices that have to be made — such as how to allocate our limited resources — are not presented to the people for their ultimate decision.[1]

Reich and Marshall take us back to the themes of democracy and administrative efficiency. Their conclusion is that we have neither. Their call for democracy and efficiency not only reminds us that these values are strongly desired in this country; it also underscores the fundamental problem they present for institutional design. Strategies to further the one goal often conflict or undermine strategies to further the other.

If there is a crisis of public authority in America today, I believe that it centers on the intertwined problems of democracy and efficiency. Citizens and public officials alike feel deeply frustrated by the government's apparent inability to plan and to solve policy problems. On the other hand, they feel that democratic norms — the avoidance of the abuse of power, the importance of hearing citizens' voices, an open, participatory policymaking process — are often weakly upheld. Increasingly, both indictments focus on the public bureaucracies.

What is to be done? Can we after all improve democracy and efficiency at once, and particularly in bureaucratic settings? If we only had a clear public philosophy, a clearly articulated definition of the public interest, then government might more easily combine democracy and management. We would be closer to Wilson's happy reconciliation of democracy and bureaucracy. The public and its officials would strongly and clearly express their will and bureaucrats would carry it out. But this is not the case in reality. Instead of a clear public philosophy, we have sharp conflict and competition among different views, and this political conflict permeates the bureaucracy.

A Constrained Approach to Institutional Reform

If we cannot make the Wilsonian vision work, must we drift toward weak democracy and low administrative efficiency? I believe that there are strategies available to increase democracy and efficiency but that they must be applied on the basis of a careful organizational diagnosis so that government is not pulled in opposite directions in the name of conflicting values. In this chapter I will call attention to the features of the democracy and efficiency models that seem most in need of bolstering. Then I will determine to what extent these strategies can be incorporated compatibly into a design for government. The key step toward making them compatible is to revise certain norms of the efficiency model in light of my earlier analysis of public bureaucracies.

First let us identify what features the man on the street, as well as the two law professors, would like to see in American government. One desirable feature would be an improved capacity for planning, for problem solving. Policy should be coordinated better and, especially, implemented effectively so that plans achieve tangible results. The man on the street also certainly wants government not to grow aimlessly at the taxpayer's expense. The frequently heard call for "leadership" reflects these concerns as well as a need for a focal point for coherent government action. All these desired features of government summon up the norms and aspirations of the efficiency model.

At the same time, the man on the street wants someone in government to listen to his concerns: he wants to be represented. He wants policymakers to be responsive to his individual or community needs. He would like to know what is going on in government, and he may want to participate actively in government at some level. He worries that bureaucrats and experts do not care what the ordinary citizen thinks. He may not know how to approach government if he has a problem, and he is likely to be unaware of what services are available to him. He wants to be sure that government does not listen only to the big interests—he wants to keep the bureaucracy from being dominated by business or other interest groups he cannot compete against. These concerns are all related to the norms of the pluralist democracy model.

To summarize this discourse with the hypothetical man on the street, we have the following desired features of government on the administrative efficiency side:

planning and problem solving
coordination
implementation
reduction of excess spending
leadership

and on the pluralist democracy side:

representation
responsiveness
openness
participation
control of experts
competition (and balance) among interest groups.

At first glance, it appears that we have managed to wind up back where we started. If the democracy and efficiency models conflict, then do not the two sets of desired features conflict as well? I believe that with careful institutional reforms and with a revision of the efficiency model, these features are not necessarily incompatible.

The key step lies in the revision of the norms of the efficiency model, and the revision I propose is one that reflects what I have outlined so far about the central features of the politics of bureaucracy. Some critics of government still might say that the bureaucracy must be completely overhauled and made to live up to the

Wilsonian vision of it as a neutral, hierarchical machine. This view is often expressed by businessmen: If only government were run like a business . . . I prefer to ask how to improve the bureaucracy in terms of both democracy and efficiency. Others may choose to charge the walls of Jericho, but they should do so with the full knowledge that the politics of bureaucracy, with its features of fragmentation, loose control, silent politics, and valuative decision, is deeply embedded and resilient. My approach to reform is strategic in that it seeks institutional changes that are feasible. The strategy of frontal assault may be gallant, but even Joshua needed his trumpet.

The critical revision of the efficiency model is to bring the conception of the public manager's job in line with the bureaucratic environment he actually inhabits. In the Wilsonian vision, the job of the public manager, be he president, cabinet secretary, assistant secretary, or police chief, is remarkably simple in administrative terms. He receives a policy from the political sphere and then plugs it into his hierarchical bureaucracy. You drop the specification for a quarter in at the top and a quarter comes out at the bottom. This is a world free of politics but it is also a world free or nearly free of administrative conflicts. It is certainly not a world of valuative decision, guild professionalism, policy subgovernments, and intense interest-group conflict. If we redraw the map of the public manager's job in accordance with our analysis of bureaucratic politics, we can depict it as in figure 7.1.

There are several major points to be made about this map of the public manager's job. First, he inhabits an intensely political environment. As earlier students of administration have pointed out, political processes do not abruptly stop at the door of bureaucracy. This point is true but weak, for in fact the public manager's job and environment are essentially political, requiring a primary emphasis on the task of managing political and administrative conflict.

The second point reinforces the first one. Not only is the public manager's job highly political, but it contains a variety of political dimensions, including building support with the chief executive, dealing with related departments and interest groups, bargaining with Congress, managing and coordinating a fragmented structure of bureaucratic subunits, and trying to oversee and coordinate policy subgovernments extending to the operations of state and city governments.

Third, these multidimensional tasks lead directly into a vortex of

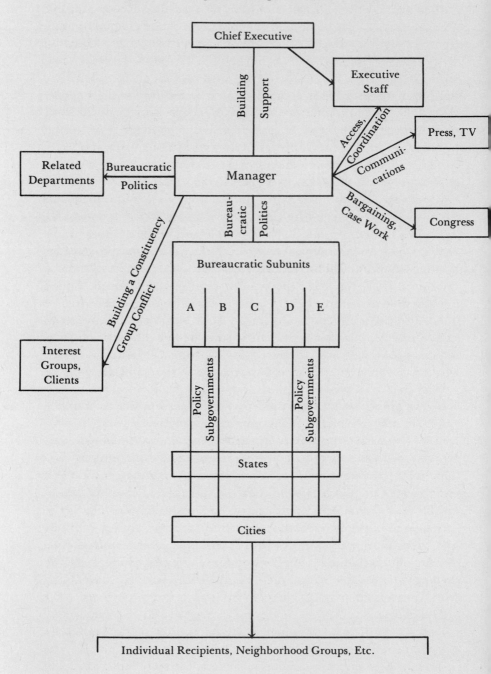

Figure 7.1 The public manager and his environment.

political and administrative conflict: the manager's primary role is to deal with competing organizational pressures and to manage political conflict. In some cases the manager will employ strategies of conflict resolution, including bargaining and zero-sum decisions. At other times his task will be to convert the negative, adversary features of conflict into something more positive, namely, cooperation, compromise, and coalition building among both political and administrative actors. This process of conversion is often, I believe, what we have in mind when we speak of leadership.

Fourth, in managing this political conflict the administrative executive faces many of the same issues that worry an advocate of pluralist democracy and, in a general way, would-be controllers of the bureaucracy. He has to worry about the fragmentation of bureaucratic activity, particularly where it leads to strongly segmented bureaucratic structures and insulated concentrations of power. He must be concerned too about loose control, silent politics, guild professionalism, and valuative decisions. No less than the ordinary citizen, the public manager needs to open up "his" bureaucracy in order to achieve any real penetration into its operations. Finally, given the number of different political and administrative interests that enter into his realm of conflict management, the public manager, along with the pluralist democrat, must worry about the balance of power among different groups: whether desirable levels of competition and bargaining exist, whether certain interests overwhelm other groups in the policymaking process, whether citizens' complaints and demands are heard and registered.

Thus the public manager's job calls into play many of the concerns of pluralist democracy as well as those of administrative efficiency. This is not to say that the two models converge to a point where their internal differences dissolve. It is to say that the public manager, far from being the clerk of a narrow efficiency, faces the problems of both pluralist democracy and administrative efficiency. This is because many of the administrative problems he faces concerning competition, secrecy, and valuative decisions are the same problems he would face if he were an external agent, say in the Congress, concerned primarily with increasing democratic control of bureaucracy.

If bureaucratic problems do not necessarily divide dichotomously into the proprietary concerns of the democracy model and the efficiency model, it is logically possible that remedies to such problems will satisfy the norms of both pluralist democracy and administrative efficiency. This will not always be true, but the point opens the way to institutional reform strategies that will promote both sets of goals at once.

I will consider a number of such strategies for reform. The remedies are directed at what I take to be the bedrock problems of government, including issues of planning, leadership, openness, fragmentation, and participation. To locate each reform strategy within the structure of American government, I present a simplified blueprint of that structure in figure 7.2. More precisely, this is a map of bureaucratic democracy, focusing on the two principal institutions of the chief executive and the bureaucracy and displaying some of the features of bureaucracy that I analyzed earlier. Each circled letter in figure 7.2 indicates what part of the structure of government a particular institutional reform strategy is designed to affect.

A. *The role of the chief executive.* Here I do not propose a particular institutional reform but simply underscore the importance of strong, centralized executive leadership, as enunciated in the administrative efficiency model. In a structure of authority as divided as that in the United States, there must be a focal point for setting a national agenda and balancing priorities for reasons of both democracy and efficiency. The pattern of structural fragmentation in administrative policymaking is so great that the need for a central coordinating figure is compelling. Considering congressional and intergovernmental policymaking as well reinforces this point. The advocates of the efficiency model conceived of the chief executive as the locus for planning and setting a strategic agenda, and I believe they were right on that score. The centripetal thrust of the chief executive is deliberately designed to compete with the centrifugal thrust created by the fragmented structure of Congress and of subnational governments. Competition between the two thrusts may be desirable on Madisonian checking-and-balancing grounds, but leaving that argument aside, it is hard to see where a focal point for governance would exist without a strong chief executive. The legislative system, the interest-group system, and subnational governments all contribute to a fragmented expression of political interests. A viable, coherent public policy is possible only if some kind of a governing coalition supports it. And here the historical aspirations

Figure 7.2 A blueprint of bureaucratic democracy.

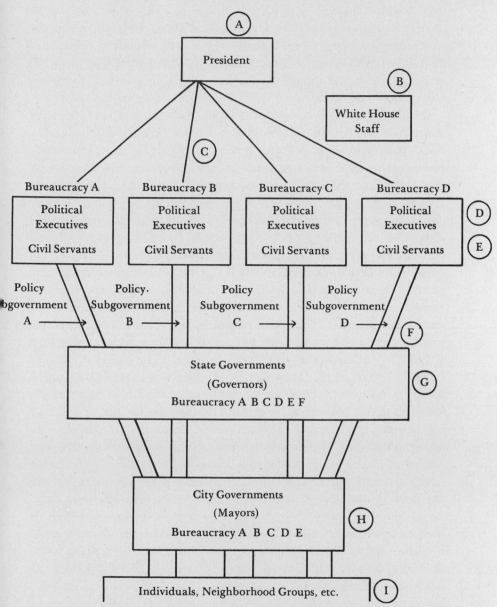

for a strong president, government, or mayor seem to be analytically well founded, especially given the decline of party organizations. A chief executive might try to forge a New Deal coalition, a middle American coalition, a right-wing coalition, a coalition of joggers. The only alternatives to some kind of national coalition-building seems to me to be something-for-everyone politics, single-interest atomization, or stalemate.

B. *Long-range planning and competitive budgeting.* Planning is alternately a talisman and an anthema for citizens and public officials. We routinely call for government planning but then worry about the possible loss of personal liberty or market efficiency it implies. The decentralized bargaining system of pluralist democracy is notably weak in establishing long time-horizons in policy. This is partly due to the short-term political pressures that exist for a mayor with a two-year term or for a congressman preoccupied with reelection. So a key institutional reform located at B on the map is to increase the president's capacity for long-range planning. My idea is not that such planning activities would lead to fixed five-year plans implemented by statute and administered by formal bureaucratic machinery. Rather, long-range planning would combat the existing fragmentation of bureaucratic policymaking — would put the pieces of policy together — and would set a policy course that would look beyond the traditional one-year budget-planning cycle. This lengthening of the time-horizon is called for in foreign and military affairs, economic planning, energy planning, urban planning, and perhaps social service planning. It would constitute an extension of activities currently performed by the National Security Council, the Domestic Policy Staff, and the Economic Policy Board. Such an emphasis on planning would constitute an explicit counterweight to the piecemeal bargaining currently practiced by both the legislature and the bureaucracy; it would create a competitive policy debate in which incremental and decentralized initiatives would be pitted against a single set of planning goals. National planning may be viewed as a way of disciplining the centrifugal forces inherent in other parts of the system. To reiterate, planning of this sort would stimulate competitive policy debate, in a Madisonian spirit; it would not completely override or eliminate the pluralist bargaining features of the policy process.

The suggestion that long-range planning should be strengthened raises the question of how and whether government can set goals, can specify an agenda for public action. A common argument is that given its inherent diversity of goals, interests, and values and given the difficulty of measuring the impact of government programs, it is impossible for government to establish clear and consistent goals. Usually this point is made in comparison to a private-sector emphasis on a clear "bottom line," with critics of government calling for a functional equivalent and defenders of government noting all the differences between public and private organizations and hence the difficulty of organizational goal-setting in a public context. To say that government cannot decide on goals as easily as some imagined firm can pursue profits is not to say that government cannot set goals. To say that government has to listen to competing legitimate interests does not mean that it cannot set goals. It may have to approach goal-setting differently from the way business firms do, but governmental goal-setting is both possible and important.

The main points then are (*a*) that central government should set a stable set of policy goals and (*b*) that it must approach this task in a way that deals directly with the central governmental problem of of managing political conflict. Executive leadership is a way of strengthening the coordination of goals, and long-range planning is a way of disciplining the goal- or agenda-setting process. Many of the proposals below will present other devices for goal-setting and conflict management — devices that meet head-on the fragmentation of public decisionmaking.

One such strategy I will call *competitive budgeting* at the highest levels of the policy process. It is commonly called "strategic planning" in the private context. What it entails is an emphasis by chief executives and their planners on fighting out primary questions of resource allocation with the major segments of the bureaucracy through the budgetary process. This involves the establishment of expenditure limits and a concomitant allocation of budget shares among major policy arenas, such as foreign policy and defense, economic policy, urban policy, and social service policy. Accomplishing this kind of strategic, competitive budgeting would require a greater centralization of presidential and bureaucratic budget-making across major policy arenas (see proposal C below). The hoped-for outcome would be a definition of broad administration policy, in budgetary terms, which would guide policymaking down the line. This competitive budgeting proposal envisions a de facto planning group, composed of the president, a small number of key planners such as the director of the OMB, and representatives of the major bureaucratic policy segments, which would meet regularly to fight out conflicts among competing priorities.

This central budgeting process would be highly competitive; the political task of leadership would be to arrive at a stable agreement on policy. The task might well involve bargaining at times, intense conflict at times, for example between military and urban policy representatives. So too, presidential staff planners and bureaucratic claimants would conflict over the use of resources. In no sense is this a strategy for getting politics and political conflict out of administration. Rather, it seeks to centralize and focus that conflict in a planning group that makes aggregate strategic choices and that in so doing counters the present fragmentation of administrative decisionmaking.

This form of centralized competitive budgeting is doubtless practiced by many governments and therefore may not appear especially novel or innovative. But in the American setting this kind of aggregate fighting-out of budgeting allocation at the center is thwarted by a deeply embedded process of piecemeal, incremental budgeting. Although there is a stage of presidential review at the end of the process, the impact of that review is highly variable. Some presidents, such as Truman and Ford, have enjoyed poring over the details of budget items. Others, such as Nixon, have delegated much of the work of presidential review to their budget directors. No president has focused the budgeting process in this sustained, competitive, and centralized way.

This proposal constitutes a way of increasing the planning capacity of government (an efficiency norm) through the explicit use of open conflict and competition (a pluralist norm). The hope is again for a latter-day Madisonian approach that will channel and check bureaucratic conflict in an open way that avoids the "here a billion, there a billion" cutting-and-pasting exercise that now passes for executive budgeting.

C. *Minicabinets.* The establishment of a more centralized, competitive executive budgeting process requires a greater coordination of bureaucratic functioning. For no planning and budgetary overview is possible as long as presidents are locked into a piecemeal, episodic approach to goal-setting. Here too, the institutional reform strategy I propose confronts head-on the problems that the existing structure and functioning of bureaucratic organizations pose for administrative efficiency. The patterns of fragmentation, conflict, guild professionalism, silent politics, valuative decision, power conservation, and so forth that add up to segmented pluralism all make it enormously difficult for the administrative reformer to put together the pieces of his department or agency or for a chief executive to establish interdepartmental relationships. In the Wilsonian view of administration these problems simply do not exist, by definition, but they are at the heart of the problem for any contemporary manager. My proposal is to create a number of policy-area "minicabinets" that would fight out and coordinate decisionmaking in a relatively broad sphere of government activity. I have mentioned military and foreign policy, economic policy, urban policy, and social services policy. There are other candidates for inclusion, such as natural resource policy, and the lines between the different arenas would not be clearly drawn. The idea of policy-oriented minicabinets speaks first to the long-observed incapacity of the cabinet as a whole to serve as an effective policymaking instrument. Various presidents, especially Eisenhower and Carter, have sought to bolster the policymaking role of the cabinet. But few analysts would disagree that the cabinet is both too cumbersome and too multifaceted to perform a major policy role.

The minicabinets are designed to break up bureaucratic segmentation and to improve the management of existing political conflict. It is impossible to have a coherent policy in any domain if the different segments are left alone to pursue their self-protective, inching-ahead strategy. So the different segments relevant to a policy problem have to be brought into the same room. Further, no coherent policy can be hammered out if existing patterns of conflict and competition lead to end-runs, freezing out tactics, deliberately misleading communications, and secrecy as so often is the case in the present politics of bureaucracy. Once the major parties in a policy area are in the same room, functioning as a minicabinet, their natural high levels of conflict and competition are more likely to be conducted in a way that forces an explicit policy debate. As with centralized competitive budgeting, the various bureaucracies may well go at it hammer and tong but the stage has been set for bargaining and accommodation. Since presidential assistants (and long-range planners) would be involved in the minicabinets, there would also be a potential for considerable conflict between departmental and Presidential perspectives. But again this would add a Madisonian checking-and-balancing feature by deliberately opening up bureaucratic policy debate and conflict in the minicabinet.

There is no guarantee that the creation of minicabinets would transform well-fortified bureaucratic segments into a smooth structure of coordinated policy planning. But I believe that bringing together the segments is a necessary condition of coherent policy-making. The resulting open conflict is a necessary condition of policy debate in which there is even a chance of positive resolution of conflict. At the least, open conflict and open policy debate would increase competition in bureaucracy and serve the Madisonian value of checking bureaucratic power. More than that, to the extent that minicabinets would prove capable of cooperating and working out shared goals, the administrative quality of bureaucratic governance would be substantially enhanced. Notice too that the members of a minicabinet would have at least one powerful incentive to cooperate. That is, in dealing with the next level up in the process of centralized, competitive budgeting, it would clearly be in their interest to present a united front—and especially if their adversaries, other minicabinets and presidential planners, had achieved one.

In short, the development of an open competitive policy debate in government draws strength from both conflict and cooperation. Conflict bolsters the Madisonian checking process. Cooperation permits movement toward shared goal-setting. The task of successful public management is one of converting conflict to cooperation —be it straight-out agreement, reduction of jurisdictional disputes, or negotiation.

The advantages of this form of interdepartmental policymaking are not completely unknown to government officials. Movement in this direction is already manifest in the roles of the National Security Council and the Domestic Policy Staff. An executive committee structure of the making of foreign policy, which resembles the idea of minicabinets, has been proposed by Graham Allison and Peter Szanton.[2] But the proposal has not been tested across a range of policy areas, nor has it been linked to a proposal for executive-level long-range planning and competitive budgeting.

D. *The executive secretariat.* Nowhere do the bureaucratic features of fragmentation, power conservation, guild professionalism, and valuative decision impinge more directly than at the level of management within a bureaucracy. Institutional reform proposal D reflects B and C in that it seeks a mechanism to bring diverse segments together and to force a focused competitive debate over the stakes of policymaking in a particular bureaucracy. The first step is to get the various contestants into the same room with the cabinet secretary, whose role is that of the central manager of policy debate. A version of this forum for internal bureaucratic debate was once developed by Elliot Richardson and called an "executive secretariat," and I will use that label for my proposed reform.[3] (The same system has been called, more grandiosely, a Cooperative Agency Management System or CAMS.)[4] The first purpose of Richardson's secretariat was to combat bureaucratic insularity and infighting. As one participant described the process, "one of our main objectives was to set up a decision-making process that would exclude *ex parte* special pleading and give everyone a fair opportunity to be heard . . . with an executive secretariat your bureaucratic enemy can no longer sneak in the boss' side door with a proposal to abolish your office. Instead, he has to send the proposal through the executive secretariat which would send it to you for comment."[5]

Having eliminated many features of backstairs bureaucratic conflict, the departmental secretariat would proceed to a competitive debate over which program or subunit should receive what kind of priority and budget allocation. The different components of the bureaucracy would have to argue the case for their program openly in the context of competing claims. At root, this is what zero-based budgeting is about. In my proposal, each subunit would make its oral argument to the secretary and the other contestants, and the secretary would perform a judge-like role, hearing claims and counterclaims and then trying to negotiate an agreement on departmental policy. Again there would be a strong incentive to bargain out conflicts, since each bureaucracy would have a clear interest in having a specified set of goals and policies when called to argue its case in the minicabinets. Bureaucratic subunits would have the same incentive to resolve conflicts in order to present a united front in policy debate with other subunits within the secretariat.

The establishment of an executive secretariat seeks the same opening up of competitive debate discussed above and aims at the same Madisonian process of managing bureaucratic conflicts. At the departmental level, it is also concerned with a more deliberate strengthening of the norms of pluralist democracy. The secretariat relies on some of these norms concerning competition, checking and balancing, and an explicit representation of diverse policy interests, but it does so only for administrative actors within the bureaucracy. One way of bolstering democratic norms is for the cabinet secretary to make an open, public accounting of major policy decisions as discussed in the last chapter. A second proposal is that the secretary hold a monthly question period, in the British style, at which he accounts for bureaucratic decisions or uncovers questions about his department's functioning in a public forum—open to the press, interest groups, and other interested citizens. A third proposal, designed to sharpen and focus the representation of outside interests, is the creation of a citizens' panel that would meet with the secretary and give its reactions to the secretary's definition of departmental programs and policies. Like the secretariat, this panel would be openly and explicitly competitive. Its membership would include representatives of the department's major constituencies as well as business, labor, consumer groups, and minorities. The purpose of this panel would not be to make policy but rather to ensure that a wide range of citizen interests were expressed directly to the secretary and that salient matters of conflict and agreement were identified. Because there is no way of guaranteeing a perfect range and balance of representation of interests on this panel, a supplement to its policy debate is proposed in E below.

E. *Office of public service.* In the last chapter I argued for a general strengthening of administrative process values in bureaucracy, such as accessibility, accountability, responsiveness, and participation. I also noted that numerous strategies to strengthen these values exist and call for a case-by-case fitting of process technique to administrative structure since remedies suited to the school system may not work as well in a fire department. In Chapter 5 I argued that bureaucracies differ along a spectrum of institutional characteristics, and that whereas some bureaucracies need to be opened up to public scrutiny, others need to be more tightly integrated and coordinated. These arguments supply general guidance about the reform of any particular bureaucracy, but they do not capture one set of democratic concerns and possible reforms in concrete institutional terms. Thus I propose the establishment in any given bureaucracy of an office of public service, whose general mission would be to bolster the norms of representation and openness.

The office of public service would have three major functions. First, it would address the problem that citizens and public officials often do not know what a bureaucracy actually does—what programs and services are available and how they relate to one another. The office would make an inventory of tasks performed and programs supplied by a department. This seems an obvious thing to do, but it would be no mean feat to achieve. Such an inventory, a "guide to government," would, it is hoped, illuminate bureaucratic functioning for citizens' groups, legislators, state and city officials, and perhaps, equally important, for members of the departmental secretariat themselves. This proposal is a simple one, but it would constitute a dramatic form of public accounting to the world outside of government. (This proposal is linked to a proposal for coordinating citizens' demands and neighborhood-level needs in proposal I below.)

The second function of the office would be to increase the capacity for ombudsman-style activity. The proposal envisions a centralized role in bureaucracy for agents whose job it is to respond to complaints and grievances about bureaucratic functioning. At present, complaints and grievances are typically handled in an informal, "who do you get on the telephone" basis. Congressional staffs and lower-level officials spend an enormous amount of time doing constituent casework involving complaints about the bureaucracy. The office of public service would focus the ombudsman role; its job would be to satisfy complaints, or at least to account explicitly for the bureaucracy's actions. Centralizing the ombudsman role in this way should also uncover patterns of grievance and thus provide a more systematic form of Kaufman's "administrative feedback" for public managers than exists in the present case-by-case approach to grievances.

The third task of the office of public service may well be, in terms of democratic theory, the most important. That task is the creation of "citizen advocates" whose job it is to represent interests that would otherwise be either weakly represented or simply ignored. The citizen advocate would provide a focal point for outside groups who wished to make claims on or express a view about government policy. The more active role of the citizen advocate would be to create a network of communication with interests of all kinds — mayors, women's groups, neighborhood groups, chambers of commerce, public interest groups, and so forth—so as to stimulate open debate about policy in the bureaucracy. Having sought to broaden the range of policy perspectives entering the bureaucracy, the advocate would distill and report his findings to the department secretariat and the citizens' panel and to the ombudsman. Thus the creation of citizen advocates is designed to meet head-on the problem of representing the weakly represented or unrepresented—a problem that is central to pluralist democracy in any context and that is especially severe in bureaucracy when its functioning is (or is perceived by citizens to be) remote, closed, or bewildering.

The Political Economy of Reform

My proposals for centralized planning and competitive policy debate rest on a strategy of reducing the transaction and information costs of policymaking and at the same time increasing the institutional incentives for policy coordination and conflict resolution. It is hoped that having the main parties to bureaucratic disputes fight it out in the same room will make easier the public manager's task of piecing together different bureaucratic segments. Easier at least than the frustrating task of trying to be a policy detective and track down the multifaceted operations of a bureaucracy.

In terms of incentives, centralized planning and competitive policy debate would have five main effects. First, the existing incentives to engage in backstairs bureaucratic maneuvering would be reduced by the establishment of an open competitive debate where each unit would know that it had an opportunity to make its voice heard. Second, bureaucratic units would have an incentive to argue their positions fully and explicitly. This incentive would work to flesh out and clarify policy options, assumptions, and evidence—in general to increase the level of communication. Third, at the presidential level, the minicabinet level, and the secretariat level, bureaucratic players would know that they would be at a disadvantage if their own unit remained divided in its policy advice while other units had worked out a shared position. This is an incentive posed in terms of horizontal bargaining. The fourth incentive, posed in terms of vertical bargaining, works in the same way: if a bureaucratic unit carried a divided position up to a higher level and there encountered other players who had hammered out a strong, shared position, it would also be at a disadvantage in competitive bargaining. The final incentive, related to both the horizontal and vertical bargaining incentives, concerns timing. This multilevel competitive policy debate would work much in the fashion of a tournament. In order to advance to a higher round in the debate, bureaucratic actors would first have to hammer out their differences in the preceding round. A given bureaucratic unit would have to resolve its internal conflicts before moving on to the higher-level debate in the minicabinet, and similarly, the minicabinet would arrive at its own unity before taking its proposals to the president for decision. At the presidential level, the planning process could well be continuous, but planners would appraise competitive claims only after the earlier rounds had been played. This use of timing and sequence sounds like a very simple thing, but the tournament concept should create powerful incentives to conflict resolution, including coordination and cooperation within the bureaucracy, as the ever more centralized policy debate moves upward in the system.

F. *Policy subgovernments and administrative decentralization.* My next proposal attacks the maze of programs and regulations overseen by policy subgovernments in the intergovernmental policymaking system. Here, perhaps more than anywhere else in American government, a detached observer would perceive a chaotic policy process characterized both by red tape and by the largely hidden insular power of the policy subgovernments. If there is one place a reformer needs to use an axe rather than a scalpel, it is in this intergovernmental arena, which in its current functioning poses glaring problems for both pluralist democracy and administrative efficiency. In democratic terms, the workings of policy subgovernments are problematic in that they fall outside of the range of public scrutiny and control. Also, policy subgovernments give a power advantage to bureaucrats that conflicts with and weakens the power and authority of elected officials in state and local government. This leads to the dependency effect, whereby mayors and legislators are forced to rely on their bureaucrats to write grant proposals, interpret regulations, and in general unravel the complexities of intergovernmental policymaking. The current intergovernmental system is also problematic in terms of administrative efficiency. Policy sub-governments undermine the central, coordinating role of the chief executive. To the extent that policy subgovernments function semi-autonomously, they constitute a strong force toward fragmentation of policy. To the extent that they practice silent politics and guild professionalism, they present major problems of administrative control.

Most important, the current intergovernmental system presents massive problems of policy implementation from the perspectives of both coordination and the complexity (and administrative costs) of government action. Problems of coordination are inherent in the fragmentation created by policy subgovernments. They are also created by the simple number of bureaucratic actors who are in-volved in implementing policy in its journey from Washington to the street level. The multiplicity of points at which decisions are made leads Pressman and Wildavsky to characterize the implementation problem in terms of the complexity of joint action.[6] Given the num-ber of actors involved, the probability that a policy will be stopped, stalled, diverted or distorted is enormously high. Also, given frag-mentation and the obstacle-course character of intergovernmental policymaking, the system imposes heavy information and transac-tion costs on public officials seeking to manage it, and makes it highly likely that the policy that comes at the bottom is not going to be the one designed at the top. I have likened this implementation process elsewhere to the playing of a pinball machine. Once the ball is launched, it will inevitably be bounced around from one obstruc-tion to another, and it is very difficult to predict where it will land.

If this appraisal of the present intergovernmental system is cor-rect, what is to be done to improve democracy and/or administra-tive efficiency? If we accept a strict dichotomy between centraliza-tion and decentralization, we are left, even if we wield an axe and not a scalpel, with two unhappy choices. We could dramatically centralize intergovernmental policymaking, but that would greatly increase the burdens and responsibilities of central bureaucracy and, more important, extend the impact of whatever policymaking problems already exist within national bureaucracies. It is also likely that a highly centralized intergovernmental system would accrue very high transaction and information costs. Many democratic countries, including Britain and Sweden, have taken a centralized approach to intergovernmental policymaking, but they do not have to deal with the highly decentralized design of government found in the United States.

The other extreme solution would be to decentralize government administration radically and return dominant power and financial resources to subnational governments. Such a solution would represent a turning back of the clock to the pre-New Deal era and perhaps even to the era of the Articles of Confederation. Such a radical decentralization would greatly increase the burden on local governments, whose policymaking abilities are, as I have argued elsewhere,[7] already faulty at best. Extreme decentralization would also completely vitiate the proposals for central and goal-setting discussed above.

Having rejected simple and extreme reforms of the intergovernmental system, we are left where we should be, with the more difficult task of designing a multilevel system that combines desirable features of centralization and decentralization. Such a combination of features may not always be fully compatible—indeed we may deliberately seek to create elements of conflict. A balancing act of some kind is unavoidable.

I will attempt to build a viable intergovernmental structure on the foundation of three premises: (1) Strong central government planning and budgeting are necessary for national goal-setting and coordination. (2) Policy subgovernments present severe problems for democracy and administrative efficiency. (3) Local governments are closer than the national government to citizens in terms of democratic control. Citizens are most likely to participate in government at the local level given the higher transaction costs of dealing with more distant governments. Local governments are likely to be more responsive to variations in individual needs because they perceive such variations at close hand, and they may be more efficient in service delivery because of the lower transaction and information costs inherent in the physical proximity between the services and the served at the local level. These three premises call for a system with a strong planning and coordinating capacity at the center and a strong capacity for service delivery at the local level. They also call for eliminating as far as possible, the cumbersome implementation process and multiple points of decision that now characterize policy subgovernments.

The design that follows is one in which broad choices about programs and budgeting are made at the center and in which local governments possess greater authority for implementing policy and providing daily services. The first part of this design has already been set up by the reform proposals aimed at central planning and competitive budgeting. The second part of the design requires a major decentralization of administrative power to governors and mayors—a decentralization typified in a small-scale way by existing revenue-sharing programs. On this strategy, governors and mayors would, in turn, adopt the reforms concerning central planning and competitive policymaking recommended above in order to improve the coordination at their levels (see proposals G and H below). A final step in the reform of the intergovernmental system would be the creation of neighborhood service centers designed to enhance both the efficiency norm of coordination and the democracy norms of participation and responsiveness (see I below).

This combination of centralized planning and goal-setting and decentralized implementation and service delivery would cut surgically through the present administrative tangle. The national government would decide that certain programs and policies should be adopted, and local governments would have the authority and obligation to spend their revenue-sharing money on these specified programs.

In essence, this proposal constitutes a new use of the Madisonian doctrine concerning the separation of government functions. Here we are not dividing functions called legislative or executive but rather policymaking functions called long-range planning, evaluation, and service delivery. The "feds" would devote their energies to the first two functions, the localities to the third. Thus the central government would concern itself with broad issues of distribution and equalization as well as with broad-scale policy evaluation (on the assumption, argued for by Wildavsky, among others, that it is difficult for any organization to evaluate its own performance).[8] What the central government would not do is to "micromanage" the entire process of implementation. This Madisonian separation of policy functions would have the double advantage of (*a*) freeing localities from the transaction costs of higher-level micromanagement (as well as from the fragmentation and regulatory tangle caused by policy subgovernments) and (*b*) empowering local govvernments to pursue their institutional advantage of responding to variations in local needs.

This proposal represents a dramatic simplification and clarification of functions in the intergovernmental system; for this reason it holds the promise of greatly reducing the transaction and information costs of policymaking. The traditionally held virtue of the Madisonian separation-of-functions doctrine is that it would provide checks and balances and contribute to the management of political conflict. I hope that the intergovernmental separation of functions called for in my proposal would have this advantage too, for I certainly do not imagine that institutional simplification would produce a conflict-free intergovernmental system. Even if a simplified intergovernmental system were erected in which the national government set broad policy and localities concentrated on day-to-day delivery of services, there would be inevitable tension between high-level goal-setting and the implementation and adaptation of policy at the local level. National government might naturally and properly believe there was too much variation from plan at the local level, in the name of responsiveness to community needs. As defenders of regularity and consistency, the "feds" would fight to maintain the integrity of basic national policies. Equally, localities might naturally and properly believe there was too little concern for local needs at the national level. Accordingly, localities would fight hard in favor of variations and flexibility. I believe that this tension between broad rules and the desire for local variations is a healthy one — especially if there are strong channels of communication between central and local governments through which disputes can flow. For this tension between central and local interests would serve to check and balance both the power of governments and the design of policy. If, for example, the national government became overbearing or attempted to micromanage the policy process, it would encounter the organized resistance of local governments, now possessing increased political resources because of administrative decentralization. At the same time, if local governments tried to adopt discriminatory policies (in the earlier States' Rights spirit), they would encounter powerful opposition from federal standard-setters, who as now could cut off funds to jurisdictions that violated basic national standards of equal treatment. In policy terms, the central-local tension would create a competitive policy debate in which rules would be tested against particular cases. No national plan could be too rigid and mechanical, for that would stir up a local outcry. Nor could a national plan dissolve into endless variations; that would stir up an outcry among national planners. In this scenario, which draws in part on the adversary procedure of the judicial process, general rules would be continuously tested against particular cases and vice versa. Doubtless the resulting balance between rule maintenance and variation would not always be optimal, any more than it is in the judicial process. But this kind of intergovernmental policy debate offers, in my view, the best hope for an institutional balancing process that would provide for the careful weighing of the claims of consistency and variation while avoiding the worst features of either micromanagement by Washington or fragmentation of public authority among thousands of local jurisdictions.

There is another sense in which this simplified intergovernmental system would produce competition within government and provide another element of Madisonian checks and balances in bureaucratic policymaking. With administrative decentralization, local governments would play a stronger *political* as well as administrative role in the policy process. As the chief operating officers of the intergovernmental system, localities would express themselves strongly about the broad shape of policy and would be a significant part of the goal-setting policy debate at the national level. I noted earlier that states and cities have already intensified their efforts to lobby the federal government. In a system of centralized planning they would further intensify those efforts, since the competitive policy debate at the center over resource allocation would be more focused, decisive, and visible. Rather than wandering the corridors of Washington in search of grants and other favors, representatives of local governments would target their lobbying efforts at the presidential-level planning process, at the minicabinets, and at the executive secretariats, all of which would be structured as focal points of policy debate. If the system worked well, localities would check any national tendency either to underestimate the importance of urban problems or to slight particular regional or local perspectives. In addition, different regions, cities, and suburbs would press competing claims, and the expression of those claims would extend the range of interests represented at the national bargaining table. The key to this feature of intergovernmental checks and balances is that local governments would have clear access to the major forums of competitive policy debate. Without delving into the details of institutional design, we can predict that a president would continue to have an office charged with dealing with intergovernmental affairs and that similar communication posts could be simply established at the minicabinet and executive secretariat levels. As a further safeguard, representatives of localities could turn to the citizen advocate to be sure their voices were heard.

G. and H. *State and local governments.* My proposals for the reform of state and local governments mirror those for the federal government. In particular, state and local governments would institute the design features of high-level competitive budgeting, minicabinets, and executive secretariats within a given bureaucracy, and an office of public service (with its "guide to government," ombudsmen, and citizen advocates).

In addition, as Lipsky has shown, there is a special need in urban governments to coordinate and control the work of street-level bureaucrats, such as policemen, teachers, welfare workers, and judges.[9] Street-level bureaucrats have special significance for two main reasons. First, they are the visible manifestation of government for most citizens, and therefore any attempt to forge a better relationship between the servers and the served must focus sharply at the street level. Second, they carry out public policy at the final point of impact in the long journey of implementation. Given the discretion they exercise and the sensitivity of their jobs, the monitoring and coordination of street-level bureaucrats must have special prominence in any analysis of the success and failure of policy implementation. For these reasons I propose an additional institutional reform at the local level, namely, the creation of neighborhood service cabinets. Such a cabinet would be composed of neighborhood-level administrators in urban service bureaucracies — school superintendents, police station house commanders, and the like. Their task would be to inspect the functioning of public policy in a given neighborhood or subcommunity, taking into account the many interrelationships among the different services. In addition, they would monitor policy implementation at its point of impact. Finally, they would be closely linked to an institutional design for citizen participation, which is described below. The idea of neighborhood service cabinets was developed with promising results by the Office of Neighborhood Government in New York City.[10] Its purpose would be to provide a final forum for policy coordination and debate in what at present is an enormously fragmented system of policymaking and implementation. Neighborhood service cabinets of this sort would receive their policy guidance from the central policy forums of urban government and higher-level governments, but they would provide a significant checking and balancing feature for City Hall, which like Washington might not always be sensitive to variations in community needs. At the very least, neighborhood service cabinets would provide an additional source of administrative feedback that is not strongly manifest in the present intergovernmental system.

I. *Neighborhood service centers.* My final proposal for institutional reform involves the creation of neighborhood service centers at the street level. These centers give citizens visible outpost of government where they could seek information and register complaints. Like the neighborhood service cabinets, such neighborhood centers would provide a focal point for communication about service problems and a linkage mechanism for problems of policy coordination. The service centers would have a residents' council which would represent major community groups in the neighborhood. They would also meet with the neighborhood service cabinets to provide an established formum for policy debate between the servers and the served. Problems and disputes arising at the neighborhood level would be channeled upward through the urban policymaking apparatus. The neighborhood centers would work closely with the various offices of public service at higher levels of government. This would create a final link in the channel of communication between government and citizens, a further way of providing for the democratic values of accessibility and participation, and implicitly, a final ombudsman-like device to press citizen concerns within the bureaucracy. It is likely that neighborhood service centers could be administratively simple, since their primary role would be not to deliver services but to strengthen communication about service opportunities and service problems. Experiments of this kind, sometimes called Little City Halls or neighborhood task forces, have been tried in numerous cities. My own research has shown that many of these experiments have been deemed effective by both officials and citizens. In analytical terms, their main purpose is to reduce the transaction, information, and participation costs for citizens seeking to do business with government.

It is easy to talk about increasing citizen participation, but if simple means of entering into a dialogue with government representatives do not exist, such talk is often empty. The farther the ordinary citizen must travel, in physical and psychological terms, to find a bureaucratic listening post, the more likely participation is to be a hollow exercise in protest or merely an occasional foray "downtown" to confront the mayor, police chief, or board of education. When the costs of participation involve having to organize citizens to deal with the state capitol or Washington, it should be no surprise that citizens, unless professionally represented, reach the familiar conclusion that bureaucracy is inaccessible and unresponsive.

Implications for Pluralist Democracy and Administrative Efficiency

The proposals presented above represent strategies for improving both the democratic functioning and the efficiency of bureaucratic policymaking. In democratic terms, many of the proposals involve a checking and balancing of bureaucratic power and hence, as I have said, constitute a latter-day Madisonian approach for increasing political competition and countering many of the existing tendencies to bureaucratic segmentation and isolation. The proposals for citizens' panels, offices of public services, and neighborhood service centers also have the obvious intent of opening up all levels of the workings of bureaucracy to participation by citizens.

In terms of administrative efficiency, I believe that the strategies of strong executive leadership, centralized planning, and competitive policy debate will enhance the ability of public managers to govern their bureaucracies. The proposed simplification of the intergovernmental system and the establishment of neighborhood service cabinets have the same aspiration and for the same reasons: they are intended to reduce transaction and communication costs and to increase the institutional forums and incentives for policy coordination.

It is too much to expect that these proposals, if enacted, would be a panacea or would work perfectly. They are a beginning.

Notes

1. Bureaucracy and American Democratic Theory

1. James Q. Wilson, "The Rise of the Bureaucratic State," in Nathan Glazer and Irving Kristol, eds., *The American Commonwealth—1976* (New York: Basic Books, 1976), pp. 77-78.

2. Alexander Hamilton, John Jay, James Madison, *The Federalist Papers*, Mentor Edition (New York: New American Library, 1961), p. 300.

3. Lynton K. Caldwell, *The Administrative Theories of Hamilton and Jefferson* (Chicago: University of Chicago Press, 1949), p. 120.

4. Ibid., p. 134.

5. Ibid., p. 133.

6. David Truman, *The Governmental Process* (New York: Alfred A. Knopf, 1955), p. 502.

7. Ibid., pp. 45, 524, 437, 467-468.

8. Robert A. Dahl, *A Preface to Democratic Theory* (Chicago: University of Chicago Press, 1956), p. 145.

9. Charles E. Lindblom, *The Intelligence of Democracy* (New York: The Free Press, 1965), p. 88.

10. See Charles S. Hyneman, *Bureaucracy in a Democracy* (New York: Harper and Row, 1950); Carl J. Friedrich, "Public Policy and the Nature of Administrative Responsibility," *Public Policy* (1940): 3-24; Herbert Finer, "Administrative Responsibility in Democratic Government," *Public Administration Review*, no. 1 (1941): 335-350; Vincent Ostrom, *The Intellectual Crisis in American Public Administration* (University, Ala.: University of Alabama Press, 1973).

2. The Rise of Bureaucratic Democracy

1. Andrew Hacker, *The Study of Politics* (New York: McGraw-Hill, 1963), p. 73; Dahl, *A Preface*, p. 145; Truman, *Governmental Process*, p. 524.

2. Alexander Hamilton, John Jay, James Madison, *The Federalist Papers*, no. 51, pp. 320, 321-322.

3. Ibid., no. 39, p. 246.

4. Alexis de Tocqueville, *Democracy in America*, ed. Richard Heffner (New York: New American Library, Mentor Edition, 1956), p. 60.

5. Saul K. Padover, ed., *The Forging of American Federalism: Selected Writings of James Madison* (New York: Harper and Row, 1965), p. 101; Dahl, *A Preface*, p. 146.

6. Dahl, *A Preface*, p. 150.

7. Ibid., p. 145.

8. Bernard Bailyn, *The Ideological Origins of the American Revolution* (Cambridge, Mass.: Harvard University Press, 1967), p. 86; Wilson, "Bureaucratic State," p. 101.

9. Robert A. Dahl, *Polyarchy* (New Haven: Yale University Press, 1971), pp. 7, 6.

10. Philippe C. Schmitter, "Still the Century of Corporatism?," in Frederick B. Pike and Thomas Stritch, eds., *The New Corporatism: Social-Political Structures in the Iberian World* (Notre Dame: University of Notre Dame Press, 1974), pp. 93-94.

11. See Arthur F. Bentley, *The Process of Government* (Chicago: University of Chicago Press, 1908), John Kenneth Galbraith, *American Capitalism: The Concept of Counter-vailing Power* (Boston: Houghton Mifflin, 1952), and V. O. Key, *Politics, Parties, and Pressure Groups*, 3rd ed. (New York: Thomas Crowell, 1952).

12. Woodrow Wilson, "The Study of Administration," *Political Science Quarterly* 2, no. 2 (June 1887): 197; Dwight Waldo, *The Administrative State* (New York: Ronald Press, 1948), p. 19.

13. Wilson, "The Study of Administration," pp. 209-210.

14. Ibid., p. 210.

15. Ibid., p. 213.

16. Woodrow Wilson, *Congressional Government* (1885) (New York: Meridian Books, 1956), p. 187; U.S. President's Committee on Administrative Management, *Report with Special Studies* (Washington, D.C.: U.S. Government Printing Office, 1937).

17. Wilson, "The Study of Administration," p. 216.

18. Herbert Kaufman, "Emerging Conflicts in the Doctrines of Public Administration," in Alan Altshuler, ed., *The Politics of the Federal Bureaucracy* (New York: Dodd, Mead, 1968), p. 75.

19. Waldo, *Administrative State*, p. 29; Lowell is cited in Martin J. Schiesl, *The Politics of Efficiency* (Berkeley: University of California Press, 1977), p. 150.

20. Frederick Mosher, *Democracy and the Public Service* (New York: Oxford University Press, 1968), pp. 101, 109.

21. Michael B. Katz, *Class, Bureaucracy, and Schools* (New York: Praeger, 1971), p. 68.

22. Robert A. Dahl and Charles E. Lindblom, *Politics, Economics and Welfare*, 2nd ed. (Chicago: University of Chicago Press, 1976), p. 236.

23. For an extended analysis of the planning idea, see Otis L. Graham, *Toward a Planned Society* (New York: Oxford University Press, 1976).

24. Schiesl, *Politics of Efficiency*, pp. 99, 100.

25. Kaufman, "Emerging Conflicts," pp. 80-81.

26. Frederick C. Mosher, *Democracy and the Public Service* (New York: Oxford University Press, 1968), pp. 103-110.

27. Wilson, "The Study of Administration," p. 200.

28. Waldo, *The Administrative State*, p. 44.

29. Allan Schick, "Systems Politics and Systems Budgeting," in *Public Administration Review*, March/April 1969, pp. 137-151.

30. *New York Times*, Oct. 14, 1979, E19.

31. These quotes are from Richard Polenberg, *Reorganizing Roosevelt's Government, 1936-39* (Cambridge, Mass.: Harvard University Press, 1966), pp. 55, 51.

32. Robert A. Dahl, *Who Governs?* (New Haven: Yale University Press, 1961).

33. Phillip Singerman, "Politics, Bureaucracy, and Public Policy" (Ph.D. diss., Yale University, 1980).

34. For an account of the evolution of Community Progress, Inc., see Douglas Yates, *Neighborhood Democracy* (Lexington, Mass.: D. C. Heath, 1973), ch. 4.

35. The most extensive and controversial appraisal of Moses's career has been provided in Robert Caro, *The Power Broker: Robert Moses and the Fall of New York* (New York: Knopf, 1974).

36. Annmarie Hauck Walsh, *The Public's Business* (Cambridge, Mass.: MIT Press, 1978), p. 89.

37. Ibid., p. 103.

38. See David R. Mayhew, *Congress: The Electoral Connection* (New Haven: Yale University Press, 1974), p. 53.

39. Aaron Wildavsky, "The Two Presidencies," in *The Revolt against the Masses* (New York: Basic Books, 1971), pp. 332-337.

40. For an incisive historical review of presidential relationships with the cabinet, see Thomas E. Cronin, "Conflict over the Cabinet," *New York Times Magazine*, August 12, 1979, p. 24 passim.

41. Marver H. Bernstein, *Regulating Business by Independent Commission* (Princeton: Princeton University Press, 1955), p. 24.

42. Wilson, "The Study of Administration," pp. 210, 212.

43. Ibid., p. 216.

44. Frank J. Goodnow, *Politics and Administration* (New York: Macmillan, 1900), pp. 22, 14.

45. Alan Altshuler, "The Study of American Public Administration," in Altshuler, ed., *The Politics of the Federal Bureaucracy*, p. 62.

46. James M. Burns, *Presidential Government* (Boston: Houghton Mifflin, 1966), pp. 326-327.

47. William A. McClenaghan, *Magruder's American Government* (Boston: Allyn and Bacon, 1962), p. 262.

48. Robert Carr, Marver Bernstein, and Walter Murphy, *American Democracy in Theory and Practice*, 4th ed. (New York: Hold, Rinehart and Winston, 1965), p. 447.

49. Clinton Rossiter, *The American Presidency*, rev. ed. (New York: New American Library, 1960), p. 250.

50. Thomas Cronin, "The Textbook Presidency," in Stanley Bach and

George T. Sulzner, eds., *Perspectives on the Presidency* (Lexington, Mass.: D. C. Heath, 1974), pp. 34-74; Burns, *Presidential Government*; James M. Burns, *Roosevelt: The Lion and the Fox* (New York: Harcourt, Brace, and World, 1956); Thomas A. Bailey, *Presidential Greatness* (New York: Appleton, 1966); Joseph A. Califano, Jr., *A Presidential Nation* (New York: Norton, 1975).

51. Francis Rourke, *Bureaucracy, Politics, and Public Policy*, 2nd ed. (Boston: Little, Brown, 1976), p. 144.

52. Waldo, *The Administrative State*, p. 106.

53. Samuel Beer, "In Search of a New Public Philosophy," in Anthony King, ed., *The New American Political System* (Washington, D.C.: American Enterprise Institute, 1978), p. 8.

54. Altshuler, "American Public Administration," p. 4.

55. Richard Nathan, *The Plot That Failed: Nixon and the Administrative Presidency* (New York: Wiley, 1975).

56. Hugh Heclo, "Issue Networks and the Executive Establishment," in King, ed., *The New American Political System*, p. 100.

57. For a discussion of the growth of these new congressional institutions, see James Fesler, *Public Administration* (Englewood Cliffs, N.J.: Prentice-Hall, 1980), pp. 179ff.

58. Terry Sanford, *Storm over the States* (New York: McGraw-Hill, 1967), p. 80.

59. An example of a broader definition of democracy—in this case grounded in the notion of social justice—is presented by C. B. MacPherson in *The Real World of Democracy* (Oxford: Oxford University Press, 1966).

60. Theodore Lowi, *The End of Liberalism* (New York: Norton, 1969).

61. Charles E. Lindblom, *Politics and Markets* (New York: Basic Books, 1977).

62. Lindblom, *The Intelligence of Democracy*; Norton Long, *The Polity* (Chicago: Rand McNally, 1962), pp. 52ff.

3. An Analysis of Public Bureaucracy

1. James Q. Wilson, "The Bureaucracy Problem" in *The Public Interest*, no. 6 (Winter 1967), p. 5.

2. See Lindblom, *The Intelligence of Democracy*, esp. pt. 4.

3. Long, *The Polity*, p. 74; Dahl, *A Preface*.

4. Graham T. Allison, *Essence of Decision* (Boston: Little, Brown, 1971).

5. Paul Appleby, *Policy and Administration* (University, Alabama: University of Alabama Press, 1949); Rourke, *Bureaucracy, Politics, and Public Policy*; Peter Woll, *American Bureaucracy* (New York: Norton, 1977), p. 7.

6. Allison, *Essence of Decision*, p. 176.

7. Mark V. Nadel and Francis Rourke, "Bureaucracies" in Fred I. Greenstein and Nelson Polsby, eds., *Handbook of Political Science: Governmental Institutions and Processes*, vol. 5 (Reading, Mass.: Addison-Wesley, 1975), p. 394.

8. James Q. Wilson, *Political Organizations* (New York: Basic Books, 1973), p. 334.

9. R. Douglas Arnold, *Congress and the Bureaucracy* (New Haven: Yale University Press, 1979), p. 207.

10. For a good description of the iron triangle system at work, see Harold Seidman, *Politics, Position, and Power*, 2nd ed. (New York: Oxford University Press, 1976), p. 34.

11. Leon V. Sigal, *Reporters and Officials* (Lexington, Mass.: D. C. Heath, 1973), p. 181.

12. Hugh Heclo, *A Government of Strangers* (Washington, D.C.: The Brookings Institution, 1977), pp. 128-130, 158; Samuel Huntington, *The Common Defense* (New York: Columbia University Press, 1961), p. 397.

13. Seidman, *Politics, Position, and Power*, p. 123.

14. Graham Allison and Peter Szanton, *Remaking Foreign Policy* (New York: Basic Books, 1976), pp. 42-43.

15. Heclo, *A Government of Strangers*, pp. 116-120.

16. Samuel Beer, "Political Overload and Federalism" *Polity* 10 (Fall 1977), p. 9.

17. Ibid., p. 10.

18. Mosher, *Democracy and the Public Service*, pp. 108-109.

19. Sanford, *Storm over the States*, p. 80.

20. See Heclo, *A Government of Strangers*, chs. 3 and 4.

21. James David Barber, "Some Consequences of Pluralization in Government," in Harvey Perloff, ed., *The Future of the U.S. Government: Toward the Year 2000* (New York: George Braziller, 1971), p. 243.

22. Jeffrey L. Pressman and Aaron B. Wildavsky, *Implementation* (Berkeley: University of California Press, 1973), p. 107.

23. Martha Derthick, *Policymaking for Social Security* (Washington, D.C.: The Brookings Institution, 1979).

24. Graham Allison and Morton Halperin, *Bureaucratic Politics: A Paradigm and Some Policy Implications* (Washington, D.C.: The Brookings Institution, 1972), p. 49.

25. Ibid., p. 35.

26. Arnold J. Meltsner, *Policy Analysts in the Bureaucracy* (Berkeley: University of California Press, 1976), pp. 11-12.

27. Thomas Cronin, *The State of the Presidency*, 1st ed. (Boston: Little, Brown, 1975), p. 202.

28. Heclo, *A Government of Strangers*, pp. 142 ff.

29. The development of these organizational traits in the Forest Service is presented in Herbert Kaufman's classic administrative study, *The Forest Ranger* (Baltimore: Johns Hopkins Press, 1960).

30. The concept of the street-level bureaucrat has been developed by Michael Lipsky. The most complete statement of his perspective and analysis is contained in *Street-Level Bureaucracy* (New York: Russell Sage Foundation, 1980).

31. Huntington, *The Common Defense*, p. 369.

32. Barber, "Pluralization in Government," p. 44.

33. For the full treatment of this point, see Jeffrey Pressman, *Federal Programs and City Politics* (Berkeley: University of California Press, 1975).

34. For a useful account of this intergovernmental tension, see Donald Kettl, *Managing Community Development in the New Federalism* (New York: Praeger, 1980).

35. Herbert Simon, *Administrative Behavior* (New York: Macmillan, 1957), p. 149.

36. Ibid., pp. 57, 58.

37. Ibid., pp. 51, xxxv.

38. Cited in Martin Albrow, *Bureaucracy* (London: Macmillan, 1970), p. 55.

39. Reinhard Bendix, *Higher Civil Servants in American Society* (Boulder: University of Colorado Press, 1949), p. 12.

40. Charles F. Lindblom, *Strategies for Decision Making* (Urbana: University of Illinois Bulletin, 1971), p. 13.

41. Martha Derthick, *Uncontrollable Spending for Social Services* (Washington, D.C.: The Brookings Institution, 1975).

42. Richard Blumenthal, "The Bureaucracy: Antipoverty and the Community Action Program" in Allan Sindler, ed., *American Political Institutions and Public Policy* (Boston: Little, Brown, 1969), pp. 129-179.

43. Nadel and Rourke, "Bureaucracies," p. 386.

44. James Q. Wilson, *Varieties of Police Behavior* (Cambridge, Mass.: Harvard University Press, 1968), p. 6.

45. Douglas Yates, *The Ungovernable City* (Cambridge, Mass.: MIT Press, 1977).

46. Rourke, *Bureaucracy, Politics, and Public Policy*, p. 136.

47. See Anthony Downs, *Inside Bureaucracy* (Boston: Little, Brown, 1967) and William Niskanen, *Bureaucracy and Representative Government* (Chicago and New York: Aldine-Atherton, 1971).

48. Louis K. Bragaw, *Managing a Federal Agency* (Baltimore: Johns Hopkins University Press, 1980), p. 246.

49. James Q. Wilson, *The Investigators* (New York: Basic Books, 1978), p. 14.

50. Heclo, *A Government of Strangers*, p. 143.

51. Derthick, *Policymaking for Social Security*, p. 372.

52. Samuel Huntington, "The Marasmus of the I.C.C.: The Commission, the Railroads, and the Public Interest," *Yale Law Journal* 61 (1952): 467-509.

53. Herbert Kaufman, *Administrative Feedback* (Washington, D.C.: The Brookings Institution, 1973), p. v.

54. Beer, "Political Overload," pp. 8-9.

55. Daniel P. Moynihan, *Maximum Feasible Misunderstanding* (New York: Free Press, 1970); Beer, "Political Overload," p. 10.

56. See Paul W. MacAvoy, *The Regulated Industries and the Economy* (New York: Norton, 1979).

57. See Robert Yin and Douglas Yates, *Street-Level Governments* (Lexington, Mass.: D. C. Heath, 1975).

58. Daniel Bell and Virginia Held, "The Community Revolution," *The Public Interest*, no. 16 (Summer 1969): 142-177.

59. Herbert Kaufman, *Red Tape* (Washington, D.C.: The Brookings Institution, 1977), p. 30.

4. The Politics of Bureaucracy

1. Downs, *Inside Bureaucracy;* Niskanen, *Bureaucracy and Representative Government*, p. 42.
2. Derthick, *Policymaking for Social Security.*
3. Lowi, *End of Liberalism*, ch. 3.
4. King, ed., *The New American Political System*, p. 291.
5. Dahl, *Who Governs?*, p. 184.
6. Huntington, "Marasmus."
7. Long, *The Polity*; Lindblom, *The Intelligence of Democracy*, pp. 294-295.

5. Institutional Differences

1. Wilson, *The Investigators.*
2. Edward K. Hamilton, "On Nonconstitutional Management of a Constitutional Problem," *Daedalus* 107, no. 1 (Winter 1978), pp. 122ff.
3. Yates, *Ungovernable City*, pp. 38-40.
4. Ibid.
5. See Arthur Levin, *The Satisficers* (New York: McCall, 1970).
6. Downs, *Inside Bureaucracy*, p. 264.
7. Nelson Polsby, "The Institutionalization of the U.S. House of Representatives," *American Political Science Review* 62 (March 1968): 144-168.
8. Yates, *Ungovernable City*, ch. 3; Robert H. Wiebe, *The Search for Order* (New York: Hill and Wang, 1967).
9. Huntington, "Marasmus."
10. See Lipsky, *Street-Level Bureaucracy*, and Yates, *Ungovernable City* for an elaboration of this argument.
11. Kaufman, *The Forest Ranger.*
12. See Douglas Yates, *Neighborhood Democracy* (Lexington, Mass.: D. C. Heath, 1973) for a classification of different degrees and extent of participation in terms of the power and control delegated to citizen participants.
13. Ibid., ch. 5.
14. The Ocean Hill-Brownsville situation is chronicled in detail in Naomi Levine, *Ocean Hill-Brownsville: A Case Study of Schools in Crisis* (New York: Popular Library, 1969).
15. Lindblom, *Strategies for Decision Making*, p. 12.
16. A useful clarification of the meaning of a political structure or system being "institutionalized" is provided by Samuel P. Huntington in *Political Order in Changing Societies* (New Haven: Yale University Press, 1968), pp. 12-24.
17. Yin and Yates, *Street-Level Governments.*

6. The Search for Control of Bureaucracy

1. "Will the 96th Become the 'Oversight Congress,' " *National Journal*, no. 2 (Jan. 13, 1979), pp. 44, 49.

2. The experience of this youth commissioner in Massachusetts is chronicled in P. Heyman et al., *Jerome Miller and the Massachusetts Department of Youth Services*, Cases in Public Policy and Management, Intercollegiate Case Clearing House, no. 9-378-586. The efforts of Gordon Chase to launch methadone maintenance programs in New York City is described in Mark Moore and Mark Ziering, *Methadone Maintenance: The Entrepreneur's View* (case material, John F. Kennedy School of Government, Harvard University, 1976).

3. Dahl and Lindblom, *Politics, Economics, and Welfare*, p. 94.

4. Cited in James Fesler, *Public Administration* (Englewood Cliffs, N.J.: Prentice-Hall, 1980), p. 312.

5. Ibid.

6. See Richard Rose, "Implementation and Evaporation: The Record of MBO," *Public Administration Review* 37, no. 1 (Jan.-Feb. 1977), p. 64-71.

7. See Robert Wood, "When Government Works," *The Public Interest*, no. 18 (Winter 1970), pp. 42-43.

8. "Will the 96th Become the 'Oversight Congress,' " p. 48.

9. Fesler, *Public Administration*, p. 329.

10. Aberbach is cited in "Will the 96th Become the 'Oversight Congress,' " p. 45.

11. Fesler, *Public Administration*, p. 321.

12. Cited in Nadel and Rourke, *Bureaucracies*, p. 420.

13. I attribute this depiction of "big loose control" to C. E. Lindblom in a comment made at a faculty seminar on American Democratic Institutions held at the Institution for Social and Policy Studies, Yale University.

14. Michael Malbin and Michael Andrew Scully, "Our Unelected Representatives," *The Public Interest*, no. 47 (Spring 1977), pp. 16-48.

15. Herbert Kaufman, *Administrative Feedback*, p. 4.

16. Kaufman, *Are Government Organizations Immortal?* (Washington, D.C.: The Brookings Institution, 1976), p. 24.

17. Yin and Yates, *Street-Level Governments*, ch. 3, pp. 187-190.

18. U.S. Department of Transportation, The Secretary's Decision on Concorde Supersonic Transport, Washington, D.C., Feb. 4, 1976, p. 7.

19. Lindblom, *Strategies for Decision Making*, p. 14.

20. Ibid., p. 13.

21. For the multitudinous interpretations of values, see Douglas Rae and Douglas Yates, Jennifer Hochschild, Joseph Morone, Carol Fessler, *Equalities* (Cambridge, Mass.: Harvard University Press, 1981).

22. For a fuller account of the "utility" of redundancy in administration, see Martin Landau, "Redundancy, Rationality, and the Problem of Duplication and Overlap," *Public Administration Review* 29 (July-Aug. 1969): 346-358.

7. Strategies for Democracy and Efficiency

1. Charles A. Reich and Burke Marshall, "Needed: A Government that Governs," in Frederick S. Lane, ed., *Current Issues in Public Administration* (New York: St. Martin's Press, 1978), p. 430.

2. Allison and Szanton, *Remaking Foreign Policy.*

3. Charles Peters, "How to Take over the Government," *The Washington Monthly,* Sept. 1974, pp. 19-21.

4. Lawrence Lynn, Jr., and John Seidl, " 'Bottom-Line' Management for Public Agencies," *Harvard Business Review* 55, no. 1 (Jan.-Feb. 1977), pp. 144-153.

5. Peters, "How to Take Over the Government," p. 20.

6. Pressman and Wildavsky, *Implementation.*

7. Yates, *The Ungovernable City.*

8. For a thoughtful discussion of this issue, see Aaron Wildavsky, "The Self-Evaluating Organization," in Wildavsky, *Speaking Truth to Power* (Boston: Little, Brown, 1979), ch. 9.

9. See Lipsky, *Street-Level Bureaucracy.*

10. The most thorough analysis of the neighborhood government experience in New York has been provided in John Mudd, *Government in Urban Neighborhoods* (New Haven: Yale University Press, forthcoming).

Index

Bureaucratic Democracy
The Search for Democracy and Efficiency in American Government

Douglas Yates

Although everyone agrees on the need to make government work better, few understand public bureaucracy sufficiently well to offer useful suggestions, either theoretical or practical. In fact, some consider bureaucratic efficiency incompatible with democratic government.

Douglas Yates places the often competing aims of efficiency and democracy in historical perspective and then presents a unique and systematic theory of the politics of bureaucracy, which he illustrates with examples from recent history and from empirical research. He argues that the United States operates under a system of "bureaucratic democracy," in which governmental decisions increasingly are made in bureaucratic settings, out of the public eye. He describes the rational, self-interested bureaucrat as a "minimaxer," who inches forward inconspicuously, gradually accumulating larger budgets and greater power, in an atmosphere of segmented pluralism, of conflict and competition, of silent politics.

To make the policy process more competitive, democratic, and open, Yates calls for strategic debate among policymakers and bureaucrats and insists that bureaucrats should give a public accounting of their significant decisions rather than bury them in incremental changes. He offers concrete proposals, applicable to federal,